EXAM✓CRAM

CompTIA® A+ Practice Questions Exam Cram Core 1 (220-1001) and Core 2 (220-1002)

PEARSON IT
CERTIFICATION

CompTIA® A+ Practice Questions Exam Cram
Core 1 (220-1001) and Core 2 (220-1002)

David L Prowse

Copyright© 2020 Pearson Education, Inc.

Published by:
Pearson Education
221 River St.
Hoboken, NJ 07030 USA

Library of Congress Control Number:2019908203

 1 2019

ISBN-13: 978-0-13-556626-8

ISBN-10: 0-13-556626-6

Warning and Disclaimer

This book is designed to provide information about the CompTIA A+ Core 1 (220-1001) and Core 2 (220-1002) exams for the CompTIA A+ certification. Every effort has been made to make this book as complete and as accurate as possible, but no warranty or fitness is implied.

The information is provided on an "as is" basis. The author and publisher shall have neither liability nor responsibility to any person or entity with respect to any loss or damages arising from the information contained in this book or from the use of the discs or programs that may accompany it.

The opinions expressed in this book belong to the author.

Microsoft and/or its respective suppliers make no representations about the suitability of the information contained in the documents and related graphics published as part of the services for any purpose all such documents and related graphics are provided "as is" without warranty of any kind. Microsoft and/or its respective suppliers hereby disclaim all warranties and conditions with regard to this information, including all warranties and conditions of merchantability, whether express, implied or statutory, fitness for a particular purpose, title and non-infringement. In no event shall Microsoft and/or its respective suppliers be liable for any special, indirect or consequential damages or any damages whatsoever resulting from loss of use, data or profits, whether in an action of contract, negligence or other tortious action, arising out of or in connection with the use or performance of information available from the services.

The documents and related graphics contained herein could include technical inaccuracies or typographical errors. Changes are periodically added to the information herein. Microsoft and/or its respective suppliers may make improvements and/or changes in the product(s) and/or the program(s) described herein at any time. Partial screen shots may be viewed in full within the software version specified.

Trademark Acknowledgments

All terms mentioned in this book that are known to be trademarks or service marks have been appropriately capitalized. Pearson IT Certification cannot attest to the accuracy of this information. Use of a term in this book should not be regarded as affecting the validity of any trademark or service mark.

Microsoft® Windows®, and Microsoft Office® are registered trademarks of the Microsoft Corporation in the U.S.A. and other countries. This book is not sponsored or endorsed by or affiliated with the Microsoft Corporation.

Special Sales

For information about buying this title in bulk quantities, or for special sales opportunities (which may include electronic versions; custom cover designs; and content particular to your business, training goals, marketing focus, or branding interests), please contact our corporate sales department at corpsales@pearsoned.com or (800) 382-3419.

For government sales inquiries, please contact governmentsales@pearsoned.com.

For questions about sales outside the U.S., please contact intlcs@pearson.com.

Editor-in-Chief
Mark Taub

Product Line Manager
Brett Bartow

Executive Editor
Paul Carlstroem

Managing Editor
Sandra Schroeder

Development Editor
Christopher A. Cleveland

Project Editor
Mandie Frank

Copy Editor
Chuck Hutchinson

Technical Editor
Chris Crayton

Editorial Assistant
Cindy Teeters

Designer
Chuti Prasertsith

Composition
codeMantra

Proofreader
Karen Davis

Contents at a Glance

Table of Contents

About the Author

David L. Prowse is the author of more than a dozen computer training books and video products. He has worked in the computer field for 25 years and loves to share his experience through teaching and writing.

He runs the website https://dprocomputer.com, where he gladly answers questions from readers and students.

About the Technical Reviewer

Chris Crayton (MCSE) is an author, technical consultant, and trainer. He has worked as a computer technology and networking instructor, information security director, network administrator, network engineer, and PC specialist. Chris has authored several print and online books on PC repair, CompTIA A+, CompTIA Security+, and Microsoft Windows. He has also served as technical editor and content contributor on numerous technical titles for several of the leading publishing companies. He holds numerous industry certifications, has been recognized with many professional teaching awards, and has served as a state-level SkillsUSA competition judge.

Acknowledgments

I'd like to give special recognition to Paul Carlstroem, Chris Cleveland, Chris Crayton, and Mandie Frank. Without you, this book wouldn't have made it to the presses. I'm serious here—writing a book is tough work, and this edition of the *A+ Practice Questions Exam Cram* was the toughest to date. Thank you.

Publishing a book takes a team of professional and talented people. My thanks to everyone at Pearson for your expertise and help throughout this project.

We Want to Hear from You!

As the reader of this book, *you* are our most important critic and commentator. We value your opinion and want to know what we're doing right, what we could do better, what areas you'd like to see us publish in, and any other words of wisdom you're willing to pass our way.

We welcome your comments. You can email or write to let us know what you did or didn't like about this book—as well as what we can do to make our books better.

Please note that we cannot help you with technical problems related to the topic of this book.

When you write, please be sure to include this book's title and author as well as your name and email address. We will carefully review your comments and share them with the author and editors who worked on the book.

Email: community@pearsonITcertification.com

Reader Services

Register your copy of *CompTIA A+ Practice Questions Exam Cram Core 1 (220-1001) and Core 2 (220-1002)* at www.pearsonitcertification.com for convenient access to downloads, updates, and corrections as they become available. To start the registration process, go to www.pearsonitcertification.com/register and log in or create an account*. Enter the product ISBN 9780135566268 and click Submit. When the process is complete, you will find any available bonus content under Registered Products.

*Be sure to check the box that you would like to hear from us to receive exclusive discounts on future editions of this product.

Introduction

Welcome to *CompTIA A+ Core 1 (220-1001) and Core 2 (220-1002) Practice Questions Exam Cram*. The sole purpose of this book is to provide you with practice questions that are complete with answers and explanations to help you learn, drill, and review for the CompTIA A+ certification exams. The book offers 480 questions that help you practice each exam domain and help you assess your knowledge before you take the real exams. The detailed answers to every question aid in reinforcing your knowledge about the concepts associated with the 1000 series of the CompTIA A+ exams.

Who This Book Is For

The CompTIA A+ exams are designed for individuals with at least 12 months of hands-on experience in the lab or field. If you have that experience, this book will be an excellent late-stage study tool. However, if you have not acquired that experience, I recommend that you register for a hands-on A+ course or, at the very least, purchase an A+ study guide such as the *CompTIA A+ Core 220-1001 and Core 220-1002 Exam Cram* textbook or consider my *A+ Complete Video Course*. After you take the course and/or read the study guide, return to this book as your late-stage test preparation to be used just before taking the real exams.

What You Will Find in This Book

In every chapter devoted to practice exams, you will find the following three elements:

- ▶ **Practice Questions:** There are 480 questions that help you learn, drill, and review for the exams. All of the questions in this section are multiple choice.

- ▶ **Quick-Check Answer Key:** After you finish answering the questions, you can quickly grade your exam from this section. Only correct answers are given in this section. No explanations are offered yet. Even if you answered a question incorrectly, do not be discouraged. Keep in mind that this is not the real exam. You can always review the topic and revisit the questions again.

- ▶ **Answers and Explanations:** This section provides you with correct answers as well as further explanations about the content posed in that question. Use this information to learn why an answer is correct and to reinforce the content in your mind for exam day.

The book also comes with a companion website. It contains a simulated testing environment where you can take all the exams on a computer in study mode or in full practice test mode. It also includes a "Real-World Scenarios" document and supporting performance-based exercises and videos, as well as two bonus exams. Create an account and register this book at http://www.pearsonitcertification.com/ to get access to the bonus content. (Access to the test engine is print version only.)

Hints for Using This Book

Complete your exams on a separate piece of paper so that you can reuse the practice questions again if necessary. Also, plan to score 90 percent or higher on each exam before moving on to the next one. The higher you score on these practice questions, the better your chances for passing the real exams.

I am available for questions at my website:

https://dprocomputer.com

I answer questions Monday through Friday, usually in the mornings.

Companion Website

Register this book to get access to the Pearson IT Certification test engine and other study materials plus additional bonus content. Check this site regularly for new and updated postings written by the author that provide further insight into the more troublesome topics on the exam. Be sure to check the box that you would like to hear from us to receive updates and exclusive discounts on future editions of this product or related products.

To access this companion website, follow these steps:

1. Go to www.pearsonitcertification.com/register and log in or create a new account.

2. Enter the ISBN: **9780135566268**.

3. Answer the challenge question as proof of purchase.

4. Click the **Access Bonus Content** link in the Registered Products section of your account page, to be taken to the page where your downloadable content is available.

Please note that many of our companion content files can be very large, especially image and video files.

If you are unable to locate the files for this title by following the steps at left, please visit www.pearsonITcertification.com/contact and select the **Site Problems/ Comments** option. Our customer service representatives will assist you.

Pearson Test Prep Practice Test Software

As noted previously, this book comes complete with the Pearson Test Prep practice test software containing two full exams. These practice tests are available to you either online or as an offline Windows application. To access the practice exams that were developed with this book, please see the instructions in the card inserted in the sleeve in the back of the book. This card includes a unique access code that enables you to activate your exams in the Pearson Test Prep software.

Accessing the Pearson Test Prep Software Online

The online version of this software can be used on any device with a browser and connectivity to the Internet, including desktop machines, tablets, and smartphones. To start using your practice exams online, simply follow these steps:

Step 1. Go to https://www.PearsonTestPrep.com.

Step 2. Select **Pearson IT Certification** as your product group.

Step 3. Enter your email/password for your account. If you don't have an account on PearsonITCertification.com, you will need to establish one by going to PearsonITCertification.com/join.

Step 4. In the **My Products** tab, click the **Activate New Product** button.

Step 5. Enter the access code printed on the insert card in the back of your book to activate your product.

Step 6. The product will now be listed in your My Products page. Click the **Exams** button to launch the exam settings screen and start your exam.

Accessing the Pearson Test Prep Software Offline

If you wish to study offline, you can download and install the Windows version of the Pearson Test Prep software. There is a download link for this software on the book's companion website, or you can just enter this link in your browser:

http://www.pearsonitcertification.com/content/downloads/pcpt/engine.zip

To access the book's companion website and the software, simply follow these steps:

Step 1. Register your book by going to PearsonITCertification.com/register and entering the ISBN: **9780135566268**.

Step 2. Answer the challenge questions.

Step 3. Go to your account page and click the **Registered Products** tab.

Step 4. Click the **Access Bonus Content** link under the product listing.

Step 5. Click the **Install Pearson Test Prep Desktop Version** link under the Practice Exams section of the page to download the software.

Step 6. After the software finishes downloading, unzip all the files on your computer.

Step 7. Double-click the application file to start the installation, and follow the onscreen instructions to complete the registration.

Step 8. After the installation is complete, launch the application and click the **Activate Exam** button on the My Products tab.

Step 9. Click the **Activate a Product** button in the Activate Product Wizard.

Step 10. Enter the unique access code found on the card in the sleeve in the back of your book and click the **Activate** button.

Step 11. Click **Next** and then click **Finish** to download the exam data to your application.

Step 12. Start using the practice exams by selecting the product and clicking the **Open Exam** button to open the exam settings screen.

Note that the offline and online versions will synch together, so saved exams and grade results recorded on one version will be available to you on the other as well.

Customizing Your Exams

Once you are in the exam settings screen, you can choose to take exams in one of three modes:

- **Study mode:** Allows you to fully customize your exams and review answers as you are taking the exam. This is typically the mode you would use first to assess your knowledge and identify information gaps.

- **Practice Exam mode:** Locks certain customization options, as it is presenting a realistic exam experience. Use this mode when you are preparing to test your exam readiness.

- **Flash Card mode:** Strips out the answers and presents you with only the question stem. This mode is great for late-stage preparation when you really want to challenge yourself to provide answers without the benefit of seeing multiple-choice options. This mode does not provide the detailed score reports that the other two modes do, so you should not use it if you are trying to identify knowledge gaps.

In addition to these three modes, you will be able to select the source of your questions. You can choose to take exams that cover all of the chapters or you can narrow your selection to just a single chapter or the chapters that make up specific parts in the book. All chapters are selected by default. If you want to narrow your focus to individual chapters, simply deselect all the chapters and then select only those on which you wish to focus in the Objectives area.

You can also select the exam banks on which to focus. Each exam bank comes complete with a full exam of questions that cover topics in every chapter. The two exams printed in the book are available to you as well as two additional exams of unique questions. You can have the test engine serve up exams from all four banks or just from one individual bank by selecting the desired banks in the exam bank area.

There are several other customizations you can make to your exam from the exam settings screen, such as the time of the exam, the number of questions served up, whether to randomize questions and answers, whether to show the number of correct answers for multiple-answer questions, and whether to serve up only specific types of questions. You can also create custom test banks by selecting only questions that you have marked or questions on which you have added notes.

Updating Your Exams

If you are using the online version of the Pearson Test Prep software, you should always have access to the latest version of the software as well as the exam data. If you are using the Windows desktop version, every time you launch the software while connected to the Internet, it checks whether there are any updates to your exam data and automatically downloads any changes that were made since the last time you used the software.

Sometimes, due to many factors, the exam data may not fully download when you activate your exam. If you find that figures or exhibits are missing, you may need to manually update your exams. To update a particular exam you have already activated and downloaded, simply click the **Tools** tab and click the **Update Products** button. Again, this is only an issue with the desktop Windows application.

If you wish to check for updates to the Pearson Test Prep exam engine software, Windows desktop version, simply click the **Tools** tab and click the **Update Application** button. Taking this step ensures that you are running the latest version of the software engine.

Need Further Study?

Consider a hands-on A+ course, and be sure to see the following companion products to this book:

CompTIA A+ Core 220-1001 and Core 220-1002 Exam Cram by David L. Prowse (ISBN: 9780789760579)

CompTIA A+ 220-1001 Complete Video Course by David L. Prowse (ISBN: 978-0-13-530535-5)

CompTIA A+ 220-1002 Complete Video Course by David L. Prowse (ISBN: 978-0-7897-6054-8)

CHAPTER ONE

Introduction to the 220-1001 Exam

The CompTIA A+ 220-1001 exam is all about mobile devices, PC hardware, computer networking, and troubleshooting of those technologies. It also contains a small percentage of cloud computing and virtualization.

In this chapter, I briefly discuss how the exam is categorized, give you some test-taking tips, and then prepare you to take the three 220-1001 practice exams that follow this chapter.

Exam Breakdown

The CompTIA A+ 220-1001 exam objectives are divided by domain. Each domain makes up a certain percentage of the test. The five domains of the A+ 220-1001 exam and their respective percentages are listed in Table 1.1.

TABLE 1.1   220-1001 Domains

Domain	Percentage of Exam
1.0 Mobile Devices	14
2.0 Networking	20
3.0 Hardware	27
4.0 Virtualization and Cloud Computing	12
5.0 Hardware and Network Troubleshooting	27
Total	100

Chances are that when you take the real CompTIA exam, the questions will be based on these percentages, but you never know. The questions are chosen at random, so you have to be prepared for anything, and study all of the objectives.

Each domain has several objectives. There are far too many to list in this book, but I recommend you download a copy of the objectives for yourself. You can get them from CompTIA's A+ web page or from my website: https://dprocomputer.com.

Let's talk about each domain briefly.

Domain 1.0: Mobile Devices (14%)

CompTIA refers to any portable computers as mobile devices, including laptops, tablets, smartphones, and hybrid versions of those devices. This domain comprises only 14 percent of the exam, but remember that every domain is important. You should be able to demonstrate the ability to install and configure laptop hardware and software. You also should know how to operate laptops' special functions, such as dual displays, wireless, and Bluetooth. Finally, because of the explosion of mobile devices in the tech world and the increased adoption of bring your own device (BYOD) policies by companies, you need to understand the hardware side of smartphones and tablets for the 220-1001 exam.

Domain 2.0: Networking (20%)

The Networking domain covers network standards, cabling, connectors, and tools. TCP/IP is also a big portion of this domain; you will undoubtedly see questions on IP addresses, ports, and protocols. You should be able to install and configure a basic wired or wireless SOHO network and use the appropriate networking tools. Plus, you should be able to describe the various types of servers and networking hardware available.

Domain 3.0: Hardware (27%)

The Hardware domain concerns building a computer and upgrading it. The core of a desktop computer includes the motherboard, CPU, and RAM. Those are the guts of the computer, so to speak. They are installed inside a computer case.

You are required to understand motherboard form factors and compatibility concerns as well as the ports, connectors, buses, and expansion slots of a motherboard. You should also know how to access, configure, and update the BIOS and understand the relationship between the BIOS, CMOS, and lithium battery.

NOTE

I might refer to the BIOS as UEFI or as BIOS/UEFI or UEFI/BIOS. You might see any of these terms on the exams or in the IT field. Remember that the UEFI is a newer technology that augments the BIOS and allows for more security and better communication with the operating system.

Then there's everything that connects to the motherboard: CPU and fan, RAM, expansion cards, hard drives, and optical drives. Plus, there are all of the ports on a computer, such as USB, video, and audio ports. Next are the peripherals such as monitors, printers, USB flash drives, and other devices that interact with the computer. Finally, you should know some custom PC configurations, such as virtualization workstations, gaming PCs, and design/CAD/CAM workstations, and the hardware that those different types of systems require.

Domain 4.0: Virtualization and Cloud Computing (12%)

The Virtualization and Cloud Computing domain is new to the A+ Core 1 (220-1001) exam. Coming in at 12% of the exam—but still quite important—is virtualization and the cloud. If you are not using virtual machines now, you will be. And chances are that you already make use of some type of cloud-based services. This domain is considered to be an introduction to the cloud, but you should study it carefully because you will be dealing with the cloud and VMs often.

Domain 5.0: Hardware and Network Troubleshooting (27%)

Troubleshooting is key; it is the most vital ability a technician should possess. You need to understand how to troubleshoot hardware failures, bootup issues, no-display obstacles, network connectivity difficulties, and, of course, printing problems. This is the crux of the exam (both exams, to be accurate), and you need to study and practice accordingly.

Expect one question out of four (or more) to be based on a troubleshooting scenario. Practice the questions in this book, understand the concepts, and more importantly, practice the topics on real computers in a hands-on way whenever possible. This is where hands-on experience plays a big role and is one of the reasons that CompTIA recommends that a test-taker have 12 months of hands-on experience in the lab or field.

Remember this: Troubleshooting is a huge portion of what you do as a computer technician. To increase your job security, you need to be a good troubleshooter. Today's CompTIA A+ exams reflect that concept by incorporating many paragraph-based, scenario-oriented troubleshooting questions. You need to imagine yourself in the situation and think carefully about how to fix the problem. One thing that can aid you in this process is the CompTIA A+ six-step troubleshooting process. Memorize it!

Step 1.   Identify the problem.

Step 2.   Establish a theory of probable cause. (Question the obvious.)

Step 3.   Test the theory to determine cause.

Step 4.   Establish a plan of action to resolve the problem and implement the solution.

Step 5.   Verify full system functionality and, if applicable, implement preventative measures.

Step 6.   Document findings, actions, and outcomes.

I really can't stress enough the importance of this domain. Practice on real systems and be ready to troubleshoot!

Test-Taking Tips

My first recommendation is to take the exams slowly. Don't rush through, especially on the first exam. Carefully read each question. Some questions are tricky by design. Others may seem tricky if you lack knowledge in certain areas. Still other questions are somewhat vague, and that is intentional as well. You need to place yourself in the scenario of the question. Think of yourself actually installing a CPU and heat sink, or imagine that you are upgrading a video card. Picture in your head the steps you must take to accomplish what the question is asking of you. Envision what you do with computers step by step, and the answers will come more easily to you.

Next, read through *all* of the answers. Don't just jump on the first one that seems correct to you. Look at each answer and ask yourself whether it is right or wrong. And if it is wrong, define why it is wrong. Using this approach helps you eliminate wrong answers in the search for the correct answer. When you have selected an answer, be confident in your decision.

Finally, don't get stuck on any one question. You can always mark it and return to it later. This advice especially applies to performance-based questions and longer questions. I offer more tips as we progress through the book, and I summarize all test-taking tips at the end of this book.

Getting Ready for the Practice Exams

The next three chapters feature practice exams based on the 220-1001 exam. Every exam is followed by in-depth explanations. Be sure to read them carefully. Don't move on to another exam until you have mastered the first one. And by "mastered," I mean you should be scoring 90 percent or higher on the exam (without memorizing the answers). Really understand the concepts before moving on to another exam. This makes you an efficient test-taker and allows you to benefit the most from this book.

Consider timing yourself. Give yourself 90 minutes to complete each exam. Write down your answers on a piece of paper. When you are finished, if there is still time left, review your answers for accuracy.

Each exam gets progressively more difficult. Don't get overconfident if you do well on the first exam; your skills will be tested more thoroughly as you progress. And don't get too concerned if you don't score 90 percent on the first try. This just means you need to study more and try the test again later. Keep studying and practicing!

After each exam is an answer key, followed by the in-depth answers/explanations. Don't skip the explanations, even if you think you know the concept. I often insert little tidbits of knowledge that are on the periphery of the concept; these serve to build you a stronger foundation of knowledge in general. In other words, I might branch off the main topic, but this is done so you can get a clearer, bigger picture of the 220-1001 exam and of the tech world in general.

So take a deep breath, and let's go!

CHAPTER TWO

220-1001 Practice Exam A

Welcome to the first 220-1001 practice exam. This is the easiest of the 220-1001 exams. The subsequent exams will get progressively harder.

Take this first exam slowly. The goal is to make sure you understand all of the concepts before moving on to the next test.

Write down your answers, and check them against the Quick-Check Answer Key, which immediately follows the exam. After the answer key, you will find the explanations for all of the answers. Good luck!

Practice Questions

1. Which of the following are components you might find inside a PC? (Select the three best answers.)

   ❏ **A.** CPU
   ❏ **B.** Motherboard
   ❏ **C.** Keyboard
   ❏ **D.** Printer
   ❏ **E.** RAM
   ❏ **F.** Cable modem

Quick Answer: **24**
Detailed Answer: **25**

2. Which device stores data over the long term?

   ○ **A.** CPU
   ○ **B.** RAM
   ○ **C.** Hard drive
   ○ **D.** Video card

Quick Answer: **24**
Detailed Answer: **25**

3. To which type of technology would you install a x16 card?

○ **A.** Thunderbolt

○ **B.** PCIe

○ **C.** USB

○ **D.** DisplayPort

4. Which process of the computer checks all your components during boot?

○ **A.** CMOS

○ **B.** POST

○ **C.** BIOS

○ **D.** Lithium battery

5. Tim installs a new CPU in a computer. After a few hours, the processor starts to overheat. Which of the following might be the cause?

○ **A.** The CPU is not locked down.

○ **B.** The CPU is not properly seated.

○ **C.** Thermal compound was not applied.

○ **D.** The CPU is not compatible with the motherboard.

6. Which of the following could cause the POST to fail? (Select the two best answers.)

❏ **A.** CPU

❏ **B.** Power supply

❏ **C.** Optical drive

❏ **D.** Memory

❏ **E.** Hard drive

7. Which of the following might you find as part of a tablet computer? (Select the two best answers.)

❏ **A.** Flash memory

❏ **B.** SATA hard drive

❏ **C.** Multi-touch touchscreen

❏ **D.** 24-inch display

8. Which kind of socket incorporates "lands" to ensure connectivity to a CPU?

Quick Answer: **24**
Detailed Answer: **26**

- ○ **A.** PGA
- ○ **B.** Chipset
- ○ **C.** LGA
- ○ **D.** Copper

9. How should you hold RAM when installing it?

Quick Answer: **24**
Detailed Answer: **26**

- ○ **A.** By the edges
- ○ **B.** By the front and back
- ○ **C.** With tweezers
- ○ **D.** With a punchdown tool

10. You have been tasked with setting up a specialized computer for video editing. Which of the following should you include with the computer? (Select the two best answers.)

Quick Answer: **24**
Detailed Answer: **26**

- ❏ **A.** Gigabit NIC
- ❏ **B.** Hypervisor
- ❏ **C.** SSD
- ❏ **D.** Docking station
- ❏ **E.** Dual monitors
- ❏ **F.** NAS

11. How many pins are inside an SATA 3.0 data connector?

Quick Answer: **24**
Detailed Answer: **27**

- ○ **A.** 15
- ○ **B.** 7
- ○ **C.** 24
- ○ **D.** 127

12. What is the delay in the RAM's response to a request from the memory controller called?

Quick Answer: **24**
Detailed Answer: **27**

- ○ **A.** Latency
- ○ **B.** Standard deviation
- ○ **C.** Fetch interval
- ○ **D.** Lag

13. What is the minimum number of hard drives necessary to implement RAID 5?

Quick Answer: **24**
Detailed Answer: **27**

- ❍ **A.** Two
- ❍ **B.** Five
- ❍ **C.** Three
- ❍ **D.** Four

14. A user's time and date keep resetting to January 1, 2012. Which of the following is the most likely cause?

Quick Answer: **24**
Detailed Answer: **27**

- ❍ **A.** The BIOS needs to be updated.
- ❍ **B.** Windows needs to be updated.
- ❍ **C.** The Windows Date and Time Properties window needs to be modified.
- ❍ **D.** The lithium battery needs to be replaced.

15. Which type of adapter card is normally plugged into a PCIe x16 adapter card slot?

Quick Answer: **24**
Detailed Answer: **27**

- ❍ **A.** Modem
- ❍ **B.** Video
- ❍ **C.** NIC
- ❍ **D.** Sound

16. Which of the following is a common type of CPU for a smartphone?

Quick Answer: **24**
Detailed Answer: **28**

- ❍ **A.** LGA 2011
- ❍ **B.** SoC
- ❍ **C.** Core i7
- ❍ **D.** LPDDR

17. Which of the following components could cause the POST to beep several times and fail during boot?

Quick Answer: **24**
Detailed Answer: **28**

- ❍ **A.** Sound card
- ❍ **B.** Power supply
- ❍ **C.** Hard drive
- ❍ **D.** RAM

18. Which of the following are ports you might find on smartphones and tablets? (Select the two best answers.)

   ❏ **A.** eSATA

   ❏ **B.** USB-C

   ❏ **C.** Lightning

   ❏ **D.** DVI

19. Which of the following has the fastest data throughput?

   ◯ **A.** CD-ROM

   ◯ **B.** Hard drive

   ◯ **C.** RAM

   ◯ **D.** USB

20. Which of the following CPU cooling methods is the most common?

   ◯ **A.** Heat sink

   ◯ **B.** Heat sink and fan

   ◯ **C.** Liquid cooling

   ◯ **D.** Liquid nitrogen

21. You are tasked with fixing a problem with a video editing workstation. There is an unexpected clicking noise every time the video editing program is started. The case fans have been replaced, but the noise remains. Diagnostics have also been run on the video card, and it appears to be operating normally. What action should you take first?

   ◯ **A.** Perform a System Restore.

   ◯ **B.** Replace the video card.

   ◯ **C.** Replace the hard drive.

   ◯ **D.** Perform a full data backup.

   ◯ **E.** Scan for malware.

22. Which of the following is not a video port?

   ◯ **A.** DVI

   ◯ **B.** HDMI

   ◯ **C.** DisplayPort

   ◯ **D.** S/PDIF

23. Which of the following is necessary for a CAD/CAM workstation? (Select the two best answers.)

Quick Answer: **24**
Detailed Answer: **29**

- ❏ **A.** SSD
- ❏ **B.** HDMI output
- ❏ **C.** Surround sound
- ❏ **D.** High-end video

24. Which of the following technologies allows two mobile devices to transfer data simply by touching them together?

Quick Answer: **24**
Detailed Answer: **30**

- ○ **A.** USB
- ○ **B.** NFC
- ○ **C.** Bluetooth
- ○ **D.** Wi-Fi

25. What type of power connector is used for a x16 video card?

Quick Answer: **24**
Detailed Answer: **30**

- ○ **A.** Molex 4-pin
- ○ **B.** SATA 15-pin
- ○ **C.** PCIe 6-pin
- ○ **D.** P1 24-pin

26. Which of the following are output devices? (Select the three best answers.)

Quick Answer: **24**
Detailed Answer: **30**

- ❏ **A.** Speakers
- ❏ **B.** Keyboard
- ❏ **C.** Mouse
- ❏ **D.** Printer
- ❏ **E.** Display
- ❏ **F.** Touchpad

27. What does the b in 1000 Mbps stand for?

Quick Answer: **24**
Detailed Answer: **30**

- ○ **A.** Megabytes
- ○ **B.** Bits
- ○ **C.** Bytes
- ○ **D.** Bandwidth

28. When running cable through drop ceilings, which type of cable do you need?

Quick Answer: **24**
Detailed Answer: **30**

○ **A.** PVC

○ **B.** Category 5

○ **C.** Strong cable

○ **D.** Plenum

29. Which device connects multiple computers in a LAN?

Quick Answer: **24**
Detailed Answer: **31**

○ **A.** Modem

○ **B.** Router

○ **C.** Switch

○ **D.** Firewall

30. Which of the following is the default subnet mask for IP address 192.168.1.1?

Quick Answer: **24**
Detailed Answer: **31**

○ **A.** 255.255.0.0

○ **B.** 255.255.255.0

○ **C.** 255.0.0.0

○ **D.** 255.255.255.255

31. Which of the following is the minimum category cable needed for a 1000BASE-T network?

Quick Answer: **24**
Detailed Answer: **31**

○ **A.** Category 3

○ **B.** Category 5

○ **C.** Category 5e

○ **D.** Category 6

32. Which of the following IP addresses can be routed across the Internet?

Quick Answer: **24**
Detailed Answer: **31**

○ **A.** 127.0.0.1

○ **B.** 192.168.1.1

○ **C.** 129.52.50.13

○ **D.** 10.52.50.13

33. Which port number is used by HTTPS by default?

Quick Answer: **24**
Detailed Answer: **31**

○ **A.** 21

○ **B.** 25

○ **C.** 80

○ **D.** 443

34. Which of the following cable types have a copper medium? (Select the three best answers.)

- ❏ **A.** Twisted pair
- ❏ **B.** Coaxial
- ❏ **C.** Fiber optic
- ❏ **D.** Cat 7
- ❏ **E.** Multimode

Quick Answer: **24**
Detailed Answer: **32**

35. Which of the following cable types can protect from electromagnetic interference (EMI)? (Select the two best answers.)

- ❏ **A.** UTP
- ❏ **B.** STP
- ❏ **C.** Fiber optic
- ❏ **D.** Cat 6

Quick Answer: **24**
Detailed Answer: **32**

36. You are configuring Bob's computer to access the Internet. Which of the following are required? (Select all that apply.)

- ❏ **A.** DNS server address
- ❏ **B.** Gateway address
- ❏ **C.** Email server name
- ❏ **D.** DHCP server address
- ❏ **E.** Domain name

Quick Answer: **24**
Detailed Answer: **32**

37. Which of the following translates a computer name into an IP address?

- ○ **A.** TCP
- ○ **B.** UDP
- ○ **C.** DNS
- ○ **D.** FTP

Quick Answer: **24**
Detailed Answer: **32**

38. A customer wants to access the Internet from many different locations in the United States. Which of the following is the best technology to enable the customer to do so?

- ○ **A.** Infrared
- ○ **B.** Cellular WAN
- ○ **C.** Bluetooth
- ○ **D.** 802.11ac

Quick Answer: **24**
Detailed Answer: **32**

39. You just configured the IP address 192.168.0.105 in Windows. When you press the Tab key, Windows automatically configures the default subnet mask of 255.255.255.0. Which of the following IP addresses is a suitable gateway address?

Quick Answer: **24**
Detailed Answer: **33**

- O **A.** 192.168.1.100
- O **B.** 192.168.1.1
- O **C.** 192.168.10.1
- O **D.** 192.168.0.1

40. A wireless network is referred to as which of the following?

Quick Answer: **24**
Detailed Answer: **33**

- O **A.** SSID
- O **B.** WPA
- O **C.** DMZ
- O **D.** DHCP

41. You have been tasked with blocking remote logins to a server. Which of the following ports should you block?

Quick Answer: **24**
Detailed Answer: **33**

- O **A.** 21
- O **B.** 23
- O **C.** 80
- O **D.** 443
- O **E.** 587

42. Which of the following connector types is used by fiber-optic cabling?

Quick Answer: **24**
Detailed Answer: **33**

- O **A.** LC
- O **B.** RJ45
- O **C.** RG-6
- O **D.** RJ11

43. Which protocol uses port 53?

Quick Answer: **24**
Detailed Answer: **33**

- O **A.** FTP
- O **B.** SMTP
- O **C.** DNS
- O **D.** HTTP

44. Which of the following Internet services are wireless? (Select the two best answers.)

Quick Answer: **24**
Detailed Answer: **33**

- ❏ **A.** Cable Internet
- ❏ **B.** Satellite
- ❏ **C.** DSL
- ❏ **D.** Cellular
- ❏ **E.** Fiber optic

45. Which of the following terms best describes two or more LANs connected over a large geographic distance?

Quick Answer: **24**
Detailed Answer: **34**

- ○ **A.** PAN
- ○ **B.** WAN
- ○ **C.** WLAN
- ○ **D.** MAN

46. Which device connects to the network and has the sole purpose of providing data to clients?

Quick Answer: **24**
Detailed Answer: **34**

- ○ **A.** NAS
- ○ **B.** NAT
- ○ **C.** NAC
- ○ **D.** IaaS

47. You are making your own networking patch cable. You need to attach an RJ45 plug to the end of a twisted-pair cable. Which tool should you use?

Quick Answer: **24**
Detailed Answer: **34**

- ○ **A.** Tone and probe kit
- ○ **B.** Cable tester
- ○ **C.** Crimper
- ○ **D.** Multimeter

48. Which port is used by RDP?

Quick Answer: **24**
Detailed Answer: **34**

- ○ **A.** 80
- ○ **B.** 110
- ○ **C.** 443
- ○ **D.** 3389

49. Which key on a laptop aids in switching to an external monitor?

Quick Answer: **24**
Detailed Answer: **34**

- ○ **A.** Fn
- ○ **B.** Ctrl
- ○ **C.** Alt
- ○ **D.** Shift

50. Which of the following printer failures can be described as a condition in which the internal feed mechanism stopped working temporarily?

Quick Answer: **24**
Detailed Answer: **35**

- ○ **A.** No connectivity
- ○ **B.** Corrupt driver
- ○ **C.** Paper jam
- ○ **D.** Power cycle

51. A customer can barely hear sound from the speakers on her laptop. What should you do first?

Quick Answer: **24**
Detailed Answer: **35**

- ○ **A.** Install a new sound driver.
- ○ **B.** Tap the speakers.
- ○ **C.** Search for a volume key.
- ○ **D.** Reinstall Windows.

52. After you replace a motherboard in a PC, the system overheats and fails to boot. Which of the following is the most likely cause?

Quick Answer: **24**
Detailed Answer: **35**

- ○ **A.** The GPU is not compatible with the CPU.
- ○ **B.** The new motherboard's firmware is out of date.
- ○ **C.** Thermal paste was not applied between the heat sink and the CPU.
- ○ **D.** The case fan failed.

53. You use your laptop often. Which of the following is a simple, free way to keep your laptop running cool?

Quick Answer: **24**
Detailed Answer: **35**

- ○ **A.** Keep the laptop on a flat surface.
- ○ **B.** Put the laptop in the freezer when not in use.
- ○ **C.** Direct a fan at the laptop.
- ○ **D.** Keep the laptop turned off whenever possible.

54. Which of the following are important factors when purchasing a replacement laptop AC adapter? (Select the two best answers.)

- ❏ **A.** Current and voltage
- ❏ **B.** Connector size and shape
- ❏ **C.** Battery type
- ❏ **D.** Inverter type

55. Eric uses an external monitor with his laptop. He tells you that his laptop will boot, but the system won't display anything on the external screen. Which of the following solutions enables the display?

- ○ **A.** Connect the laptop to another external monitor.
- ○ **B.** Press the Fn and Screen keys one or more times until an image appears on the screen.
- ○ **C.** Press the Enter and Esc keys while the laptop is booting.
- ○ **D.** Press the Fn key while the laptop is booting.

56. Which type of printer uses a toner cartridge?

- ○ **A.** Inkjet
- ○ **B.** Laser
- ○ **C.** Impact
- ○ **D.** Thermal

57. Which of the following should *not* be connected to a UPS?

- ○ **A.** PCs
- ○ **B.** Monitors
- ○ **C.** Laser printers
- ○ **D.** Speakers

58. Terri finishes installing a printer for a customer. What should she do next?

- ○ **A.** Verify that the printer prints by using Microsoft Word.
- ○ **B.** Print a test page.
- ○ **C.** Restart the spooler.
- ○ **D.** Set up a separator page.

59. Which of the following best describes printing in duplex?

Quick Answer: 24
Detailed Answer: 37

- ○ **A.** Printing on both sides of the paper
- ○ **B.** Printer collation
- ○ **C.** Full-duplex printer communication
- ○ **D.** Printing to file

60. Special paper is needed to print on which type of printer?

Quick Answer: 24
Detailed Answer: 37

- ○ **A.** Impact
- ○ **B.** Thermal
- ○ **C.** Laser
- ○ **D.** Inkjet
- ○ **E.** 3D

61. Which of the following channels should you select for an 802.11 wireless network?

Quick Answer: 24
Detailed Answer: 37

- ○ **A.** 6
- ○ **B.** 21
- ○ **C.** 802
- ○ **D.** 8080

62. Which environmental issue affects a thermal printer the most?

Quick Answer: 24
Detailed Answer: 37

- ○ **A.** Moisture
- ○ **B.** ESD
- ○ **C.** Dirt
- ○ **D.** Heat

63. Which of the following occurs last in the laser printing process?

Quick Answer: 24
Detailed Answer: 38

- ○ **A.** Charging
- ○ **B.** Exposing
- ○ **C.** Developing
- ○ **D.** Fusing
- ○ **E.** Cleaning

64. Which type of printer uses impact to transfer ink from a ribbon to the paper?

- ○ **A.** Laser
- ○ **B.** Inkjet
- ○ **C.** Impact
- ○ **D.** Thermal

65. Which of the following steps enables you to take control of a network printer from a remote computer?

- ○ **A.** Installing the printer locally and accessing the Sharing tab
- ○ **B.** Installing the printer locally and accessing the spool settings
- ○ **C.** Installing the printer locally and accessing the Ports tab
- ○ **D.** Connecting to the printer via FTP

66. A color laser printer produces images that are tinted blue. Which of the following steps should be performed to address this problem?

- ○ **A.** Clean the toner cartridge
- ○ **B.** Calibrate the printer
- ○ **C.** Change the fusing assembly
- ○ **D.** Clean the primary corona

67. A laptop cannot access the wireless network. Which of the following statements best describes the most likely causes for this? (Select the two best answers.)

- ❏ **A.** The function key for wireless was pressed by accident.
- ❏ **B.** The user installed a new web browser.
- ❏ **C.** The wireless network was forgotten in Windows.
- ❏ **D.** The computer is obtaining an IP address automatically.

68. A desktop computer does not have a lit link light on the back of the computer. Which of the following is the most likely reason for this?

- ○ **A.** Wi-Fi was disabled.
- ○ **B.** USB is malfunctioning.
- ○ **C.** The system did not POST correctly.
- ○ **D.** The network cable is disconnected.

69. Which of the following IP addresses would a technician see if a computer running Windows is connected to a multifunction network device and is attempting to obtain an IP address automatically but is not receiving an IP address from the DHCP server?

- ○ **A.** 172.16.10.10
- ○ **B.** 192.168.0.10
- ○ **C.** 169.254.10.10
- ○ **D.** 192.168.10.10

70. For which type of PC component are 80 mm and 120 mm common sizes?

- ○ **A.** Case fans
- ○ **B.** CPUs
- ○ **C.** Heat sinks
- ○ **D.** Memory modules

71. An exclamation point next to a device in the Device Manager indicates which of the following?

- ○ **A.** A driver is not properly installed for this device.
- ○ **B.** The device is disabled.
- ○ **C.** The driver is not digitally signed.
- ○ **D.** The device driver needs to be upgraded.

72. Beep codes are generated by which of the following?

- ○ **A.** CMOS
- ○ **B.** RTC
- ○ **C.** POST
- ○ **D.** Windows

73. Which of the following indicates that a printer is network-ready?

- ○ **A.** An RJ11 jack
- ○ **B.** A USB connector
- ○ **C.** An RJ45 jack
- ○ **D.** An SCSI connector

74. You just turned off a printer to maintain it. Which of the following should you be careful of when removing the fuser?

Quick Answer: **24**
Detailed Answer: **40**

- ○ **A.** The fuser being hot
- ○ **B.** The fuser being wet
- ○ **C.** The fuser being fragile
- ○ **D.** The fuser releasing toner

75. Which of the following connectors is used for musical equipment?

Quick Answer: **24**
Detailed Answer: **40**

- ○ **A.** MIDI
- ○ **B.** HDMI
- ○ **C.** DVI
- ○ **D.** DisplayPort

76. Which of the following tools is not used as often as a Phillips screwdriver but is sometimes used to remove screws from the outside of a computer case or from within a laptop?

Quick Answer: **24**
Detailed Answer: **41**

- ○ **A.** Monkey wrench
- ○ **B.** Torx screwdriver
- ○ **C.** Spudger
- ○ **D.** Pliers

77. Moving your CPU's speed beyond its normal operating range is called _____.

Quick Answer: **24**
Detailed Answer: **41**

- ○ **A.** Overclocking
- ○ **B.** Overdriving
- ○ **C.** Overpowering
- ○ **D.** Overspeeding

78. Which of the following is the most important piece of information needed to connect to a specific wireless network?

Quick Answer: **24**
Detailed Answer: **41**

- ○ **A.** Channel
- ○ **B.** MAC address
- ○ **C.** SSID
- ○ **D.** Administrator password

79. You are considering a cloud-based service for file storage and synchronization. Which of the following resources is the most critical to your design?

    ○ **A.** Disk speed

    ○ **B.** RAM utilization

    ○ **C.** CPU utilization

    ○ **D.** I/O bandwidth

Quick Answer: **24**
Detailed Answer: **41**

80. Which of the following statements describes why the display on a laptop gets dimmer when the power supply from the AC outlet is disconnected?

    ○ **A.** The laptop cannot use full brightness when on battery power.

    ○ **B.** Power management settings on the laptop are configured for power-saving.

    ○ **C.** To operate properly, laptop displays require an alternating current power source.

    ○ **D.** Security settings on the laptop are configured to dim the display.

Quick Answer: **24**
Detailed Answer: **42**

Quick-Check Answer Key

1. A, B, E	**28.** D	**55.** B
2. C	**29.** C	**56.** B
3. B	**30.** B	**57.** C
4. B	**31.** C	**58.** B
5. C	**32.** C	**59.** A
6. A, D	**33.** D	**60.** B
7. A, C	**34.** A, B, D	**61.** A
8. C	**35.** B, C	**62.** D
9. A	**36.** A, B	**63.** E
10. C, E	**37.** C	**64.** C
11. B	**38.** B	**65.** C
12. A	**39.** D	**66.** B
13. C	**40.** A	**67.** A, C
14. D	**41.** B	**68.** D
15. B	**42.** A	**69.** C
16. B	**43.** C	**70.** A
17. D	**44.** B, D	**71.** A
18. B, C	**45.** B	**72.** C
19. C	**46.** A	**73.** C
20. B	**47.** C	**74.** A
21. D	**48.** D	**75.** A
22. D	**49.** A	**76.** B
23. A, D	**50.** C	**77.** A
24. B	**51.** C	**78.** C
25. C	**52.** C	**79.** D
26. A, D, E	**53.** A	**80.** B
27. B	**54.** A, B	

Answers and Explanations

1. Answers: A, B, and E

Explanation: Common components inside a PC include the CPU, motherboard, and RAM, along with the power supply, adapter cards, and hard drives.

Incorrect answers: Keyboards (and mice) are input devices that are located outside the PC. Printers (and displays) are output devices that are located outside the PC. A cable modem is an Internet communication device that is outside the PC. *Know the internal components of a PC!*

2. Answer: C

Explanation: The hard drive stores data over the long term. The hard drive stores the OS and data in a nonvolatile fashion, meaning the data won't be erased when the computer is turned off.

Incorrect answers: The CPU calculates data and sends it to RAM for temporary storage; the RAM (which is volatile) is cleared when the computer is turned off. The video card stores temporary video data within its onboard memory, but this, like RAM, is volatile and is cleared when the computer is turned off.

3. Answer: B

Explanation: PCI Express (PCIe) expansion slots accept x1, x4, and x16 cards (pronounced "by one", "by four", and "by sixteen" respectively).

Incorrect answers: PCIe is by far the most common expansion slot for video cards (which are usually x16). Thunderbolt is a technology used primarily with Mac computers for displays and for data transfer. USB stands for universal serial bus; it is a standard for connecting external equipment to a computer, not an expansion bus for use with cards. DisplayPort is a video technology that acts as connectivity between the video card and the monitor.

4. Answer: B

Explanation: The POST (power-on self-test) is part of the Basic Input/Output System (BIOS) or Unified Extensible Firmware Interface (UEFI). It runs a self-check of the computer system during boot and stores many of the parameters of the components within the CMOS.

Incorrect answers: BIOS is known as firmware. The lithium battery powers the CMOS while the computer is off. It remembers settings such as the time and date and passwords. The CMOS, BIOS, and the lithium battery are not processes, but they do work hand in hand with each other.

5. Answer: C

Explanation: Without the thermal compound applied, the processor might overheat after a few hours.

Incorrect answers: If the CPU is not locked down or is not properly seated, the PC will simply fail to boot. If the CPU is not compatible with the motherboard, either it will not fit the socket or the PC will not boot.

6. **Answers: A and D**

   Explanation: The CPU and memory need to be installed properly for the POST to run (and to pass).

   Incorrect answers: The hard drive and optical drive may or may not be installed properly, but they are not necessary for the POST to complete. If the power supply is defective, the system simply will not boot and will not even get to the POST stage.

7. **Answers: A and C**

   Explanation: A tablet computer will almost always contain flash memory as main storage and a multi-touch touchscreen.

   Incorrect answers: SATA hard drives and 24-inch displays are more likely to be found on PCs, not tablet computers.

8. **Answer: C**

   Explanation: LGA (land grid array) is the type of socket that uses "lands" to connect the socket to the CPU.

   Incorrect answers: PGA (pin grid array) sockets have pinholes that make for connectivity to the CPU's copper pins. The chipset is either a single chip or the combination of the northbridge and southbridge on the motherboard. LGA sockets are often a brass alloy or have gold contacts; although copper might be a possibility for some sockets, such sockets don't fit the description of "lands" in the question. LGA is the best answer.

9. **Answer: A**

   Explanation: Hold RAM by the edges to avoid contact with the pins, chips, and circuitry.

   Incorrect answers: Touching the front and back is not advised because it requires touching the chips on the RAM module. Tools are not needed, and if they are used, metallic ones could be damaging to the module. Plastic tweezers are used to remove screws that fall into tough-to-reach places in the case. A punchdown tool is used to terminate networking cables to patch panels or to punch blocks.

10. **Answers: C and E**

    Explanation: You should incorporate a solid-state drive (SSD) and dual monitors for the video editing workstation. Video files, such as .MP4 and .AVI, are considerable; they are big files that require a decent-size hard drive. An SSD, possibly an M.2 or similar drive, helps to work with these files efficiently, especially in the video rendering stage. And having dual monitors (or more than two) is important when editing. You will generally want to have an editing window and a separate playback window.

    Incorrect answers: A gigabit NIC is quite common. Chances are that the computer will have it already, but this, and especially 10 Gbit NICs, are more important for servers. The hypervisor is the type of virtualization software manager that you are using—for example, VMware or VirtualBox. A docking station is a device used with a laptop to charge it and to replicate video and other peripherals. Network-attached storage (NAS) is a storage device with multiple hard drives that connects directly to the network. It often uses magnetic drives; SSDs are not required. It doesn't use a screen; instead, you remotely administer it, usually from a browser.

11. **Answer: B**

    Explanation: The SATA version 3.0 data connector has seven pins. Note: SATA Express uses a triple connector with 18 pins (7 + 7 + 4).

    Incorrect answers: The SATA power connector has 15 pins. ATX 12V 2.0 and higher power connections have 24 pins. Among other things, 127 is the maximum number of USB devices you can connect to the computer.

12. **Answer: A**

    Explanation: Memory latency or CAS (column address strobe) latency happens when a memory controller tries to access data from a memory module. It is a slight delay (usually measured in nanoseconds) while the memory module responds to the memory controller. It is also known as *CL*. The memory controller (also known as the northbridge) has a specific speed at which it operates. If the CPU asks the chip for too much information at once, this might increase latency time while the memory controller works.

    Incorrect answers: The terms *standard deviation* and *fetch interval* deal with CPUs. *Lag* is a term that is similar to latency but is more commonly associated with network connections.

13. **Answer: C**

    Explanation: Because RAID 5 uses striping with parity, a third disk is needed. You can have more than three disks as well.

    Incorrect answers: Two disks are enough for plain RAID 0 striping, so two is the exact number you need for RAID 1 mirroring. RAID 6 and RAID 10 require four disks.

14. **Answer: D**

    Explanation: If the time and date keep resetting—for example, to a date such as January 1, 2012—chances are that the lithium battery needs to be replaced. These are usually nickel-sized batteries; most PCs use a CR2032 lithium battery.

    Incorrect answers: Updating the UEFI/BIOS allows the PC to "see" new devices and communicate with them better, but it will not fix the time issue. Updating Windows will not fix this problem, but it should be done often to keep the computer secure. Other date and time synchronization problems can be fixed in the clock settings within the Notification Area. Windows client computers should be configured to synchronize to a time server.

15. **Answer: B**

    Explanation: The PCI Express (PCIe) x16 expansion slot is used primarily for video.

    Incorrect answers: Modems, network interface cards (NICs), and sound cards usually connect to a PCIe x1 slot. Sometimes, cards require a minimum of PCIe x4.

16. **Answer: B**

    Explanation: System on a chip (SoC) is a type of CPU used in smartphones and tablet computers. The 64-bit versions are common in mobile devices; they incorporate a variety of functionality within the CPU.

    Incorrect answers: LGA 2011 is a type of CPU socket used in PCs. It is designed for Intel Core i7 and other Intel CPUs. LPDDR is a common type of RAM used in mobile devices.

17. **Answer: D**

    Explanation: RAM is one of the big four (RAM, CPU, motherboard, and video) that can cause the POST to fail. Different RAM errors can cause the POST to make a different series of beeps. Consult your motherboard documentation for more information about the different beep codes.

    Incorrect answers: The sound card does not have an effect on the POST. If the power supply has a problem, the computer either will not boot at all (and not even enter POST) or will have intermittent problems—for example, shutting down unpredictably. Hard drive problems result in a variety of errors. Although the POST will complete in these cases, the operating system will not boot.

18. **Answers: B and C**

    Explanation: Mobile devices such as smartphones and tablets commonly incorporate ports such as USB-C (and micro USB) and Apple's Lightning connector.

    Incorrect answers: eSATA (used by external storage devices) and DVI (used by video cards) are commonly found on PCs.

19. **Answer: C**

    Explanation: RAM is much faster than the rest of the options listed. For instance, if you have PC4-25600 DDR4 RAM (aka DDR4-3200), your peak transfer rate is 25,600 MB/s.

    Incorrect answers: The rest of the devices in the incorrect answers are listed in descending order of data throughput:

    Hard drive: for example, 600 MB/s for SATA 3.0, 1969 MB/s for SATA Express, and 3500 MB/s for typical M.2 drives. M.2 is very fast but still a fraction of RAM speeds (as of the writing of this book in 2019).

    USB: for example, 5 Gbps for version 3.0 and 20 Gbps for version 3.2 (which equates to 2.5 GB/s)

    CD-ROM (typically 7.5 MB/s).

20. **Answer: B**

Explanation: The most common CPU cooling method is the heat sink and fan combination. The heat sink helps the heat to disperse away from the CPU, whereas the fan blows the heat down and through the fins; the power supply exhaust fan and possibly additional case fans help the heat escape the case. Heat sink and fan combinations are known as active cooling methods.

Incorrect answers: The heat sink by itself is called passive cooling; it requires no power but is not enough to cool most desktop PCs. Liquid cooling is a more extreme method used in custom PCs such as gaming computers and possibly audio/video workstations and virtualization machines. It uses a coolant similar to the way an automobile does. Liquid nitrogen would be plain foolish and is not a legitimate answer.

21. **Answer: D**

Explanation: The first action you should take is to perform a full data backup. Clicking noises can indicate that the computer's magnetic-based hard drive is damaged and might fail. Immediately back up the drive's contents before taking any other action.

Incorrect answers: It is less likely, but the clicking noise can also be caused by a fan. However, the case fans have already been replaced, and it is uncommon for a video card fan to make that noise unless a cable is brushing against it (which is also unlikely). As you gain experience, you will find that fan noise and hard disk drive clicking are usually two different sounds. The damage to the hard drive could possibly be caused by malware. After backing up data, scan the drive, and if necessary, run a System Restore. The video card should not need to be replaced because the diagnostics indicate that it is running normally. After the backup, you should strongly consider replacing the hard drive, for two reasons: (1) the drive is clicking and is probably going to fail, and (2) video editing workstations require faster hard drives. The scenario implies that the system is using a magnetic-based hard drive. A solid-state drive (SATA or M.2) would run the video editing program more efficiently and would be better in the file-rendering phase.

22. **Answer: D**

Explanation: S/PDIF is not a video port. It stands for Sony/Philips digital interface format—a digital audio interconnect that can be used with fiber-optic TOSLINK connectors or coaxial RCA connectors.

Incorrect answers: DVI is the Digital Visual Interface, one of the most common outputs on PC video cards. HDMI is the High-Definition Multimedia Interface, another common video standard, especially in laptops, home theaters, and home theater PCs (HTPCs). DisplayPort is another video standard used by some PCs that has the ability to display high resolutions.

23. **Answers: A and D**

Explanation: A computer-aided design/computer-aided manufacturing workstation requires an SSD, high-end video, and as much RAM as possible. The CPU can also be important to run the latest design applications such as AutoCAD. Always check the minimum and *recommended* requirements for applications.

Incorrect answers: HDMI output and surround sound are often necessary on gaming computers and home theater PCs (HTPCs).

24. **Answer: B**

Explanation: Near field communication (NFC) allows two mobile devices such as smartphones to transfer data simply by touching them together (or bringing them in very close proximity of each other).

Incorrect answers: A USB port (for example, micro USB) allows for the transfer and synchronization of data, but to and from a mobile device and a PC or laptop. Bluetooth and Wi-Fi enable wireless connectivity but do not require that the devices touch or be in close proximity.

25. **Answer: C**

Explanation: A x16 card is a PCI Express card. It can have one or two PCIe 6-pin power connectors (or 8-pin).

Incorrect answers: Molex 4-pin power connectors are used by secondary devices, such as fans, monitoring devices, and older IDE hard drives. SATA 15-pin power connections are used by SATA-compliant hard drives and optical drives. P1 24-pin power is the main power connection that the motherboard gets from the power supply.

26. **Answers: A, D, and E**

Explanation: Speakers, printers, and displays are output devices. A speaker outputs sound. A printer outputs paper with text and graphics. A display (or monitor) displays video.

Incorrect answers: Keyboards, mice, and touchpads are input devices. Another input device used by mobile devices is the stylus. A stylus is used on mobile devices that incorporate touchscreens. This pen-like device is used to manipulate the display, similar to a mouse. However, most mobile devices now allow a person to simply use a finger and tap on the screen.

27. **Answer: B**

Explanation: The *b* in 1000 Mbps stands for bits: 1000 Mbps is 1000 megabits per second or 1 gigabit per second. Remember that the lowercase *b* is used to indicate bits when measuring network data transfer rates, USB data transfer rates, and other similar serial data transfers.

Incorrect answers: *Bytes* and *megabytes* refer to parallel data transfers or the calculation and storage of data where 8 bits equal a standard byte of information. Network data transfer rates are also known as speed or bandwidth.

28. **Answer: D**

Explanation: Plenum-rated cable needs to be installed wherever a sprinkler system is not able to spray water. This includes ceilings, walls, and plenums (airways). Plenum-rated cable has a protective covering that burns slower and gives off fewer toxic fumes than regular PVC-based cable.

Incorrect answers: PVCs in regular cable give off toxic fumes in the case of a fire. Category 5 cable can be obtained in regular or plenum-rated versions. "Strong cable" is rather vague.

29. **Answer: C**

Explanation: A switch connects computers together in a local-area network (LAN). In SOHO networks, it is usually a part of a multifunction network device. In larger networks, the switch is an individual device that has 24, 48, or 96 ports.

Incorrect answers: A modem connects a PC to the Internet either by way of a coaxial cable connection (as in a cable modem) or a dial-up connection over a plain old telephone service (POTS) line (as in a dial-up modem). A router connects one network to another. Though a SOHO multifunction device is often referred to as a *router*, it is not the router portion of that device that connects the computers in the LAN. A firewall protects all the computers on the LAN from intrusion.

30. **Answer: B**

Explanation: 192.168.1.1, by default, has the subnet mask 255.255.255.0, which is the standard subnet mask for class C IP addresses. However, remember that some networks are classless, which means that a network can use a different subnet mask.

Incorrect answers: 255.255.0.0 is the class B default subnet mask. 255.0.0.0 is the class A default subnet mask. 255.255.255.255 is the broadcast address for IP. It is not usable as a subnet mask for typical computers on the LAN.

31. **Answer: C**

Explanation: The minimum cable needed for 1000BASE-T networks is Category 5e. Of course, Cat 6 would also work, but it is not the minimum of the listed answers. 1000BASE-T specifies the speed of the network (1000 Mbps), the type (baseband, single shared channel), and the cable to be used (T = twisted pair).

Incorrect answers: Cat 3 is an older type of cable that is suitable for 10 Mbps networks. Cat 5 is typically suitable for 100 Mbps networks. Another type of cable, Category 7, is a newer and even faster version of twisted pair; it is used in 1 Gbps and 10 Gbps networks.

32. **Answer: C**

Explanation: The only listed answer that is a public address (needed to get onto the Internet) is 129.52.50.13.

Incorrect answers: All the other answers are private IPs, meant to be behind a firewall. 127.0.0.1 is the IPv4 local loopback IP address. 192.168.1.1 is a common private IP address used by SOHO networking devices. 10.52.50.13 is a private address. Note that the 10 network is common in larger networks.

33. **Answer: D**

Explanation: The Hypertext Transfer Protocol Secure (HTTPS) uses port 443 (by default).

Incorrect answers: Port 21 is used by the File Transfer Protocol (FTP). Port 25 is used by the Simple Mail Transfer Protocol (SMTP). Port 80 is used by regular HTTP, which is considered to be insecure.

34. Answers: A, B, and D

Explanation: Twisted-pair, coaxial, and Category 7 cable are all examples of network cables with a copper medium. They all send electricity over copper wire.

Incorrect answers: Multimode is a type of fiber-optic cable; it uses light to send data over a glass or plastic medium. Twisted pair is the most common type of cabling used in today's networks.

35. Answers: B and C

Explanation: Shielded twisted pair (STP) and fiber optic can protect from EMI.

Incorrect answers: Unshielded twisted pair (UTP) cannot protect from EMI. Unless otherwise mentioned, Category 6 cable is UTP. STP is shielded twisted pair. Unlike UTP (unshielded twisted pair), STP provides an aluminum shield that protects from EMI. UTP and coaxial have no such protection. Fiber optic uses a different medium altogether, transmitting light rather than electricity; therefore, EMI cannot affect fiber-optic cables.

36. Answers: A and B

Explanation: To get on the Internet, the DNS server address is required so that the computer can get the resolved IP addresses from the domain names that are typed in. The gateway address is necessary to get outside the network.

Incorrect answers: Email server information is not necessary if the person is just looking to get on the Internet. A DHCP server address is not necessary either; however, it is an easier method. The beauty of DHCP is that you don't need to know the DHCP server's address to acquire an IP address. The domain name for your network is normally not needed, either; it is necessary only if you want to add the computer to the organization's domain.

37. Answer: C

Explanation: The Domain Name System (DNS) protocol translates a computer name into an IP address. Whenever you type a web server name such as dprocomputer.com, a DNS server translates that name to its corresponding IP address.

Incorrect answers: The Transmission Control Protocol (TCP) is used to send data from one computer to another utilizing a guaranteed delivery system. User Datagram Protocol (UDP), on the other hand, sends data in a streaming format, without the need for guaranteed delivery. The File Transfer Protocol (FTP) allows you to send files between computers over the Internet.

38. Answer: B

Explanation: Cellular WAN uses a phone or other mobile device to send data over standard cellular connections.

Incorrect answers: By themselves, the other options don't offer a direct connection to the Internet. Infrared is used more often for very short distance connections, allowing data to be "beamed" from one device to another. Bluetooth is also for short distances, but not as short as infrared. Bluetooth headsets are commonly used with smartphones. 802.11ac is a Wi-Fi technology for the LAN.

39. **Answer: D**

    Explanation: 192.168.0.1 is the only suitable gateway address. Remember that the gateway address must be on the same network as the computer. In this case, the network is 192.168.0, as defined by the 255.255.255.0 subnet mask.

    Incorrect answers: 192.168.1.100 is on the 192.168.1.0 network; so is 192.168.1.1. 192.168.10.1 is on the 192.168.10.0 network. Don't forget that a zero at the end of an IP address denotes the network number.

40. **Answer: A**

    Explanation: The Service Set Identifier (SSID) is the name of the wireless network. This is the name you look for when locating a wireless network.

    Incorrect answers: WPA stands for Wi-Fi Protected Access, a connectivity protocol for wireless networks. A demilitarized zone (DMZ) is an area between the LAN and the Internet that often houses web, email, and FTP servers. The Dynamic Host Configuration Protocol (DHCP) is a service that assigns IP addresses automatically to computers and other devices.

41. **Answer: B**

    Explanation: Port 23 should be blocked. It is associated with the Telnet service, which is used to remotely log in to a server at the command line. You can block this service at the company firewall and individually at the server and other hosts. It uses port 23 by default, but it can be used with other ports as well. Telnet is considered to be insecure, so it should be blocked and disabled.

    Incorrect answers: Here are the default port numbers for the incorrect answers: Port 21 is FTP. Port 80 is HTTP. Port 443 is HTTPS. Port 587 is the default secure port for SMTP. (Keep in mind that, originally, SMTP used port 25—and sometimes still does—but it is usually not a secured port.)

42. **Answer: A**

    Explanation: The LC connector is used by fiber-optic cabling. Other fiber connectors include SC and ST.

    Incorrect answers: RJ45 is the connector used by twisted-pair networks. RG-6 is the cable used by cable Internet and TV; an F-connector is attached to the ends of an RG-6 cable. RJ11 is the standard phone line connector.

43. **Answer: C**

    Explanation: The Domain Name System (DNS) protocol uses port 53 by default.

    Incorrect answers: FTP uses port 21. SMTP uses port 25 (or 587 or 465). HTTP uses port 80.

44. **Answers: B and D**

    Explanation: Satellite and cellular are examples of wireless Internet services.

    Incorrect answers: Cable Internet, DSL, and fiber optic all use wired connections.

45. Answer: B

Explanation: A wide-area network (WAN) is a network in which two or more LANs are connected over a large geographic distance—for example, between two cities. The WAN requires connections to be provided by a telecommunications or data communications company.

Incorrect answers: A personal-area network (PAN) is a small network made up of short-distance devices such as Bluetooth. WLAN stands for wireless local-area network. This is the name that the IEEE uses for its 802.11 standards. The reason is that the term *Wi-Fi*, though widely used, is copyrighted. A MAN is a metropolitan- (or municipal-) area network; it can connect two or more LANs but does so in a small city-based area.

46. Answer: A

Explanation: Network-attached storage (NAS) devices store data for network use. They connect directly to the network.

Incorrect answers: Network Address Translation (NAT) is used on routers to take a group of computers on a private LAN and connect them to the Internet by using a single public IP. NAC stands for network access control—a group of technologies designed to allow or deny access by authenticating users. IaaS stands for infrastructure as a service, a cloud-based technology by which organizations can offload their network infrastructure to a third-party. Threw in a tougher one there—have to keep you on your toes!

47. Answer: C

Explanation: Use an RJ45 crimper tool to permanently attach RJ45 plugs to the end of a cable.

Incorrect answers: You use a tone generator and probe kit to locate individual phone lines, but you can also use it with network lines. The better tool, however, for testing and locating is a continuity cable tester. A multimeter is great for testing AC outlets and for testing wires inside a computer, but it is not often used in networking applications.

48. Answer: D

Explanation: The Remote Desktop Protocol (RDP) uses port 3389 by default. This protocol allows one computer to take control of another remote system.

Incorrect answers: Port 80 is used by HTTP. Port 110 is used by POP3. Port 443 is used by HTTP Secure (or HTTPS), a protocol used during secure web sessions.

49. Answer: A

Explanation: The Fn (Function) key is used for a variety of things, including toggling between the built-in LCD screen and an external monitor/TV. The Fn key could be a different color (for example, blue) and offers a sort of "second" usage for keys on the laptop.

Incorrect answers: Ctrl may also have secondary functions but is otherwise used the same as on a PC's keyboard. Alt and Shift work in the same manner as they do on a PC.

50. **Answer: C**

    Explanation: A failure that occurs due to the internal feed mechanism stopping is known as a paper jam. For example, an HP LaserJet might show error code 13.1 on the display, which means a paper jam at the paper feed area. You should verify that the paper trays are loaded and adjusted properly.

    Incorrect answers: A No Connectivity message means that the printer is not currently connected to the network. A corrupt driver loaded on a workstation would cause any print job from that computer either to fail or to print nonsense. A Power Cycle message means that the self-diagnostic program has encountered a problem and is telling you to shut down the printer and turn it back on. Doing so resets the printer, which can fix many of the issues that can occur.

51. **Answer: C**

    Explanation: Sometimes, the volume key(s) on laptops can be a little difficult to locate and may be muted or set to the lowest position (which might still make a slight audible noise). The volume is usually controlled by pressing the Fn key and the Volume Up or Volume Down key (or mute) simultaneously.

    Incorrect answers: Installing a new sound driver isn't necessary yet. Always check the physical volume first, and then check if the volume is low or the sound is muted in Windows. Tapping the speakers is an interesting idea, but it has no place in this discussion. If a speaker is loose, it often makes scratchy noises; however, speakers rarely become loose on today's laptops. Reinstalling Windows is the last thing you want to do. Check the simple solutions when troubleshooting problems such as no audio or video.

52. **Answer: C**

    Explanation: If the motherboard was just replaced and the system overheats when booted, there's a good chance that thermal paste was not applied to the CPU. When you install a new motherboard, the CPU must be removed from the old board and installed to the new one, or a new CPU needs to be installed. Either way, the heat sink must come off. Whenever a heat sink is connected (or reconnected) to a CPU, thermal compound (also known as thermal paste) should be applied; otherwise, overheating can easily occur.

    Incorrect answers: The GPU is the video card's processor; it is not possible for this to be incompatible with the CPU. It is possible for the video card to be incompatible with the expansion bus slots on the new motherboard, though. Even if the new motherboard's firmware has not been updated, the system should not overheat. If the case fan fails, the computer should not overheat. The CPU will still have its own fan, and the power supply will still exhaust hot air.

53. **Answer: A**

    Explanation: Laptops have airflow underneath them; if the unit is not on a flat surface, that airflow will be reduced or stopped altogether, leading to component damage.

    Incorrect answers: The freezer is not a good idea because condensation could build up inside the unit. A fan won't do much good unless the laptop is on a flat surface, and although it is plausible to keep the laptop turned off, doing so negates the reason for using the laptop.

54. **Answers: A and B**

Explanation: Make sure to purchase an AC adapter that is a true replacement. You can find one on the laptop manufacturer's website. When you enter your model number, the website will tell you everything you need to know about current, voltage, and connector type (these details are also listed on the brick portion of the power adapter).

Incorrect answers: The battery and AC adapter do need to work in conjunction with each other; because of this, they both need to be compatible with the laptop. The AC adapter does several things, including reducing voltage and converting from AC to DC, but it does not invert the signal. However, there is an inverter in the laptop; it powers the display. This question does not refer to that, but if you are ever troubleshooting a display, the inverter type is very important.

55. **Answer: B**

Explanation: The Screen key (also known as the display toggle) is one of the keys available when you use the Function (Fn) key. It enables you to switch between the laptop display and an external display (or if you want to use both).

Incorrect answers: If the display toggle doesn't work, try another external monitor. No other key combinations perform this task.

56. **Answer: B**

Explanation: Laser printers use toner cartridges.

Incorrect answers: Inkjet printers use ink cartridges. Impact printers (for example, dot-matrix printers) use a ribbon. Thermal printers use specially coated paper that is heated.

57. **Answer: C**

Explanation: Laser printers use large amounts of electricity, which in turn could quickly drain the battery of the UPS. They should be plugged in to their own individual power strips.

Incorrect answers: PCs, monitors, and speakers can be connected to a UPS. In fact, if you want to have continued use (and protection) during a power outage, they should be!

58. **Answer: B**

Explanation: Print a test page after installation. If the test page prints properly, printing a page in Word should be unnecessary.

Incorrect answers: Restarting the spooler is not necessary if the printer has just been installed. The spooler should already be running. If the spooler has failed, that would be a separate troubleshooting scenario. Separator pages are not necessary; they are optional and can be configured in the Printer Properties window.

59. Answer: A

Explanation: When you are printing "duplex," you are printing on both sides of the paper (if the printer has that capability). Some laser printers can do this, but printing this way creates a longer total paper path, which leads to more frequent paper jams.

Incorrect answers: Collation means that documents are printed in a standard order, usually numerically. Full-duplex in networking means that information can be sent and received simultaneously. A printer can have a full-duplex connection to the network, but this question refers to printing in duplex. Printing to file is a process that Windows can perform. Instead of selecting a physical printer when printing a document, Windows prints to a special file and saves that file to a location of your choice with a .prn extension.

60. Answer: B

Explanation: Regular paper can be used on all the listed printers except for thermal printers, which use specially coated paper that is heated to create the image.

Incorrect answers: A dot-matrix printer might use tractor-feed paper, but that is standard for many impact printers; it is also still considered regular paper. A laser printer or dot-matrix printer might use two-part paper, but two-part paper isn't necessary for laser printers or dot-matrix printers to operate; thermal printers won't work unless you use specially coated paper. Inkjet printers normally use standard copy paper for printing. Finally, 3D printers use a plastic filament, not paper.

61. Answer: A

Explanation: Of the listed answers, use channel 6 for 802.11 wireless networks. That would imply a 2.4 GHz connection using either 802.11n, g, or b. The 2.4 GHz frequency range in the United States allows for channels 1 through 11.

Incorrect answers: Of these answers, 21 is outside the allowable 2.4 GHz range for any country. On a separate note, it is a port number used with FTP. Here, 802 has no meaning other than it is the name of the IEEE protocol suite that includes wireless protocols such as 802.11ac. Also, it is far beyond the range of 5 GHz wireless networks, which range between 36 and 165. 8080 is a less commonly used HTTP port.

62. Answer: D

Explanation: Heat is the number-one enemy to a thermal printer. Keeping a thermal printer or the thermal paper in a location where the temperature is too high could cause failure of the printer and damage to the paper.

Incorrect answers: Excessive moisture can cause rubber rollers and separation pads to fail over time, especially in laser printers. Electrostatic discharge (ESD) is always a foe, but only if you are working inside the printer. Dirt can clog up the works over time in any device. But by far, heat is what you have to watch for with thermal printers.

63. Answer: E

Explanation: In the laser printing process, also known as the imaging process, the cleaning stage happens last.

Incorrect answers: The printing process includes the following steps in order: processing, charging, exposing, developing, transferring, fusing, and cleaning.

64. Answer: C

Explanation: Impact is a type of impact printer. It uses a printhead to physically impact the ribbon and transfer ink to the paper.

Incorrect answers: Laser printers apply toner to paper through varying voltages. Inkjet printers spray ink from a cartridge onto the paper. Thermal paper is specially coated and forms text when it is heated properly.

65. Answer: C

Explanation: After you install the driver for the printer locally, you can then take control of it by going to the properties of the printer and accessing the Ports tab. Then click the Add Port button and select the Standard TCP/IP Port option. You have to know the IP address of the printer or the computer that the printer is connected to.

Incorrect answers: The Sharing tab enables you to share the printer so that remote users can use it; however, the remote user would then somehow have to connect to the printer. The spool settings can be set so that the computer spools documents before sending pages to the printer, which helps with less powerful printers and printer congestion. Some printers can be accessed via FTP, but usually they are controlled and accessed in another way. Either way, making a connection to the printer is not taking control of the printer.

66. Answer: B

Explanation: After you install a printer, it is important to calibrate it for color and orientation, especially if you are installing a color laser printer or an inkjet printer. These calibration tools are usually built in to the printer's software and can be accessed from Windows, or you can access them from the printer's display.

Incorrect answers: If a toner cartridge needs to be cleaned, it probably has a leak and should be replaced. The fusing assembly needs to be changed only when it fails. Many printers will indicate when the fuser is at 20 percent life and needs to be replaced soon. If the fuser fails, the toner will fail to stick to the paper. The primary corona wire can be cleaned; it is near the drum. Cleaning it can help with other types of print quality problems, such as lines and smearing, though on many printers this is not necessary.

67. Answers: A and C

Explanation: Most laptops have a special function key (for example, F12) that allows you to enable or disable the Wi-Fi connection just by pressing it. Also, a wireless network can be "forgotten" in the operating system. If this happens, the laptop has to be reconnected to the wireless network.

Incorrect answers: After you are connected to a network, you can typically use whatever web browser you want, as long as the browser is compatible with the operating system in question. Client computers (such as laptops) normally obtain their IP addresses automatically from a DHCP server, so this is not a likely problem.

68. **Answer: D**

    Explanation: The most likely answer in this scenario is that the network cable is disconnected. If the desktop computer is using a wired connection, it is most likely a twisted-pair Ethernet connection. When this cable is connected to the computer on one end and to a switch or other central connecting device on the other end, it initiates a network connection over the physical link. This link then causes the network adapter's link light to light up. The link light is directly next to the RJ45 port of the network adapter. The corresponding port on the switch (or other similar device) is also lit. If the cable is disconnected, the link light becomes unlit, though there are other possibilities for this link light to be dark—for example, if the computer is off or if the switch port is disabled.

    Incorrect answers: The Wi-Fi connection might have its own link light (for example, on the front of a laptop), but this is separate from the wired connection link light. Although it is unlikely, a malfunctioning USB controller or port could possibly be the cause of the unlit link light, but only if the computer is using a USB-based network adapter. Normally, the network adapter (and corresponding RJ45 port) on a PC is either integrated into the motherboard or is installed as a PCIe x1 adapter card. If the system doesn't POST properly, it usually means a problem with the RAM, video, or other primary component of the system. Generally, a network adapter will not cause a failure during POST.

69. **Answer: C**

    Explanation: If the computer fails to obtain an IP address from a DHCP server, Windows will take over and apply an Automatic Private IP Address (APIPA). This address will be on the 169.254.0.0 network.

    Incorrect answers: All of the other addresses could possibly be obtained from a DHCP server. 172.16.10.10, 192.168.0.10, and 192.168.10.10 are all private IP addresses that could typically be obtained through DHCP.

70. **Answer: A**

    Explanation: Case fans are measured in mm (millimeters); 80 mm and especially 120 mm are very common. They are used to exhaust heat out of the case. These fans aid in keeping the CPU and other devices cool. The 120 mm is quite common in desktop and tower PCs, and the 80 mm is more common in smaller systems and 1U and 2U rackmount servers.

    Incorrect answers: CPUs commonly use a heat sink/fan combination. However, the two are often connected. Memory modules don't use fans, but they can be equipped (or purchased) with heat sinks of their own.

71. Answer: A

Explanation: If you see an exclamation point in the Device Manager, this indicates that the device does not have a proper driver.

Incorrect answers: If the device is disabled, it will have a down arrow. If a driver was not digitally signed, the device might show up in the Unknown Devices category until it is installed properly. If a device has a working driver, upgrading it will be up to you, but you won't necessarily be notified that the driver needs to be upgraded. This question may seem more like a 220-1002 question, but you have to be prepared for some overlap. Remember, some of the concepts of the 220-1001 and the 220-1002 are heavily intertwined!

72. Answer: C

Explanation: As the power-on self-test (POST) checks all the components of the computer, it may present its findings on the screen or in the form of beep codes.

Incorrect answers: The complementary metal-oxide semiconductor (CMOS) stores information such as time and date and UEFI/BIOS passwords. RTC stands for real-time clock; it is the device that keeps time on the motherboard. Windows generates all kinds of error codes but not beep codes. The beep codes come from the POST, which happens before Windows boots.

73. Answer: C

Explanation: The RJ45 jack enables a connection to a twisted-pair (most likely Ethernet) network. Printers with a built-in RJ45 connector are network-ready; so are printers that are Wi-Fi enabled.

Incorrect answers: RJ11 ports are used by modems and dial-up Internet connections. If a printer has this port, it is a multifunction printer acting as a fax machine. USB is the standard port for a printer. This port allows it to connect to a PC or to a print server. SCSI connectors are not often found on today's printers; regardless, they indicate a local connection, not a network connection.

74. Answer: A

Explanation: The fuser heats paper to around 400° Fahrenheit (204° Celsius). That's like an oven. If you need to replace the fuser, let the printer sit for 10 or 15 minutes after shutting it down and before maintenance.

Incorrect answers: The fuser is not wet or fragile, and it does not contain toner; that is contained by the cartridge.

75. Answer: A

Explanation: The Musical Instrument Digital Interface (MIDI) connector is used for musical equipment such as keyboards, synthesizers, and sequencers. MIDI is used to create a clocking signal that all devices can synchronize to.

Incorrect answers: The other three connectors, HDMI, DVI, and DisplayPort, are all video connectors.

76. **Answer: B**

Explanation: The Torx screwdriver (also known as a Torx wrench) is a special tool used to remove screws from the outside of a case; often, proprietary computer manufacturers use these screws. This tool can also be used to remove screws (albeit smaller ones) from a laptop. The standard is the size T10 Torx screwdriver, but you might also use a T8 or even a T6 on laptops.

Incorrect answers: A monkey wrench is an adjustable wrench with large jaws—something you should not typically need when working on computers! A spudger is used to separate plastic bezels and other similar plastics when working on mobile devices. Pliers have a variety of uses, but removing screws is not one of them. However, as a computer technician, you should have all these tools in your toolkit.

77. **Answer: A**

Explanation: Overclocking is the act of increasing your CPU's operating speed beyond its normal rated speed.

Incorrect answers: The rest of the terms are not used in relation to this concept.

78. **Answer: C**

Explanation: The Service Set Identifier (SSID) is the most important piece of information required to connect to a wireless network; it is the name of the wireless network.

Incorrect answers: The wireless channel number isn't necessarily needed; the wireless access point (WAP) might autonegotiate the channel. Also, MAC address filtering is not enabled by default, so the MAC address might not be needed. (In fact, the admin would enter this at the wireless access point, not from the client computer.) You need the administrator password only if you want to make configuration changes to the wireless access point. For example, if you want to implement MAC filtering, you would have to log in to the WAP with an admin password to configure it.

79. **Answer: D**

Explanation: I/O bandwidth is the most critical of the listed resources in the question. When you are considering file storage and file synchronization, you need to know the maximum input/output operations per second (IOPS) that the cloud provider can deliver. (Get actual reports of previous customers as proof!) IOPS gives you a concrete measurement of data that you can use for analysis.

Incorrect answers: Disk speed is not enough for the planning of file storage. Plus, it might not even be a factor if the cloud provider is using SSDs. RAM and CPU utilization percentages are important, but they become more vital if you will be working with virtual machines. It's also important to monitor them regularly.

80. Answer: B

Explanation: The power management settings on the laptop can cause the display to automatically dim when the AC adapter is unplugged. In fact, this is the default on many laptops to conserve battery power. These settings can be configured within Power Options in Windows.

Incorrect answers: You can certainly set the display to full brightness when on battery power; doing so just isn't recommended. Laptops can operate properly when connected to the AC power adapter or when using the battery only. The display brightness of a laptop isn't affected by any security settings.

CHAPTER THREE

220-1001 Practice Exam B

Now let's kick it up a notch. This second 220-1001 exam could be considered an intermediate practice test. I've mixed in some more difficult questions this time. You may have noticed that the first exam had some questions grouped together by A+ domain. This exam is more random.

Again, the goal here is to make sure you understand all of the concepts before moving on to the next test. If you didn't take a break already, I suggest taking one between exams. If you just completed the first exam, give yourself a half hour or so before you begin this one. If you didn't score 90 percent or higher on Exam A, go back and study; then retake Exam A until you pass with 90 percent or higher.

> **NOTE**
>
> If you feel that you are having trouble with more than 25 percent of the concepts within this exam and the first exam, I suggest purchasing the main A+ Exam Cram study guide or even considering an actual hands-on A+ course before continuing with this book.

Write down your answers and check them against the answer key that immediately follows the exam. After the answer key, you will find explanations for all of the answers. Good luck!

Practice Questions

1. Which of the following servers is responsible for resolving a name such as dprocomputer.com to its corresponding IP address?

   Quick Answer: **61**
   Detailed Answer: **62**

   ○ **A.** Web server

   ○ **B.** FTP server

   ○ **C.** DNS server

   ○ **D.** Proxy server

   ○ **E.** Syslog server

2. Which of the following statements describe advantages of using the Dynamic Host Configuration Protocol (DHCP)? (Select the two best answers.)

   Quick Answer: **61**
   Detailed Answer: **62**

   ❏ **A.** IP addresses can be managed from a central location.

   ❏ **B.** The network speed can automatically adjust based on the type of traffic being generated.

   ❏ **C.** The hosts file on the computer can be validated for proper entries.

   ❏ **D.** Media access control addresses can be changed.

   ❏ **E.** Computers can automatically get new addressing when moved to a different network segment.

3. Which of the following storage technologies is used by hard disk drives?

   Quick Answer: **61**
   Detailed Answer: **62**

   ○ **A.** Magnetic

   ○ **B.** Optical

   ○ **C.** Impact

   ○ **D.** Solid-state

4. On which type of computer is RAM the most important?

   Quick Answer: **61**
   Detailed Answer: **62**

   ○ **A.** Gaming PC

   ○ **B.** Virtualization workstation

   ○ **C.** AV editing workstation

   ○ **D.** Standard thick client

5. A client brings in a printer that is giving a paper-feed error. Which of the following is the most likely cause?

   Quick Answer: **61**
   Detailed Answer: **63**

   ○ **A.** The separation pad

   ○ **B.** The developing rollers

   ○ **C.** The paper tray

   ○ **D.** The pickup rollers

6. Which protocol uses port 389?

   ○ **A.** SMTP
   ○ **B.** POP3
   ○ **C.** LDAP
   ○ **D.** HTTPS

Quick Answer: **61**
Detailed Answer: **63**

7. What is the maximum distance at which a Class 2 Bluetooth device can receive signals from a Bluetooth access point?

   ○ **A.** 100 meters
   ○ **B.** 10 meters
   ○ **C.** 5 meters
   ○ **D.** 1 meter

Quick Answer: **61**
Detailed Answer: **63**

8. Which of the following wireless networking standards operates at 5 GHz only? (Select the two best answers.)

   ❑ **A.** 802.11a
   ❑ **B.** 802.11b
   ❑ **C.** 802.11g
   ❑ **D.** 802.11n
   ❑ **E.** 802.11ac

Quick Answer: **61**
Detailed Answer: **63**

9. Which of the following types of RAM has a peak transfer rate of 21,333 MB/s?

   ○ **A.** DDR4-1600
   ○ **B.** DDR4-2133
   ○ **C.** DDR4-2400
   ○ **D.** DDR4-2666

Quick Answer: **61**
Detailed Answer: **63**

10. Which of the following types of printers uses a print head, ribbon, and tractor feed?

   ○ **A.** Laser
   ○ **B.** Impact
   ○ **C.** Inkjet
   ○ **D.** Thermal

Quick Answer: **61**
Detailed Answer: **64**

11. Several users on your network are reporting that a network printer, which is controlled by a print server, is not printing. What is the first action you should take to fix the problem?

Quick Answer: **61**
Detailed Answer: **64**

   ○ **A.** Have the affected users restart their computers.

   ○ **B.** Replace the USB cable.

   ○ **C.** Clear the print queue.

   ○ **D.** Reinstall the printer drivers on the affected users' computers.

12. Which of the following is a possible symptom of a failing CPU?

Quick Answer: **61**
Detailed Answer: **65**

   ○ **A.** CPU is beyond the recommended voltage range.

   ○ **B.** Computer won't boot.

   ○ **C.** BIOS reports low temperatures within the case.

   ○ **D.** Spyware is installed into the browser.

13. Which of the following cable types is not affected by EMI but requires specialized tools to install?

Quick Answer: **61**
Detailed Answer: **65**

   ○ **A.** Cat 6

   ○ **B.** STP

   ○ **C.** Fiber optic

   ○ **D.** Coaxial

14. Setting an administrator password in the BIOS accomplishes which of the following?

Quick Answer: **61**
Detailed Answer: **65**

   ○ **A.** Prevents a user from rearranging the boot order

   ○ **B.** Prevents a user from reading email

   ○ **C.** Prevents a virus from infecting the MBR

   ○ **D.** Prevents an attacker from opening the case

15. Which of the following functions is performed by the external power supply of a laptop?

Quick Answer: **61**
Detailed Answer: **65**

   ○ **A.** Increases voltage

   ○ **B.** Stores power

   ○ **C.** Converts DC power to AC power

   ○ **D.** Converts AC power to DC power

16. How many pins would you see in a high-quality printhead on a dot-matrix printer?

- ○ **A.** 24
- ○ **B.** 15
- ○ **C.** 8
- ○ **D.** 20

17. What is an LCD display's contrast ratio defined as?

- ○ **A.** Power consumption
- ○ **B.** Display resolution and brightness
- ○ **C.** The brightest and darkest outputs
- ○ **D.** Power savings

18. Which of the following tools can protect you in the case of a surge?

- ○ **A.** Torx screwdriver
- ○ **B.** Antistatic strap
- ○ **C.** Voltmeter
- ○ **D.** Antistatic mat

19. Which of the following connectors can have audio *and* video pass through it?

- ○ **A.** VGA
- ○ **B.** RGB
- ○ **C.** DVI
- ○ **D.** HDMI

20. Which of the following devices limits network broadcasts, segments IP address ranges, and interconnects different physical media?

- ○ **A.** Switch
- ○ **B.** WAP
- ○ **C.** Firewall
- ○ **D.** Router

21. Which of the following technologies can be used to make wireless payments?

Quick Answer: **61**
Detailed Answer: **67**

- ○ **A.** Bluetooth
- ○ **B.** IR
- ○ **C.** NFC
- ○ **D.** LTE

22. You just upgraded the CPU. Which of the following issues can make your computer shut down automatically after a few minutes? (Select the best answer.)

Quick Answer: **61**
Detailed Answer: **67**

- ○ **A.** Wrong CPU driver.
- ○ **B.** Wrong voltage to the CPU.
- ○ **C.** Incorrect CPU has been installed.
- ○ **D.** The CPU has overheated.

23. Which of the following addresses is a valid IPv4 address for a network host?

Quick Answer: **61**
Detailed Answer: **67**

- ○ **A.** 127.0.0.1
- ○ **B.** 169.254.0.0/16
- ○ **C.** 172.17.58.254
- ○ **D.** 255.10.15.7

24. You want to upgrade memory in your computer. Which of the following is user-replaceable memory in a PC?

Quick Answer: **61**
Detailed Answer: **68**

- ○ **A.** CMOS
- ○ **B.** BIOS
- ○ **C.** DRAM
- ○ **D.** SRAM
- ○ **E.** ROM

25. Which of the following IP addresses is private?

Quick Answer: **61**
Detailed Answer: **68**

- ○ **A.** 11.58.254.169
- ○ **B.** 169.255.10.41
- ○ **C.** 172.31.1.1
- ○ **D.** 192.169.0.1

26. Which of the following is the local loopback IPv6 address?

   ◯ **A.** 127.0.0.1

   ◯ **B.** ::1

   ◯ **C.** 192.168.0.0

   ◯ **D.** FE80::/10

Quick Answer: **61**
Detailed Answer: **68**

27. Which of the following statements is correct concerning IPv6 addresses?

   ◯ **A.** They cannot be used with IPv4.

   ◯ **B.** They are supported by all routers.

   ◯ **C.** They represent addressing using 128 bits.

   ◯ **D.** They require fiber-optic connections.

Quick Answer: **61**
Detailed Answer: **68**

28. Which of the following operating CPU temperatures is typical?

   ◯ **A.** 60° Fahrenheit

   ◯ **B.** 60° Celsius

   ◯ **C.** 72° Fahrenheit

   ◯ **D.** 72° Celsius

Quick Answer: **61**
Detailed Answer: **69**

29. Which of the following printer technologies should be used to print payroll checks on paper forms that have a carbon backing?

   ◯ **A.** Impact

   ◯ **B.** Laser

   ◯ **C.** Inkjet

   ◯ **D.** Thermal

Quick Answer: **61**
Detailed Answer: **69**

30. Which of the following is *not* a configuration that can be made in the UEFI/BIOS?

   ◯ **A.** Boot sequence

   ◯ **B.** Temperature thresholds

   ◯ **C.** Overclocking

   ◯ **D.** Install drivers

   ◯ **E.** Intrusion detection

Quick Answer: **61**
Detailed Answer: **69**

31. Which of the following traits and port numbers are associated with POP3? (Select the two best answers.)

Quick Answer: **61**
Detailed Answer: **69**

- ❏ **A.** Receives inbound email on port 110
- ❏ **B.** Receives inbound email on port 25
- ❏ **C.** Sends outbound email on port 110
- ❏ **D.** Sends outbound email on port 25
- ❏ **E.** Receives inbound email on port 995
- ❏ **F.** Sends outbound email on port 587

32. Which type of cable should be used to connect a laptop directly to a PC?

Quick Answer: **61**
Detailed Answer: **69**

- ○ **A.** Cat 6 patch cable
- ○ **B.** Parallel cable
- ○ **C.** Rolled cable
- ○ **D.** Cat 5e crossover cable

33. To perform a network installation of Windows, which of the following must be supported by the computer's network interface card?

Quick Answer: **61**
Detailed Answer: **70**

- ○ **A.** PXE
- ○ **B.** PCIe
- ○ **C.** PCL
- ○ **D.** PnP

34. Which of the following devices is the least likely to be replaced on a laptop?

Quick Answer: **61**
Detailed Answer: **70**

- ○ **A.** CPU
- ○ **B.** RAM
- ○ **C.** M.2 card
- ○ **D.** Keyboard

35. If your "bandwidth" is 1000 Mbps, how many bits are you sending/receiving? (Select the two best answers.)

Quick Answer: **61**
Detailed Answer: **70**

- ❏ **A.** 100,000,000 bits per minute
- ❏ **B.** 1000 bits per second
- ❏ **C.** 1,000,000,000 bits per second
- ❏ **D.** 1 gigabit per second

36. Which of the following can send data the farthest?

   ○ **A.** Multi-mode fiber

   ○ **B.** Single-mode fiber

   ○ **C.** STP

   ○ **D.** Coaxial

Quick Answer: **61**
Detailed Answer: **70**

37. You need to expand the peripherals of a computer, but the system doesn't have enough ports. Which type of card should be installed?

   ○ **A.** Modem

   ○ **B.** Network adapter

   ○ **C.** USB card

   ○ **D.** TV tuner card

Quick Answer: **61**
Detailed Answer: **71**

38. Which of the following is the typical speed of an SATA hard disk drive?

   ○ **A.** 1000 Mbps

   ○ **B.** 3.1 GHz

   ○ **C.** 32 GB

   ○ **D.** 7200 RPM

Quick Answer: **61**
Detailed Answer: **71**

39. Which of the following best describes the differences between a switch and a router?

   ○ **A.** A switch interconnects devices on the same network so that they can communicate; a router interconnects one or more networks.

   ○ **B.** A router broadcasts all data packets that are sent on the network; a switch transmits data directly to the device.

   ○ **C.** A switch broadcasts all data packets that are sent on the network; a router transmits data directly to the device.

   ○ **D.** A switch interconnects one or more networks; a router interconnects devices on a network.

Quick Answer: **61**
Detailed Answer: **71**

40. A group of users in ABC Corp. needs to back up several gigabytes of data daily. Which of the following is the best media for this scenario?

   ○ **A.** DVD

   ○ **B.** Dual-layer DVD

   ○ **C.** USB flash drive

   ○ **D.** LTO

Quick Answer: **61**
Detailed Answer: **71**

41. The organization you work for has three locations within a city that need to be networked together. The network requirement for all three locations is a minimum data throughput of 1 Gbps. Which of the following network types are most likely to be used for internal office and office-to-office communications? (Select the two best answers.)

Quick Answer: **61**
Detailed Answer: **71**

    ❏ **A.** LAN

    ❏ **B.** PAN

    ❏ **C.** WAN

    ❏ **D.** MAN

    ❏ **E.** SAN

    ❏ **F.** WLAN

42. Which of the following is a type of virtualization software?

Quick Answer: **61**
Detailed Answer: **72**

    ○ **A.** On-demand

    ○ **B.** IaaS

    ○ **C.** Measured service

    ○ **D.** VMware

43. You need to replace and upgrade the memory card in a smartphone. Which type of memory is most likely used by the smartphone?

Quick Answer: **61**
Detailed Answer: **72**

    ○ **A.** SSD

    ○ **B.** CF

    ○ **C.** USB flash drive

    ○ **D.** SD

44. Your organization relies heavily on its server farm for resources and is less reliant on the client computers. Which type of client computer is most likely used by the organization?

Quick Answer: **61**
Detailed Answer: **72**

    ○ **A.** Virtualization workstation

    ○ **B.** Client/server

    ○ **C.** Thin client

    ○ **D.** Thick client

45. Which of the following statements describe the respective functions of the two corona wires in a laser printer? (Select the two best answers.)

Quick Answer: **61**
Detailed Answer: **73**

    ❏ **A.** Conditions the drum to be written to

    ❏ **B.** Transfers toner from the drum to the paper

    ❏ **C.** Fuses the toner to the paper

    ❏ **D.** Cleans the drum

46. Which of the following tools should be used to test a 24-pin ATX 12v power connector?

Quick Answer: 61
Detailed Answer: 73

   ○ **A.** Torx screwdriver

   ○ **B.** PSU tester

   ○ **C.** Receptacle tester

   ○ **D.** Tone and probe kit

47. Which of the following uses port 427?

Quick Answer: 61
Detailed Answer: 73

   ○ **A.** FTP

   ○ **B.** DNS

   ○ **C.** SLP

   ○ **D.** HTTPS

   ○ **E.** RDP

48. Which of the following ports is used by AFP?

Quick Answer: 61
Detailed Answer: 73

   ○ **A.** 22

   ○ **B.** 23

   ○ **C.** 80

   ○ **D.** 143

   ○ **E.** 445

   ○ **F.** 548

49. Which of the following does a laptop have yet a tablet does not?

Quick Answer: 61
Detailed Answer: 73

   ○ **A.** Touchpad

   ○ **B.** Display

   ○ **C.** Keyboard

   ○ **D.** Wireless network adapter

50. At the beginning of the workday, a user informs you that her computer is not working. When you examine the computer, you notice that nothing is on the display. Which of the following should be done first?

Quick Answer: 61
Detailed Answer: 74

   ○ **A.** Check whether the monitor is connected to the computer.

   ○ **B.** Check whether the monitor is on.

   ○ **C.** Check whether the computer is plugged in.

   ○ **D.** Reinstall the video driver.

51. A customer reports that when his computer is turned on, the screen is blank except for some text and a flashing cursor. He also tells you that there are numbers counting upward when the computer beeps and then freezes. Which of the following is the most likely cause of this problem?

Quick Answer: **61**
Detailed Answer: **74**

- ○ **A.** The computer has faulty memory.
- ○ **B.** There is a corrupt MBR.
- ○ **C.** The OS is corrupted.
- ○ **D.** The computer is attempting to boot off the network.

52. Joey's computer was working fine for weeks, yet suddenly it cannot connect to the Internet. Joey runs the command **ipconfig** and sees that the IP address his computer is using is 169.254.50.68. Which of the following statements describes the most likely issue?

Quick Answer: **61**
Detailed Answer: **74**

- ○ **A.** The computer cannot access the DHCP server.
- ○ **B.** The computer cannot access the POP3 server.
- ○ **C.** The computer cannot access the DNS server.
- ○ **D.** The computer cannot access the WINS server.

53. Which of the following could cause a ghosted image on the paper outputted by a laser printer?

Quick Answer: **61**
Detailed Answer: **74**

- ○ **A.** Transfer corona wire
- ○ **B.** Primary corona wire
- ○ **C.** Pickup rollers
- ○ **D.** Photosensitive drum

54. Mary installed a new sound card and speakers; however, she cannot get any sound from the speakers. Which of the following statements describe the most likely cause? (Select all that apply.)

Quick Answer: **61**
Detailed Answer: **75**

- ❑ **A.** The speaker power is not plugged in.
- ❑ **B.** The sound card driver is not installed.
- ❑ **C.** The sound card is plugged into the wrong slot.
- ❑ **D.** The speaker connector is in the wrong jack.

55. A laptop with an integrated 802.11 WLAN card is unable to connect to any wireless networks. Just yesterday the laptop was able to connect to wireless networks. Which of the following statements describes the most likely cause?

Quick Answer: **61**
Detailed Answer: **75**

- ○ **A.** The wireless card drivers are not installed.
- ○ **B.** The wireless card is disabled in BIOS.
- ○ **C.** The wireless card firmware requires an update.
- ○ **D.** The wireless hardware button is turned off.

56. The IP address of dprocomputer.com is 216.97.236.245. You can ping that IP address, but you cannot ping dprocomputer.com. Which of the following statements describes the most likely cause?

Quick Answer: **61**
Detailed Answer: **75**

    ○ **A.** dprocomputer.com is down.

    ○ **B.** The DHCP server is down.

    ○ **C.** The DNS server is down.

    ○ **D.** The AD DS server is down.

57. A newly built computer runs through the POST, but it doesn't recognize the specific CPU that was just installed. Instead, it recognizes it as a generic CPU. Which of the following is the first thing you should check?

Quick Answer: **61**
Detailed Answer: **75**

    ○ **A.** Whether the CPU is seated properly

    ○ **B.** The version of the firmware for the motherboard

    ○ **C.** Whether it is the correct CPU for the motherboard

    ○ **D.** The version of Windows installed

58. Which of the following commands displays a network interface card's MAC address?

Quick Answer: **61**
Detailed Answer: **76**

    ○ **A.** **ping**

    ○ **B.** **ipconfig/all**

    ○ **C.** **ipconfig**

    ○ **D.** **ipconfig/release**

59. A customer reports that print jobs sent to a local printer are printing as blank pieces of paper. Which of the following can help you determine the cause?

Quick Answer: **61**
Detailed Answer: **76**

    ○ **A.** Reload the printer drivers.

    ○ **B.** Stop and restart the print spooler.

    ○ **C.** Replace the printer cable.

    ○ **D.** Print an internal test page.

60. Signal strength for a laptop's wireless connection is low (yellow in color and only one bar). The laptop is on the first floor of a house. The wireless access point (WAP) is in the basement. Which of the following can improve signal strength? (Select the two best answers.)

Quick Answer: **61**
Detailed Answer: **76**

    ❑ **A.** Use a WAP signal booster.

    ❑ **B.** Move the WAP from the basement to the first floor.

    ❑ **C.** Download the latest driver for the NIC.

    ❑ **D.** Download the latest BIOS for the laptop.

61. You are troubleshooting a computer that can't communicate with other computers on the network. An ipconfig shows an APIPA IP address (169.254.21.184). What is the most likely problem?

   ○ **A.** DNS resolution

   ○ **B.** Duplicate IP address

   ○ **C.** DHCP failure

   ○ **D.** Cleared ARP cache

Quick Answer: **61**
Detailed Answer: **76**

62. Which of the following is the first thing you should check when a computer cannot get on the Internet?

   ○ **A.** NIC driver

   ○ **B.** Disk defrag

   ○ **C.** Patch cable

   ○ **D.** Firewall settings

Quick Answer: **61**
Detailed Answer: **77**

63. You just built a PC, and when it first boots, you hear some beep codes. If you don't have the codes memorized, which of the following are the best devices to examine first? (Select the two best answers.)

   ❏ **A.** RAM

   ❏ **B.** Optical drive

   ❏ **C.** Video card

   ❏ **D.** CPU

Quick Answer: **61**
Detailed Answer: **77**

64. Which of the following are examples of virtual printing? (Select the two best answers.)

   ❏ **A.** Start printing after the last page is spooled.

   ❏ **B.** Print to XPS.

   ❏ **C.** Print to a printer pool.

   ❏ **D.** Print to PRN.

Quick Answer: **61**
Detailed Answer: **77**

65. A coworker needs to print to a printer from a laptop running Windows. The printer has a USB and an Ethernet connector. Which of the following is the easiest way to connect the printer to the laptop?

   ○ **A.** Use the Thunderbolt port.

   ○ **B.** Use the network connection.

   ○ **C.** Use the USB connector.

   ○ **D.** Use the Ethernet connector.

Quick Answer: **61**
Detailed Answer: **77**

66. You have had several support requests for a PC located in a school
cafeteria kitchen that is experiencing a problem. You have already
reseated the PCIe and PCI cards and replaced the hard drive in the
PC. Computers located in the business office or the classrooms
have not had the same problem as the computer in the cafeteria.
Which of the following is the most likely issue?

  ○ **A.** Excessive heat

  ○ **B.** Faulty RAM

  ○ **C.** 240 V outlets

  ○ **D.** Power brownouts

67. A user complains that his network interface card (NIC) is not
functioning and has no link lights. The weather has been changing
drastically over the past few days, and humidity and temperature
have been rising and falling every day. Which of the following could be the direct cause of this problem? (Select the best
answer.)

  ○ **A.** Thermal expansion and contraction

  ○ **B.** Thermal sublimation

  ○ **C.** Chip creep

  ○ **D.** POST errors

68. Which network type enables high-speed data communication and
is the most difficult to eavesdrop on?

  ○ **A.** Satellite

  ○ **B.** DSL

  ○ **C.** Fiber optic

  ○ **D.** Cable

69. Which of the following properties of a heat sink has the greatest
effect on heat dissipation?

  ○ **A.** Connection type

  ○ **B.** Shape

  ○ **C.** Surface area

  ○ **D.** Proximity to the power supply

70. You need to set up a server system that will run in a VM. It will have the bulk of the network computers' resources and will supply much of the resources necessary to the client computers that will connect to it. You are also required to set up the client computers. Which two types of systems (server and client) will you be implementing?

   ◯ **A.** CAD/CAM workstation and PCs

   ◯ **B.** Virtualization workstation and thin clients

   ◯ **C.** Home server PC and thick clients

   ◯ **D.** AV editing workstation and laptops

71. Your boss can receive email but can't seem to send email with the installed email client software. Which protocol is not configured properly?

   ◯ **A.** SMTP

   ◯ **B.** POP3

   ◯ **C.** FTP

   ◯ **D.** HTTP

72. A customer's laptop LCD needs replacement. Which of the following tools should be used to remove the display bezel?

   ◯ **A.** Pliers

   ◯ **B.** Plastic tweezers

   ◯ **C.** Flathead screwdriver

   ◯ **D.** Plastic shim

73. One of your customers is running Windows on a PC that has a 3.0-GHz CPU, 16-GB RAM, and an integrated video card. The customer tells you that performance is slow when editing video files. Which of the following solutions increases performance on the computer?

   ◯ **A.** Increasing system RAM

   ◯ **B.** Upgrading the video card

   ◯ **C.** Increasing the hard drive capacity

   ◯ **D.** Upgrading the CPU

74. Which of the following is configured in the UEFI/BIOS? (Select the four best answers.)

- ❏ **A.** Time and date
- ❏ **B.** The registry
- ❏ **C.** Boot sequence
- ❏ **D.** Passwords
- ❏ **E.** USB drivers
- ❏ **F.** WOL

Quick Answer: **61**
Detailed Answer: **79**

75. You want to test whether IPv4 *and* IPv6 are working properly on a computer. Which of the following commands should be issued?

- ◯ **A.** **ipconfig ::1** and **ping ::1**
- ◯ **B.** **ping 127.0.0.0** and **ping :1**
- ◯ **C.** **ping 127.0.0.1** and **ping ::1**
- ◯ **D.** **ipconfig 127.0.0.1** and **ping 127::1**

Quick Answer: **61**
Detailed Answer: **79**

76. Which of the following measurements is the typical latency of an SATA hard drive?

- ◯ **A.** 300 MB/s
- ◯ **B.** 7200 RPM
- ◯ **C.** 64 MB
- ◯ **D.** 4.2 ms

Quick Answer: **61**
Detailed Answer: **80**

77. The marketing printer has been used for four years. Which of the following statements represents a best practice for ensuring the printer remains in good working order?

- ◯ **A.** You should clean the printer.
- ◯ **B.** You should install a maintenance kit.
- ◯ **C.** You should clear the counter.
- ◯ **D.** You should print a test page.

Quick Answer: **61**
Detailed Answer: **80**

78. A customer wants users to be able to store additional files in a cloud-based manner when necessary and remove them when they are not needed anymore. What is this known as?

- ◯ **A.** Resource pooling
- ◯ **B.** Virtual application streaming
- ◯ **C.** Shared resources
- ◯ **D.** On-demand
- ◯ **E.** Synchronization application

Quick Answer: **61**
Detailed Answer: **80**

79. You are troubleshooting a computer that is no longer able to browse the Internet. The user says that the computer worked before he went on vacation. However, now the user is able to navigate the local intranet but cannot connect to any outside sites. You ping a well-known website on the Internet by name, but you receive no replies. Then you ping the website's IP address, and you do receive a reply. Which of the following commands will fix the problem?

   ○ **A. ipconfig /flushdns**
   ○ **B. ipconfig /all**
   ○ **C. ipconfig /release**
   ○ **D. ipconfig /setclassid**

Quick Answer: **61**
Detailed Answer: **80**

80. Which of the following is used to measure TDP?

   ○ **A.** Volts
   ○ **B.** Watts
   ○ **C.** Ohms
   ○ **D.** Amps

Quick Answer: **61**
Detailed Answer: **81**

Quick-Check Answer Key

1. C	**28.** B	**55.** D
2. A, E	**29.** A	**56.** C
3. A	**30.** D	**57.** B
4. B	**31.** A, E	**58.** B
5. D	**32.** D	**59.** D
6. C	**33.** A	**60.** A, B
7. B	**34.** A	**61.** C
8. A, E	**35.** C, D	**62.** C
9. D	**36.** B	**63.** A, C
10. B	**37.** C	**64.** B, D
11. C	**38.** D	**65.** C
12. A	**39.** A	**66.** A
13. C	**40.** D	**67.** A
14. A	**41.** A, D	**68.** C
15. D	**42.** D	**69.** C
16. A	**43.** D	**70.** B
17. C	**44.** C	**71.** A
18. B	**45.** A, B	**72.** D
19. D	**46.** B	**73.** B
20. D	**47.** C	**74.** A, C, D, F
21. C	**48.** F	**75.** C
22. D	**49.** A	**76.** D
23. C	**50.** B	**77.** B
24. C	**51.** A	**78.** D
25. C	**52.** A	**79.** A
26. B	**53.** D	**80.** B
27. C	**54.** A, B, D	

Answers and Explanations

1. Answer: C

Explanation: A Domain Name System (DNS) server is responsible for resolving (or converting) hostnames and domain names to their corresponding IP addresses. To see this in action, open the command line and try connecting to a domain (such as dprocomputer.com) and run a ping, tracert (or traceroute in Linux and macOS), nslookup, or dig (or all of those) against the domain name. These commands can supply you with the IP address of the host. Remember, always practice in a hands-on manner on real computers to reinforce your knowledge!

Incorrect answers: A web server is in charge of storing websites and presenting them to users on the Internet or intranet. File Transfer Protocol (FTP) servers are used to upload and download files. A proxy server facilitates web page caching for client computers. A syslog server is used to send out log file information of networking devices in real time to an administrator's workstation for analysis. Know your server roles!

2. Answers: A and E

Explanation: Advantages of using DHCP include the following: IP addresses can be managed from a central location, and computers can automatically get new addressing when moved to a different network segment (perhaps one that uses a different DHCP server).

Incorrect answers: Quality of service (QoS) adjusts the network speed based on the type of traffic generated. DHCP has nothing to do with the Hosts.txt file; that file contains static entries of hostname-to-IP address conversions. Media access control addresses are usually not changed on a network adapter, although they can be masked. MAC filtering maintains a list of MAC addresses that are allowed to access a network, but once again, this is a different concept from DHCP.

3. Answer: A

Explanation: Hard disk drives (HDDs) are magnetic disks. These are the type with moving parts, as opposed to solid-state drives (SSDs) that have no moving parts.

Incorrect answers: There are optical hard drives, but they are rare; optical disc drives are commonly implemented as CD, DVD, or Blu-ray drives. Impact refers to a type of printer, such as the dot-matrix or the daisywheel printer. Solid-state hard drives do not have a *disk* and therefore have no moving parts, are quiet, and work as fast as (if not faster than) traditional magnetic hard drives. However, they are far more expensive than magnetic-based hard disk drives.

4. Answer: B

Explanation: RAM is more essential to the virtualization workstation than any of the other types of custom PCs listed. Virtual operating systems (virtual machines or VMs) require a lot of RAM to run, much more than any other application. Plus, a virtualization workstation often has more than one virtual machine running, increasing its need for RAM even further.

Incorrect answers: A gaming PC's biggest requirements are the CPU and the video card, followed by an SSD. Audio/video editing workstations require specialized audio and video cards, large and fast hard drives, and dual monitors. A standard thick client is a basic PC running typical applications that meets recommended requirements for the selected OS.

5. **Answer: D**

Explanation: Paper-feed errors are often caused by the pickup rollers, which are in charge of feeding the paper into the printer.

Incorrect answers: If a separation pad fails, it might cause more than one sheet of paper to be entered into the printer. The developing rollers transfer ink to the imaging drum. The paper tray simply holds the paper. It should not cause paper-feed errors unless the constraining tabs are too tight.

6. **Answer: C**

Explanation: Port 389 is used by the Lightweight Directory Access Protocol (LDAP). Although 389 is the default port, 636 is also used for secure LDAP.

Incorrect answers: Port 25 is the default port for Simple Mail Transfer Protocol (SMTP). Port 110 or 995 is used by POP3. Port 443 is used by HTTPS.

7. **Answer: B**

Explanation: Class 2 Bluetooth devices have a maximum range of approximately 10 meters. Class 2 devices (such as Bluetooth headsets) are the most common.

Incorrect answers: Class 1 has a 100-meter range, and Class 3's range is approximately 1 meter. The maximum length of a standard USB 2.0 cable is 5 meters. USB 3.0 can go beyond this, but with varying results as far as data transfer rate, latency, dropped frames, and so on.

8. **Answers: A and E**

Explanation: 802.11a operates at 5 GHz only; so does 802.11ac.

Incorrect answers: 802.11b and g operate at 2.4 GHz. 802.11n operates at either 2.4 or 5 GHz. The IEEE 802.11 wireless standards are collectively known as 802.11x. However, there is no actual 802.11x standard; it was not used in order to avoid confusion. 802.11x is instead a variable that you may sometimes see that refers to two or more 802.11 technologies.

9. **Answer: D**

Explanation: DDR4-2666 has a peak transfer rate of 21,333 MB/s. It runs at an I/O bus clock speed of 1333 MHz and can send 2666 megatransfers per second (MT/s). It is also known as PC4-21333.

The math: To figure out the data transfer rate of DDR4 from the name "DDR4-2666," simply multiply the 2666 by 8 (bytes) and solve for megabytes: 21,333 MB/s. To figure out the data transfer rate of DDR4 by the consumer name "PC4-21333," just look at the number within the name and add "MB/s" to the end. To figure out the data transfer rate when given only the I/O bus clock speed (for example, 1333 MHz), multiply the clock speed by 2 and then multiply that number by 8 and solve for megabytes: 1333 MHz × 2 × 8 = 21,333 MB/s. However, keep in mind that a RAM module such as DDR4-2666 is often inaccurately referred to as a 2666-MHz RAM module, but really that is the MT/s.

Incorrect answers: DDR4-1600 has a peak transfer rate of 12,800 MB/s; it is also known as PC4-12800. DDR4-2133 has a peak transfer rate of 17,066 MB/s; it is also known as PC4-17000. DDR4-2400 has a peak transfer rate of 19,200 MB/s; it is also known as PC4-19200.

10. **Answer: B**

Explanation: The impact printer uses a print head, ribbon, and tractor feed. An example of an impact printer is the dot matrix.

Incorrect answers: Laser printers are much more complex and use more parts. Inkjet printers use a print head but use an ink cartridge instead of a ribbon and don't use a tractor feed. Thermal printers use a print head and a special heating element.

11. **Answer: C**

Explanation: The first thing you should try (of the listed answers) is to clear the print queue. How this is done will vary depending on the type of print server being used. For example, if the printer is being controlled by a Windows Server, that server will have the Print Management role installed. From the Print Management console window, you can access the printer in question and locate the queue. In most client Windows operating systems (such as Windows 10), you can find the queue simply by double-clicking the printer. Regardless of the OS, it is where you would normally go to manage print jobs. Then, after you have found the queue, delete any pending or stalled jobs. One of those print jobs might have been causing a delay, possibly if the print job was too big or was corrupted. Of course, you will have to notify users that any jobs as of x time frame have been deleted and they will need to be printed again. On some printers you can clear the print queue from the onscreen display (OSD) directly on the printer. Or, if the print server is built into a SOHO router or similar device, you would have to access it from a browser.

Incorrect answers: If at all possible, try to solve problems centrally without getting users involved. Having the affected users restart their computers is probably a waste of time in this case. If only one user were affected, this could be a viable solution, but when multiple users are affected, the problem is usually located centrally—at a server or a network device. You don't even know if the printer is connected with a USB cable. It might be if it is connected directly to the server, but if not, it is probably wired to the network with a twisted-pair patch cable. Either way, cables don't usually fail out of nowhere. This potential solution should be further down your list. Reinstalling the print drivers is not the best answer because several users were affected. Again, if only one user were affected, this might be a valid option, but if several were affected, the problem is probably more centralized.

12. **Answer: A**

    Explanation: If the CPU is running beyond the recommended voltage range for extended periods of time, it can be a sign of a failing CPU. The problem could also be caused by overclocking. Check in the UEFI/BIOS to see whether or not the CPU is overclocked.

    Incorrect answers: If the computer won't boot at all, another problem might have occurred, or the CPU might have already failed. Low case temperatures are a good thing (if they aren't below freezing!), and spyware is unrelated to this issue.

13. **Answer: C**

    Explanation: Fiber-optic cable is the only answer listed that is not affected by electromagnetic interference (EMI). The reason is that it does not use copper wire or electricity, but instead uses glass or plastic fibers and light.

    Incorrect answers: Any copper cable is susceptible to EMI to a certain degree. Regular UTP cable such as Cat 5e or Cat 6 is very susceptible, coaxial slightly less, and shielded twisted pair (STP) even less than that. STP is difficult to install and must be grounded; because of this, it is found less commonly in networks. To truly protect from EMI, fiber optic is the best way to go. It often requires special tools during installation to splice the fibers properly and test the connection effectively.

14. **Answer: A**

    Explanation: Setting an admin password in the UEFI/BIOS prevents a user from rearranging the boot order. The idea behind this is to stop a person from attempting to boot off an optical disc or USB flash drive. As an administrator, you should change the BIOS boot order to hard drive first. Then apply an administrative password. That'll stop 'em right in their tracks!

    Incorrect answers: The administrator password does not prevent any of the other listed answers. To prevent a user from reading email, you would have to remove email applications (such as Outlook) and probably take away the browser, too. (Doesn't sound feasible.) To prevent a virus from infecting the MBR, you could turn on boot sector scanning in the BIOS (if the motherboard supports it). To prevent an attacker from opening the case, use a case lock. To find out if someone attempted to get into the computer itself, turn on the chassis intrusion alert in the BIOS.

15. **Answer: D**

    Explanation: The external power supply of the laptop converts AC to DC for the system to use and for charging the battery. It is known as the power adapter, and it needs to run at a very specific voltage. In fact, different make and model power adapters usually do not work with different laptops, even if the voltages are only slightly different.

    Incorrect answers: The adapter does not increase voltage. It also does not store power; that is the responsibility of the laptop battery. It is also accomplished by a UPS, though you probably wouldn't lug one of those around with your laptop while traveling.

16. **Answer: A**

    Explanation: High-quality dot-matrix printheads can come in 9, 18, or 24 pins, with 24 being the highest quality.

    Incorrect answers: 15-pin is a number associated with the power connection of SATA as well as VGA connectors. 8-pin is associated with PCIe video cards and RJ45 plugs. 20-pin is the older standard for ATX main power connections, though today they are usually 24-pin.

17. **Answer: C**

    Explanation: Contrast ratio is the brightness of the brightest color (measured as white) compared to the darkest color (measured as black). Static contrast ratio measurements are static; they are performed as tests using a checkerboard pattern. But there is also the dynamic contrast ratio, a technology in LCD displays that adjusts dynamically during darker scenes in an attempt to give better black levels. It usually has a higher ratio, but it should be noted that there is no real uniform standard for measuring contrast ratio.

    Incorrect answers: Power consumption deals with the number of watts that the display uses. Display resolution is the number of pixels on the screen, measured horizontally by vertically. Displays often have a brightness setting as well as a contrast setting. The brightness setting is used to increase or decrease the amount of light put out by the display. Power savings is another concept altogether and can be adjusted by enabling the power savings feature of the operating system, ultimately using fewer watts and conserving energy while increasing the life span of the display.

18. **Answer: B**

    Explanation: Most antistatic straps come with a 1-megaohm resistor, which can protect against surges. However, the best way to avoid a surge is to (1) make sure the computer is unplugged before working on it, (2) not touch any components that hold a charge, and (3) stay away from live electricity sources. In other words, this means: don't open power supplies or CRT monitors; don't touch capacitors on any circuit boards such as motherboards; and, of course, stay away from any other electrical devices, wires, and circuits when working on computers.

    Incorrect answers: A Torx screwdriver is used to remove specialized screws from laptops and other mobile devices. A voltmeter (or a multimeter) is used to find out how many volts are being generated by a battery or are being cycled through an AC outlet. The antistatic mat is used to keep a computer and components at the same electrical potential as the person working on the computer.

19. **Answer: D**

    Explanation: High-Definition Multimedia Interface (HDMI), as the word *multimedia* implies, can transmit video and audio signals.

    Incorrect answers: VGA, RGB, and DVI are video standards only.

20. Answer: D

Explanation: A router can limit network broadcasts through segmenting and pro-grammed routing of data. This is part of a router's job when connecting two or more networks. It is also used with different media. For example, you might have a LAN that uses twisted-pair cable, but the router connects to the Internet via a fiber-optic connec-tion. That one router will have ports for both types of connections.

Incorrect answers: A switch connects multiple computers on the LAN; it does not limit IP-based network broadcasts. However, the switch does not segment by IP address; it communicates with computers and segments the network via MAC addresses. Also, the switch normally uses one type of media—twisted pair, connecting to RJ45 ports. However, it is possible that the switch might connect to another switch by way of a specialized fiber-optic connector. A wireless access point (WAP) connects the comput-ers on the wireless LAN (WLAN). It often has only one connection, a single RJ45 port. A hardware-based firewall usually connects to the network via RJ45; regardless, it has only one or only a few connections. It doesn't deal with routing or broadcasts; instead, it prevents intrusion to a network.

21. Answer: C

Explanation: Near-field communication (NFC) is a wireless technology that allows mobile devices to transfer data simply by touching or being in close proximity to each other, as well as make payments wirelessly to some point-of-sale (POS) systems.

Incorrect answers: Bluetooth is a wireless technology that is used with peripherals such as headsets and speakers. IR stands for infrared, a technology that can be used to beam information, but today it is not used often with mobile devices. Long-Term Evolution (LTE) is a data communications technology used by cellular phones and smartphones; it is based on GSM and is often found in conjunction with 4G.

22. Answer: D

Explanation: The CPU could overheat if thermal compound has not been applied cor-rectly (which is common) or if it is not seated properly (which is rare).

Incorrect answers: As part of the boot process, power needs to verify the CPU. If the wrong voltage is running to the CPU, the system won't even boot. If an incorrect CPU has been installed, the system will probably not boot, especially if the BIOS doesn't recognize it. Finally, the CPU doesn't use a driver; instead, the BIOS recognizes it (or doesn't, if it needs a BIOS update) and passes that information to the operating system.

23. Answer: C

Explanation: Of the answers listed, 172.17.58.254 is the only valid IPv4 address for a network host. A host on the network is any computer or network device that uses an IP address to communicate with other computers or devices. 172.17.58.254 is a class B private IP address, so it fits the description of a valid IPv4 address for a network host.

Incorrect answers: 127.0.0.1 is the IPv4 local loopback address. Every computer using TCP/IP gets this address; it is used for testing. It cannot be used to communicate with other hosts on the network. 169.254.0.0/16 means an IP address of 169.254.0.0 with a default subnet mask of 255.255.0.0, indicating the network number is 169.254. It is not a valid host IP address because it ends in 0.0. The first IP address of a network is always reserved for the network number; it cannot be used by a host. Otherwise, if the address were, say, 169.254.0.1, the address would work, but because it is an APIPA address, it would be able to communicate only with other systems using APIPA addresses. 255.10.15.7 is not valid. That address is within the class E reserved range. For normal host IP addresses, the first octet is either between 1 and 126 or between 128 and 223, but not between 224 and 255.

24. **Answer: C**

Explanation: Dynamic random-access memory (DRAM) is a module (or stick) of memory that you can install into a motherboard. SDRAM, DDR, DDR2, DDR3, and DDR4 are all examples of DRAM.

Incorrect answers: The complementary metal-oxide semiconductor (CMOS) is a chip soldered onto the motherboard that works in conjunction with the Basic Input/Output System, another chip soldered onto the motherboard. Static RAM (SRAM) is memory that is nonvolatile (as opposed to DRAM); it is also soldered to the circuit board. Read-only memory (ROM) is usually not serviceable. The BIOS resides on a ROM chip, more specifically an electrically erasable programmable ROM (EEPROM) chip.

25. **Answer: C**

Explanation: 172.31.1.1 is the only address listed that is private. It is within the class B range of private addresses: 172.16.0.0–172.31.255.255.

Incorrect answers: 11.58.254.169 is not private because it is on the class A 11 network. The class A private range is within the 10.0.0.0 network. 169.255.10.41 is not private either. Microsoft's APIPA, however, uses the 169.254.0.0 network, which is private. 192.169.0.1 is public because of the second octet: 169. The class C private range is 192.168.0.0–192.168.255.255.

26. **Answer: B**

Explanation: The IPv6 loopback address used for testing is ::1. This determines if IPv6 is working correctly on the network card but does not generate network traffic. It exists on every computer that runs IPv6.

Incorrect answers: 127.0.0.1 is the IPv4 loopback address. 192.168.0.0 is simply a private IP network number. FE80::/10 is the link-local prefix—a range of auto-assigned addresses in IPv6.

27. **Answer: C**

Explanation: The only statement that is correct concerning IPv6 is that it uses 128-bit addressing. This is compared to IPv4, which uses 32-bit addresses.

Incorrect answers: IPv6 and IPv4 can cohabit a computer with no problems. IPv6 is not necessarily supported by all routers. Some routers still only support IPv4. IPv6 is a logical concept. The physical cable that connects to the computer has no bearing over which IP version is used.

28. **Answer: B**

    Explanation: A typical operating temperature for CPUs is 60° Celsius. Keep in mind that the operating range may be above or below that. Many computers hover around 30° to 35° Celsius.

    Incorrect answers: On the other hand, 72° Celsius becomes much less typical, even if the user is overclocking the system. A temperature of 60° Fahrenheit is equal to 15.5° Celsius. A processor will not run that cold (but it would be pretty efficient if it did!). A temperature of 72° Fahrenheit falls within the range of room temperature and is what you should set the room temperature for computers to run at their best.

29. **Answer: A**

    Explanation: The impact printer technology is what you want. This strikes the ribbon and consequently the paper with a printhead. The physical hammering action causes the carbon backing to apply text to the next layer of paper. Multipart forms such as these are commonly used for receipts.

    Incorrect answers: Laser printers can print to special multipart forms, but not ones with carbon backing. Inkjet and thermal printers are not used with multipart forms usually.

30. **Answer: D**

    Explanation: You cannot install drivers to the UEFI/BIOS. Drivers are software that allows the operating system to communicate with hardware; they can be configured in the Device Manager in Windows.

    Incorrect answers: The rest of the answers can be configured in the BIOS. The boot sequence (also known as boot priority or boot order) allows you to select which device will be booted off first. (The hard drive is the most secure.) Temperature thresholds allow you to set alerts and possibly shut down the system if the CPU runs too hot. Overclocking occurs when the CPU's voltage is raised and the speed is increased. Overclocking is not recommended, but if you do configure it, you should set temperature thresholds. Intrusion detection can be enabled and will log if a person opened the computer case.

31. **Answers: A and E**

    Explanation: POP3 is a protocol used by email clients to receive email. It makes use of either port 110 (considered insecure) or port 995 (a default secure port).

    Incorrect answers: SMTP is used by email clients to send email. It uses port 25 and the more secure port 587.

32. **Answer: D**

    Explanation: To connect one computer to another directly by way of network adapter cards, use a crossover cable. (The category such as 5e or 6 doesn't matter.) That cable is designed to connect *like* devices. It is wired as T568B on one end and T568A on the other. Those standards are ratified by the Telecommunications Industry Association/Electronic Industries Alliance (TIA/EIA).

Incorrect answers: A regular (and more common) Cat 6 patch cable is known as a straight-through cable. It is used to connect *unlike* devices, such as a computer to a switch. Normally, it is wired with the T568B standard on each end. A parallel cable might be used to connect an older printer to a computer or an external hard drive to a SCSI card. *Rolled cable* is a less commonly used term for a cable that administrators use to connect from a serial port on a PC to a console port on a router. Its proper name is a *null-modem cable*, but it might also be referred to as a *rollover cable* or a *console cable*.

33. **Answer: A**

    Explanation: Network installations require that the network card be configured for Preboot eXecution Environment (PXE). This allows the network card to boot off the network, locate a network installation server, and request that the installation begin. This configuration might be done in the UEFI/BIOS of the computer (if the network adapter is integrated to the motherboard), within a special program in Windows, or in one that boots from disc or other removable media (if the network adapter is an adapter card).

    Incorrect answers: Peripheral Component Interconnect Express (PCIe) is an expansion bus that accepts video cards, network adapter cards, sound cards, and so on. PCL stands for Printer Command Language, developed by HP so that a computer can properly communicate with impact or thermal printers. PnP stands for plug and play, a Windows technology that allows devices to be located and installed automatically.

34. **Answer: A**

    Explanation: The CPU is the least likely to be replaced. You would probably need to replace other equipment, too, in this case. Just like PCs, though, the CPU should rarely fail.

    Incorrect answers: However, you might upgrade, replace, or add to RAM. M.2 cards are internal cards that can be added or upgraded to incorporate better video or WLAN and Bluetooth. Laptop keyboards fall victim to spilled coffee, overuse, and other damage over time and sometimes need to be replaced.

35. **Answers: C and D**

    Explanation: 1000 Mbps is 1000 megabits per second, otherwise notated as 1,000,000,000 bits per second, or 1 gigabit per second.

    Incorrect answers: Data transfer is measured in bits per second (bps), not bits per minute. Consequently, 1000 bits per second would be very slow. At their peak, dial-up modems would transfer 56,000 bits per second, and that is considered the slowest Internet access you could find in the United States.

36. **Answer: B**

    Explanation: Single-mode fiber-optic cable can send data farther than any of the other answers—up to hundreds of kilometers.

    Incorrect answers: Multi-mode fiber-optic cable can send data about 600 meters. STP is a type of twisted pair; all twisted pair is limited to 100 meters or 328 feet. Coaxial cable is limited to 200 or 500 meters, depending on the type.

37. **Answer: C**

    Explanation: You should install a USB add-on card. This will give you more ports than the computer already has for use with peripherals. Another option—and a more common option at that—would be to purchase a USB hub.

    Incorrect answers: Modems, network adapters, and TV tuner cards all have their own purpose and do not allow additional peripherals.

38. **Answer: D**

    Explanation: A typical speed of a magnetic hard disk drive is 7200 RPM—rotational speed, that is. Other common rotational speeds include 5400 RPM, 10,000 RPM, and 15,000 RPM. Note: Solid-state hard drives do not have a magnetic disk and therefore are not given an RPM rating or a latency rating.

    Incorrect answers: A common network data transfer rate is 1000 Mbps. SATA hard drives commonly have a DTR of 6 Gb/s (600 MB/s). Note that 3.1 GHz is a common CPU frequency, and 32 GB might be the amount of RAM you install in a computer or the size of a USB flash drive.

39. **Answer: A**

    Explanation: A switch interconnects devices on the same network so that they can communicate, whereas a router interconnects one or more networks.

    Incorrect answers: All other answers are incorrect. Remember that the switch is in charge of connecting devices on the LAN, but the router is in charge of connecting the LAN to another LAN, to the Internet, or to both. Multifunction network devices make matters confusing; they combine the functionality of a switch, a router, a wireless access point, and a firewall. Physically, the four-port section of the device is the switch portion, and the single port that leads to the Internet is the router portion.

40. **Answer: D**

    Explanation: In a large corporation (or enterprise environment), tape backup such as Linear Tape-Open (LTO) or Digital Linear Tape (DLT) is the best media for backing up.

    Incorrect answers: LTO and DLT tapes have a large capacity, allowing for a huge amount of backup as compared to DVD and dual-layer DVD (4.7–17 GB) and USB flash drives (typically 16 to 256 GB as of the writing of this book).

41. **Answers: A and D**

    Explanation: The organization will most likely use local-area networks (LAN) for each office and a metropolitan-area network (MAN) to connect the three networks. The LANs meet the requirements for each office's internal communications. Most LANs operate at 1 Gbps or faster. The MAN meets the requirement for the connection between the offices within the city. A MAN is the right choice because it can harness the power of fiber-optic cables and other technologies that already exist in the city limits and provide for 1 Gbps or more throughput.

Incorrect answers: A personal-area network (PAN) is a group of Bluetooth devices that communicate with each other. A wide-area network (WAN) is one that connects multiple LANs but usually over longer distances—often between cities. Also, a WAN does not typically have as much data throughput as a MAN. A storage-area network (SAN) is a group of storage arrays, network-attached storage (NAS) devices, and so on. It could be that the offices might use one, but just having a SAN does not meet the throughput requirements; plus, a SAN can be within a LAN, cross over to a MAN, or move beyond to a WAN, so it is somewhat vague when considering the scenario. A wireless local-area network (WLAN) might be incorporated as well, but as of the writing of this book (2019), you'd be hard-pressed to get it to meet the 1 Gbps data throughput requirement for all computers.

42. Answer: D

Explanation: VMware is an example of virtualization software. Actually, VMware is the company, and it makes a multitude of software including virtualization software such as VMware Workstation and VMware ESXi.

Incorrect answers: *On-demand* is cloud-based terminology, meaning that a customer has access to cloud services 24 hours, 7 days a week. Infrastructure as a service (IaaS) is a type of cloud model that allows a company to use the cloud to host networking infrastructure, routing, and VM hosting (which includes various types of virtualization software). In measured services, the provider monitors the services rendered so that the provider can properly bill the customer and make sure that the customer's use of services is being handled in the most efficient way.

43. Answer: D

Explanation: Smartphones typically use Secure Digital (SD) cards—more to the point, microSD cards.

Incorrect answers: SSD stands for solid-state drive. This technology is implemented as flash-based hard drives or as adapter cards with DDR memory and a battery. CompactFlash (CF) cards are a bit bulkier and might be used in conjunction with older PCs, laptops, and handheld computers. USB flash drives don't fit inside a typical smartphone and so are relegated to hanging on people's key chains and acting as mobile transporters of data.

44. Answer: C

Explanation: In this scenario, the organization probably has thin client computers for its users. These computers have operating systems that are embedded in flash memory, and the rest of the information they require comes from a server. Thin clients normally have no hard drive; this is why they are referred to as *diskless* workstations.

Incorrect answers: Virtualization workstations definitely need a hard drive and require lots of other resources; they are not as dependent on servers. Client/server is a type of networking organizational technique. However, thin clients often log in to a server. Thick clients are, for the most, part PCs, the typical desktop computer.

45. **Answers: A and B**

    Explanation: Know the main steps of the laser printer imaging process: processing, charging, exposing, developing, transferring, fusing, and cleaning. In the charging step, the drum is conditioned/charged by the primary corona wire (negatively charging it) and is prepared for writing. In the transferring step, the paper is positively charged by the transfer corona wire, preparing it to accept the toner from the drum.

    Incorrect answers: In the fusing step, the toner is fused to the paper with heat and pressure. In the cleaning step (the last step), the receptacle, rollers, and other items are cleaned and readied for the next print job.

46. **Answer: B**

    Explanation: When testing the main 24-pin ATX power connector that leads from the power supply to the motherboard, use a power supply unit tester (PSU tester) or a multimeter. The multimeter can test each individual wire's voltage, but the PSU tester can test them all in one shot.

    Incorrect answers: A Torx screwdriver is used to open computers and laptops that have special Torx screws; T-10 is a common size. A receptacle tester is used to test an AC outlet, although multimeters can be used for that as well. A tone and probe kit is used to test telephone and network connections for continuity. However, it can test only one pair of the wires in the cable. For better results when testing network cables, use a proper network cable testing kit. Testing tools are a key ingredient in a computer technician's toolkit.

47. **Answer: C**

    Explanation: The Service Location Protocol (SLP) uses port 427. It enables access to network services without previous configuration of the client computer.

    Incorrect answers: FTP uses port 21 by default. DNS uses port 53. HTTPS uses port 443. RDP uses port 3389.

48. **Answer: F**

    Explanation: The Apple Filing Protocol (AFP) uses port 548. AFP offers file services for Mac computers running macOS and can transfer files across the network.

    Incorrect answers: Port 22 is used by SSH. Port 23 is used by Telnet. Port 80 is used by HTTP. Port 143 is used by IMAP. Port 445 is used by SMB.

49. **Answer: A**

    Explanation: Tablets do not have a touchpad; instead, you use your finger(s) or a stylus to tap on the display (known as a *touchscreen*).

    Incorrect answers: Tablets have displays and wireless network adapters. They also have an onscreen keyboard. The question does not specify physical or virtual keyboard. Be ready for vagaries such as those on the real exam.

50. Answer: B

Explanation: When troubleshooting a computer system, always look for the most likely and simplest solutions first. The fact that the user might not have turned on her monitor when she first came in is a likely scenario.

Incorrect answers: If the monitor *was* on, you would move on down the troubleshooting list. So afterward, you could check whether the computer is on, if the computer and monitor are plugged into the AC outlet, and whether the monitor is plugged into the computer. Reinstalling the video driver is much further down the list.

51. Answer: A

Explanation: Chances are that the computer has faulty memory or a memory module that needs to be reseated properly. The flashing cursor on the screen tells you that the system is not posting properly. The numbers counting up are the system checking the RAM. If the system beeps and freezes during this count-up, the RAM has an issue. It could also be incompatible with the motherboard.

Incorrect answers: A corrupt MBR would either give a message stating "missing OS" or "the MBR is corrupt." However, most systems today are GPT-based, not MBR-based. If the OS was corrupted, you would get a message to that effect. If the computer attempts to boot off the network, you will see gray text and a spinning pipe sign as it attempts to find a DHCP server.

52. Answer: A

Explanation: If you get any address that starts with 169.254, the computer has self-assigned that address. It is known as an APIPA (Automatic Private IP Addressing) address, a type of link-local address. Normally, DHCP servers do not use this network number. A simple **ipconfig/release** and **ipconfig/renew** might fix the problem, if a DHCP server is actually available.

Incorrect answers: The POP3 server is for incoming mail, the DNS server is for resolving domain names to IP addresses, and the WINS server is for resolving NetBIOS names to IP addresses.

53. Answer: D

Explanation: Ghosted images or blurry marks could be a sign that the drum has some kind of imperfection or is dirty, especially if the image reappears at equal intervals. Replace the drum (or toner cartridge). Another possibility is that the fuser assembly has been damaged and needs to be replaced.

Incorrect answers: Blank pages might indicate a problem with the transfer corona wire or primary corona wire; if so, replace the toner cartridge. Stuck pages, jams, or problems with feeding the paper could be due to the pickup rollers.

54. Answers: A, B, and D

Explanation: Always make sure that the speaker power (if any) is plugged into an AC outlet and that the speakers are turned on (if they have a power button). When a sound card is first installed, Windows should recognize it and either install a driver through plug and play or ask for a driver CD. For best results, use the manufacturer's driver, the latest of which you can find on its website. Make sure that you plug the speakers into the correct 1/8" jack. The speaker out is the one with concentric circles and an arrow pointing out. Or you might have 5.1 (or 7.1) surround sound; in this case, you would use the standard front speaker jack, which is often a green jack.

Incorrect answers: It's quite hard to plug a sound card into the wrong slot. For example, if you have a PCI Express (PCIe) x1 sound card (a common standard), you can plug that sound card into any of the available PCIe slots on your motherboard, and it will be recognized. (Word to the wise: If you ever remove the sound card when upgrading, make sure you put it back in the same slot.) PCIe cards will not fit in the older PCI slot.

55. Answer: D

Explanation: The wireless hardware button is turned off. Always check that Wi-Fi switch. If it is enabled, make sure that the wireless adapter is enabled in Windows. Also, check whether the laptop is within range of the wireless access point.

Incorrect answers: The drivers and the firmware should not be an issue because the laptop was able to connect yesterday. However, you never know what might have happened, so check those later on in your troubleshooting process.

56. Answer: C

Explanation: The purpose of a DNS server is to resolve (convert) hostnames and domain names to the IP address. Computers normally communicate via IP address, but it is easier for humans to type in names. If dprocomputer.com is down, you cannot ping the corresponding IP address at all.

Incorrect answers: If the DHCP server is down, your workstation will probably not have an IP on the network and again will not ping the corresponding IP address. AD DS is Active Directory Domain Services, meaning a domain controller, which doesn't have much to do with this, except that in many smaller companies, the domain controller and DNS server are one and the same.

57. Answer: B

Explanation: You must have the correct firmware to recognize the latest CPUs. A BIOS flash can fix many problems related to unidentified hardware.

Incorrect answers: If the CPU is not seated properly or if you have an incorrect CPU, the system simply won't boot. Windows does not affect the POST at all. In some cases, you might purchase a motherboard that says it can support a specific new processor. However, the firmware might not have been written yet to actually work with that processor.

58. Answer: B

Explanation: Ipconfig/all shows a lot of information, including the MAC address, as well as the DNS server, DHCP information, and more.

Incorrect answers: Plain old ipconfig shows only the IP address, subnet mask, and gateway address. **Ping** tests whether other computers are alive on the network. Ipconfig/release is used to troubleshoot DHCP-obtained IP addresses. It is often used in conjunction with ipconfig/renew.

59. Answer: D

Explanation: First, try printing an internal test page, meaning from the printer's onscreen display. If that doesn't work, you need to start troubleshooting the printer. Perhaps the toner cartridge is empty, or maybe a corona wire is malfunctioning.

Incorrect answers: If the test page prints fine, you can check the printer drivers and other settings at the computer that uses the printer. Restarting the spooler should not help in this situation. If the spooler stalled, no paper should come out of the printer. Likewise, the printer cable should not have to be replaced.

60. Answers: A and B

Explanation: The easiest and (probably) cheapest way is to move the WAP. Basements are usually the worst place for an access point because of concrete foundations and walls, electrical interference, and so on. Signal boosters might also work, but often the cost of a signal booster is the same as buying a newer, more powerful WAP.

Incorrect answers: Unfortunately, new drivers and firmware usually do not help the situation. It's possible that a new driver can make better use of the wireless network adapter hardware, but it won't necessarily offer a better connection. It's a good idea in any event, but it's not one of the best answers listed.

61. Answer: C

Explanation: The most likely issue is a DHCP failure. Link-local IP addresses such as APIPA on 169.254.0.0 usually kick in when the client computer cannot locate a DHCP server. There are several possible reasons why this might happen: lack of network connectivity, incorrect client configuration, DHCP server failure, and so on. The best way to troubleshoot this situation would be to start at the client and check its network cable (or wireless connection) and then its TCP/IP configuration. You could also try configuring a static IP address on the client to see if it allows the client to communicate over the network. If those things don't solve the problem or give you any clues, you can look at the network switch, DHCP server, and so on.

Incorrect answers: DNS resolution has to do with the translation between hostnames and IP addresses: no hostnames are a part of this scenario; we are troubleshooting at the IP level. Duplicate IP addresses happen when two computers are statically configured with the same IP address; they are uncommon (if not rare) in DHCP environments or when APIPA is involved. The Address Resolution Protocol is responsible for converting IP addresses to MAC addresses. The ARP cache is built off the current

IP address and the IP and MAC addresses of other computers. Clearing the cache won't solve the problem, but it won't make things any worse either. However, you might consider clearing the ARP cache after the problem is fixed, or you might restart the computer.

62. Answer: C

Explanation: The simplest solution is often the most common. Check cables and see whether the power is on for your devices and computers.

Incorrect answers: Afterward, you can check the driver (for example, within the Device Manager in Windows) and check the firewall settings as well. Whether or not the drive is fragmented should not affect the Internet connection.

63. Answers: A and C

Explanation: It is common to have an unseated RAM stick or video card. These are the most common culprits of beep codes during the POST.

Incorrect answers: If the CPU is not installed properly, you might not even get any beep codes at all. And the optical drive's functionality has little bearing on the POST.

64. Answers: B and D

Explanation: Two examples of virtual printing include XPS printing and print to file (one example of which saves the file as a .prn). Other examples include printing to PDF and printing to image.

Incorrect answers: "Start printing after the last page is spooled" is a spooling setting used to lessen the load on physical or virtual printers, but is a technology that printers use, not a type of virtual printing. Printing to a printer pool is another type of printer configuration used to print to a group of printers, making use of the collective whole for efficiency; but again, these could be physical or virtual printers, and it is not a type of virtual printing in and of itself.

65. Answer: C

Explanation: Use the USB connector. By far, this is the easiest method. Windows will sense the USB connection and attempt to install the print driver automatically (though you should still install the latest proper driver from the printer manufacturer's website).

Incorrect answers: Yes, the printer has an Ethernet connection as well (that is the network connection), but using it will require you to connect it to the network. What if there is no network? And even if there is, the printer would have to be configured for the network, and then the laptop would have to connect to the printer over the network. If the laptop is the only system that will use the printer, USB becomes much easier. Thunderbolt often uses the mini DisplayPort for the transmission of data or video, especially on Apple-based computers (though not limited to those). Though Thunderbolt can be used for printing, the scenario doesn't state that the laptop has a Thunderbolt port.

66. Answer: A

Explanation: Excessive heat is the most likely cause of the problem. This could be an unfortunate result of ovens and other equipment. Computers in environments such as these are often prone to dirt collecting inside the CPU fans and other devices inside the case.

Incorrect answers: Faulty RAM wouldn't cause hard drives to fail or unseat expansion cards. The cards probably moved around due to thermal expansion and contraction. You are most likely going to find 240-volt outlets in this environment, but the computer shouldn't use those; in the United States, the computer should be connected to a 120-volt outlet. The computer should be changed to 240 V only if it is brought to another country—for example, a country in Europe. Power brownouts could cause failures of the power supply and maybe even the hard drive, but they would not cause the adapter cards to be unseated.

67. Answer: A

Explanation: Thermal expansion and contraction happen when humidity changes quickly. This can lead to what some technicians refer to as "chip creep" or "card creep."

Incorrect answers: Although there might have been chip creep, the direct cause of the problem was most likely thermal expansion/contraction. POST errors would not be the cause of the error, but in some cases could give you diagnostic information leading to the cause. Thermal sublimation deals with a specific type of printing process and is not involved in the problem. While in the computer, you might want to check other adapter cards in case they also were affected by this phenomenon.

68. Answer: C

Explanation: Fiber-optic networks use fiber-optic cables that have a core of plastic or glass fibers. They are much more difficult to eavesdrop on than any copper cable.

Incorrect answers: Satellite connections and cable Internet use RG-6. DSL uses a standard phone line or other twisted-pair cable. These other options are copper-based.

69. Answer: C

Explanation: The surface area of the heat sink has the greatest effect on heat dispersion. The more solid the bond between the heat sink and CPU cap, the better the transition of heat out of the CPU. To aid in this transition, you must use thermal compound.

Incorrect answers: The other answers have little or nothing to do with heat dispersion. The shape of the heat sink is somewhat important, but most CPUs have the same shape. The key is to get the appropriate heat sink for the type of CPU you are using.

70. Answer: B

Explanation: You will be implementing a virtualization workstation and thin clients. The virtualization workstation will run virtual software that will allow you to install the server software to a virtual machine (VM). This server provides most of the resources for the clients on the network—the thin clients. Thin clients normally have very limited resources of their own and rely on the server (be it a regular or virtual server) for the additional resources they need.

Incorrect answers: A CAD/CAM workstation is used for computer-aided design and manufacturing. PCs have plenty of their own resources and do not need a server supplying those resources. A home server PC is a possibility in this scenario if it runs in a virtual environment. However, thick clients don't meet the requirements of this scenario. Thick clients have plenty of resources and are often used as another name for PCs. An AV editing workstation is an audio/video workstation, not a server, and laptops are not thin clients; they also have plenty of internal resources.

71. Answer: A

Explanation: The Simple Mail Transfer Protocol (SMTP) is not configured properly. That is the protocol used to send mail.

Incorrect answers: POP3 receives email. FTP enables two computers to upload and download files. HTTP is the protocol used by web browsers to surf the Internet.

72. Answer: D

Explanation: Use a plastic shim to open the display or remove the bezel that surrounds it.

Incorrect answers: Pliers have many uses but could cause damage to the plastic that surrounds the display of a laptop. Plastic tweezers are used to remove hard-to-reach parts such as screws from the inside of a PC. Flathead screwdrivers are not recommended because the metal can damage the plastic case of the laptop. However, after you remove the bezel, you will need a small *Phillips*-head screwdriver to unscrew the display.

73. Answer: B

Explanation: The only solution listed is to upgrade the video card. This is the only way that computer performance can be increased while editing video files.

Incorrect answers: The CPU and RAM can make the system faster when dealing with applications and calculations of many kinds, but when it comes to the video editing and rendering, an integrated video card is inadequate. No matter how much RAM you add or what CPU you put in, the video will still perform like an actor on the late, late, late movie—badly. Increasing the hard drive capacity will have no effect on video but can definitely help in other areas of system performance such as pagefile access and general data access.

74. Answers: A, C, D, and F

Explanation: The time/date, boot priority (boot sequence), passwords, and Wake-on-LAN (WOL) can all be configured in the UEFI/BIOS.

Incorrect answers: The registry and USB drivers are configured in Windows.

75. Answer: C

Explanation: To test IPv4, use the command **ping 127.0.0.1**. To test IPv6, use the command **ping ::1**.

Incorrect answers: You don't run **ipconfig** commands to particular IP addresses. There are no **ping :1** or **ping 127::1** commands.

76. **Answer: D**

Explanation: The typical latency of an SATA magnetic-based hard disk drive is 4.2 ms (milliseconds). When you are dealing with magnetic drives, latency is the delay in time before a particular sector on the platter can be read. It is directly linked to rotational speed. A hard drive with a rotational speed of 7200 RPM has an average latency of 4.2 ms.

Incorrect answers: Note that 300 MB/s is the data transfer rate of an SATA revision 2.0 hard drive; it is also expressed as 3.0 Gb/s. Also, 7200 RPM is the rotational speed of the drive, and 64 MB is a common amount of cache memory on a hard drive; it is usually DRAM.

77. **Answer: B**

Explanation: A maintenance kit includes a new fuser assembly, rollers, and more. Installing a maintenance kit is like changing a car's oil (although it isn't done as often).

Incorrect answers: Cleaning the printer might not be necessary. If you have a toner spill or work in a dirty environment, cleaning it might be a good idea. Clearing the counter is something you might do on an inkjet printer; this process clears the counter of how much ink goes through the cartridge. Printing a test page is important when first installing a printer and when you finish installing a maintenance kit.

78. **Answer: D**

Explanation: On-demand means that a customer can get access to cloud-based services 24 hours a day, 7 days a week and that the customer can get additional space if needed on a temporary basis. This links with scalability to a certain extent.

Incorrect answers: Resource pooling occurs when resources (RAM and CPU), servers, and infrastructure are shared by multiple customers. However, shared resources, in general, are resources that are shared for use by remote users. Virtual application streaming refers to applications (such as email clients) that are served from a cloud provider and run within a virtual machine or instance of some sort. Synchronization applications are programs that will aid in the synchronization of data between a client and a server on the cloud. For example, a single synchronization program might take care of the sync of data for several programs, such as email, calendar, and contacts.

79. **Answer: A**

Explanation: You should run ipconfig /flushdns in an attempt to fix the problem. The problem could be that the DNS cache on the client computer is outdated and cannot associate Internet domain names with their corresponding IP addresses. So you run ipconfig /flushdns and potentially ipconfig /registerdns (or computer restart) to fix the problem. That clears the DNS cache of name resolutions and forces the client to request new DNS information from a DNS server either on the Internet or within the company.

Incorrect answers: Ipconfig /all shows in-depth information about the network adapter's TCP/IP configuration. If there is an incorrect DNS server configuration, this information will help you identify it but won't help to solve the problem.

Ipconfig/release is used to remove a DHCP-obtained IP address from a network adapter. (**Ipconfig/renew** is often run afterward to get a new IP.) **Ipconfig/setclassid** is a potential solution because it allows for an additional set of DHCP options for each class ID, including gateway address, DNS server address, and so on. These options are often set at the DHCP server, and you would need to know the class ID number that you wish to use. However, it is unlikely from this scenario that the class ID was ever changed. Due to the time the user was away from the computer (on vacation), it is more likely that the DNS cache needs to be purged.

80. **Answer: B**

Explanation: The thermal design power (TDP) of a CPU is measured in watts. For example, a typical Core i7 CPU might be rated at 140 watts or less. The less the wattage rating, the less the computer's cooling system needs to dissipate heat generated by the CPU.

Incorrect answers: Volts is potential energy; it is a measurement commonly associated with internal PC components running at 5- or 12-volt DC and with typical household and business AC outlets running at 120 volts or 240 volts. Ohms is the measurement used for impedance, or the resistance to electricity. Amps is the measurement for electric current. A typical computer might use 4 amps of current if it has a 500-watt power supply.

CHAPTER FOUR

220-1001 Practice Exam C

This time let's turn up the gas a little further. I've increased the level of difficulty once more. This third 220-1001 exam could be considered an advanced practice exam. Be ready for more scenario-oriented and troubleshooting-based questions.

If you didn't take a break already, I suggest taking one between exams. If you did not score 90 percent or higher on the first two 220-1001 practice exams, do not take this one yet. Go back and study, and then retake those exams until you pass with 90 percent or higher. Then come back to this exam.

Write down your answers and check them against the Quick-Check Answer Key that immediately follows the exam. After the answer key, you will find the explanations for all of the answers. Good luck!

Practice Questions

1. You just installed a maintenance kit to a laser printer. Which of the following steps should you take next?

    ○ **A.** You should restore the printer to factory settings.

    ○ **B.** You should print a test page.

    ○ **C.** You should refill the paper trays.

    ○ **D.** You should restart the printer.

Quick Answer: **102**
Detailed Answer: **103**

2. Which of the following is indicated by repetitive flashing lights on the keyboard during POST?

    ○ **A.** A software error

    ○ **B.** A hardware error

    ○ **C.** A password is required

    ○ **D.** An external peripheral error

Quick Answer: **102**
Detailed Answer: **103**

3. Which of the following defines the protocols associated with the following TCP or UDP port numbers, in order?

21, 22, 25, 53, 443, 3389

- ○ **A.** FTP, Telnet, SMTP, DNS, HTTP, RDP
- ○ **B.** FTP, SSH, SMTP, DNS, HTTP, RDP
- ○ **C.** FTP, SSH, SMTP, POP3, HTTPS, RDP
- ○ **D.** FTP, SSH, SMTP, DNS, HTTPS, RDP

4. Which of the following multimeter settings should be used only when there is no electrical flow through the part being tested? (Select the two best answers.)

- ❏ **A.** Continuity
- ❏ **B.** Wattage
- ❏ **C.** Voltage
- ❏ **D.** Amps
- ❏ **E.** Resistance

5. When a PC is first booted, which of the following tests the processor, RAM, video card, hard drive controllers, drives, and keyboard?

- ○ **A.** CMOS chip
- ○ **B.** BIOS setup
- ○ **C.** POST
- ○ **D.** Bootstrap loader

6. One of your customers needs to provide the following for corporate laptops:

- ▶ User security
- ▶ Charging ability
- ▶ Access to LAN resources
- ▶ Connect removable hardware

Which of the following would be the best solution for all requirements?

- ○ **A.** Port replicator
- ○ **B.** Thunderbolt
- ○ **C.** USB hub
- ○ **D.** Docking station
- ○ **E.** Cable lock

7. You have purchased a motherboard for your new audio workstation. You have opened the computer case and are ready to install.
   What are the first and last things you should do? (Select the two
   best answers.)

   ❏   **A.** Select a motherboard.

   ❏   **B.** Install the CPU.

   ❏   **C.** Test the motherboard.

   ❏   **D.** Put on an antistatic strap.

   ❏   **E.** Connect the main power cable.

Quick Answer: **102**
Detailed Answer: **104**

8. Which of the following tools should be used to determine why a
   computer fails to boot?

   ○   **A.** Cable tester

   ○   **B.** Loopback plug

   ○   **C.** PSU tester

   ○   **D.** Tone and probe kit

Quick Answer: **102**
Detailed Answer: **104**

9. Which type of cache memory is shared by all cores of a CPU?

   ○   **A.** L1

   ○   **B.** L2

   ○   **C.** L3

   ○   **D.** DRAM

Quick Answer: **102**
Detailed Answer: **104**

10. Which technology calculates two independent sets of instructions
    simultaneously, simulating two CPUs?

    ○   **A.** Hyper-threading

    ○   **B.** HyperTransport

    ○   **C.** Turbo Boost

    ○   **D.** Multi-core

Quick Answer: **102**
Detailed Answer: **105**

11. You are tasked with plugging a network patch cable into an inactive
    drop within a user's cubicle. Which of the following tools enables
    you to find the correct network drop in the wiring closet so that
    you can make the port hot?

    ○   **A.** PSU tester

    ○   **B.** Multimeter

    ○   **C.** Cable tester

    ○   **D.** Tone and probe kit

Quick Answer: **102**
Detailed Answer: **105**

12. You think that the power supply in your PC might be failing, causing issues with an SATA drive. You decide to test the SATA drive. Which of the following are the standard voltages of an SATA connection on an ATX power supply?

Quick Answer: **102**
Detailed Answer: **105**

- ○ **A.** 3.3 V, 5 V, 12 V
- ○ **B.** −3.3 V, 5 V, −12 V
- ○ **C.** −5 V, 5 V, 12 V
- ○ **D.** 5 V and 12 V

13. Which of the following is defined as the movement of electric charge?

Quick Answer: **102**
Detailed Answer: **105**

- ○ **A.** Voltage
- ○ **B.** Wattage
- ○ **C.** Amperage
- ○ **D.** Impedance

14. Which of the following should be used to clean a laser printer's rubber rollers?

Quick Answer: **102**
Detailed Answer: **106**

- ○ **A.** Soap and water
- ○ **B.** WD-40
- ○ **C.** Isopropyl alcohol
- ○ **D.** A moist cloth

15. A user's laptop running Windows 7 has suddenly become very dim. Adjusting the brightness does not help the problem. The display's images can be seen only by shining a flashlight directly at the screen. Which component should you consider replacing?

Quick Answer: **102**
Detailed Answer: **106**

- ○ **A.** Digitizer
- ○ **B.** Inverter
- ○ **C.** Video card
- ○ **D.** LCD panel

16. A coworker at a satellite office reports that a new replacement shared workgroup printer has arrived. It is the same model as the old one. Your coworker replaced the old printer and connected all the cables to the new printer. Which of the following is the easiest way to ensure that all the client computers can connect to the new printer via IPP?

Quick Answer: **102**
Detailed Answer: **106**

- ○ **A.** Name the new printer with the old printer name.
- ○ **B.** Allow the printer to acquire a DHCP address.
- ○ **C.** In DHCP, set a reservation by MAC address.
- ○ **D.** Have your coworker print the configuration page.

17. Which of the following communications protocols is used to connect to websites over secure communications links?

   ○ **A.** SSH

   ○ **B.** SFTP

   ○ **C.** HTTPS

   ○ **D.** Kerberos

Quick Answer: **102**
Detailed Answer: **107**

18. Which of the following protocols can be used to configure and monitor network printer device status?

   ○ **A.** SMTP

   ○ **B.** SNMP

   ○ **C.** TCP/IP

   ○ **D.** IPP

   ○ **E.** DNS

Quick Answer: **102**
Detailed Answer: **107**

19. Which of the following symptoms would indicate to you that there is a power supply issue?

   ○ **A.** The CPU is overclocking.

   ○ **B.** The Wi-Fi range is reduced.

   ○ **C.** The hard drives fail frequently.

   ○ **D.** Your CD burner takes longer to write than usual.

Quick Answer: **102**
Detailed Answer: **107**

20. Which of the following custom PC configurations requires a powerful CPU and maximum RAM to run multiple operating systems at the same time?

   ○ **A.** Graphic/CAD/CAM design workstation

   ○ **B.** Audio/video editing workstation

   ○ **C.** Virtualization workstation

   ○ **D.** NAS

Quick Answer: **102**
Detailed Answer: **107**

21. You need to install a device that can read groupings of parallel lines. Which of the following devices should be selected?

   ○ **A.** Biometric scanner

   ○ **B.** Image scanner

   ○ **C.** Barcode reader

   ○ **D.** Touchpad

Quick Answer: **102**
Detailed Answer: **108**

22. You are building a new gaming PC and want to select a mother-board that supports the Scalable Link Interface (SLI) technology so you can install two SLI video cards connected by a bridge. Which of the following expansion slots should the motherboard have for your two video cards?

    ○ **A.** Two PCIe version 2 slots

    ○ **B.** Two PCIe version 3 slots

    ○ **C.** A PCIe x1 slot and a PCIe x16 slot

    ○ **D.** A USB port and PCIe slot

Quick Answer: **102**
Detailed Answer: **108**

23. Which of the following RAID arrays is fault tolerant and allows you to do striping with parity?

    ○ **A.** RAID 0

    ○ **B.** RAID 1

    ○ **C.** RAID 5

    ○ **D.** RAID 10

Quick Answer: **102**
Detailed Answer: **108**

24. Which of the following are possible reasons that an optical mouse cursor erratically jumps around the screen? (Select the two best answers.)

    ❏ **A.** It is using an incorrect mouse driver.

    ❏ **B.** The mouse trackball needs to be removed and cleaned.

    ❏ **C.** There's a conflict with the keyboard.

    ❏ **D.** It is on an uneven surface.

    ❏ **E.** The mouse needs to be charged.

Quick Answer: **102**
Detailed Answer: **108**

25. Which of the following should be disabled to significantly conserve battery power of a laptop? (Select the two best answers.)

    ❏ **A.** Cellular

    ❏ **B.** Screen orientation

    ❏ **C.** Volume

    ❏ **D.** Touchpad

    ❏ **E.** Bluetooth

    ❏ **F.** Fingerprint reader

Quick Answer: **102**
Detailed Answer: **109**

26. When you are dealing with a power issue, which of the following should be checked first?

    ○ **A.** Input devices

    ○ **B.** Network cabling

    ○ **C.** Wall outlet

    ○ **D.** Power supply

Quick Answer: **102**
Detailed Answer: **109**

27. When a computer receives the IP address 169.254.127.1, which of the following has failed?

    ○ **A.** DHCP

    ○ **B.** DNS

    ○ **C.** WINS

    ○ **D.** APIPA

28. Emergency! Your boss forgot the password to the UEFI/BIOS on a computer. Which of the following methods helps you to reset the password?

    ○ **A.** Removing the RAM from the motherboard

    ○ **B.** Removing the CMOS battery from the motherboard

    ○ **C.** Removing the RAM jumper from the motherboard

    ○ **D.** Removing the main power connection from the motherboard

29. In a RAID 5 array of eight hard drives, how many can fail without losing the entire array?

    ○ **A.** Zero

    ○ **B.** One

    ○ **C.** Two

    ○ **D.** Five

30. A company laptop has a cracked display, and it is under warranty. Which of the following steps should be taken before shipping the laptop to the manufacturer for repair?

    ○ **A.** You should remove the LCD.

    ○ **B.** You should clean it thoroughly.

    ○ **C.** You should remove the hard drive.

    ○ **D.** You should remove the WLAN card.

31. Which of the following are the Intel and AMD names for CPU virtualization? (Select the two best answers.)

    ❏ **A.** VT-x

    ❏ **B.** AMD-Vi

    ❏ **C.** VT-d

    ❏ **D.** AMD-V

32. At 16x speed, how much data can a Blu-ray drive read per second?

    Quick Answer: **102**
    Detailed Answer: **111**

    ○ **A.** 50 GB
    ○ **B.** 576 Mb/s
    ○ **C.** 4.5 MB/s
    ○ **D.** 150 KB/s

33. Which of the following video connectors accepts digital and analog video signals only?

    Quick Answer: **102**
    Detailed Answer: **111**

    ○ **A.** DVI-D
    ○ **B.** DVI-A
    ○ **C.** DVI-I
    ○ **D.** HDMI Type B

34. Which of the following can be described as a mobile device sharing its Internet connection with other Wi-Fi–capable devices?

    Quick Answer: **102**
    Detailed Answer: **111**

    ○ **A.** USB tethering
    ○ **B.** Wi-Fi sharing
    ○ **C.** Internet passthrough
    ○ **D.** Mobile hotspot

35. Which of the printers would display an error that says: "replace filament"?

    Quick Answer: **102**
    Detailed Answer: **111**

    ○ **A.** Laser
    ○ **B.** 3D
    ○ **C.** Inkjet
    ○ **D.** Thermal

36. Which of the following steps should be taken first when a printer fails to print very large documents but still prints smaller documents without a problem?

    Quick Answer: **102**
    Detailed Answer: **111**

    ○ **A.** Check if the correct type of paper is being used.
    ○ **B.** Replace the communications cable.
    ○ **C.** Change the toner cartridges.
    ○ **D.** Add memory to the printer.

37. You print an image to your printer, but the page shows a ghosted image. Which of the following could be the cause?

    ○   **A.**   The drum needs replacing.

    ○   **B.**   The printer is offline.

    ○   **C.**   There's an incorrect driver.

    ○   **D.**   There's a dirty primary corona wire.

Quick Answer: **102**
Detailed Answer: **111**

38. A coworker notices that the battery light on a laptop is flashing when the laptop is in a docking station. Which of the following steps should be performed first to fix the problem?

    ○   **A.**   Replace the laptop battery.

    ○   **B.**   Reinstall the operating system.

    ○   **C.**   Reseat in the docking station.

    ○   **D.**   Remove and reseat the battery.

Quick Answer: **102**
Detailed Answer: **112**

39. A tablet device is having trouble accessing the wireless network. Which of the following steps should be taken to troubleshoot the problem? (Select the three best answers.)

    ❏   **A.**   Power cycle the device.

    ❏   **B.**   Use GPRS instead.

    ❏   **C.**   Check if the SSID was correct.

    ❏   **D.**   Set up a static IP.

    ❏   **E.**   Forget the network and reconnect to it.

Quick Answer: **102**
Detailed Answer: **112**

40. Which of the following steps should be taken to connect a Bluetooth headset to a smartphone? (Select the two best answers.)

    ❏   **A.**   Pair the device to the phone.

    ❏   **B.**   Install Bluetooth drivers.

    ❏   **C.**   Enter a passcode.

    ❏   **D.**   Disable Wi-Fi.

Quick Answer: **102**
Detailed Answer: **112**

41. A computer's CPU overheats and shuts down the system intermittently. Which of the following steps should be taken to fix the problem? (Select the two best answers.)

    ❏   **A.**   Check if the heat sink is secure.

    ❏   **B.**   Check the BIOS temperature threshold.

    ❏   **C.**   Check if the fan is connected.

    ❏   **D.**   Check if the RAM needs to be reseated.

Quick Answer: **102**
Detailed Answer: **112**

42. A burning smell comes from the computer. Which of the following is the most likely source?

  ○ **A.** Thermal compound

  ○ **B.** Keyboard

  ○ **C.** Power supply

  ○ **D.** AC outlet

43. A user recently purchased a new wireless 802.11ac router. After connecting a laptop with an 802.11ac wireless adapter to the wireless network, he notices that the signal strength on the laptop is poor and only connects at 54 Mbps. The user moved the laptop next to the WAP but is still experiencing the same issue. Which of the following is most likely the cause?

  ○ **A.** The cable modem is faulty.

  ○ **B.** The laptop is connecting to the incorrect wireless network.

  ○ **C.** The router's wireless card drivers are faulty.

  ○ **D.** The wireless antennas on the router need to be replaced.

44. Which of the following disk arrays provide for fault tolerance? (Select the two best answers.)

  ❏ **A.** Spanned volume

  ❏ **B.** RAID 0

  ❏ **C.** RAID 1

  ❏ **D.** RAID 5

45. You have been tasked with upgrading a desktop computer's internal storage to allow for storage room for backups, videos, and photos. This storage solution should be large enough to avoid scaling it again in the next 6 months. Which of the following is the appropriate solution?

  ○ **A.** 500 TB SAN

  ○ **B.** 50 GB NAS

  ○ **C.** 3 TB HDD

  ○ **D.** 512 GB SSD

46. Which of the following terminates a coaxial cable?

  ○ **A.** F connector

  ○ **B.** DB-9

  ○ **C.** RJ11

  ○ **D.** RJ45

47. Mary's printer is printing hundreds of pages, and she can't get it to stop. She has tried to delete the job by double-clicking the printer and deleting the print job. Which of the following steps represents the best way to stop the printer?

　　○　**A.** Clearing the print spooler

　　○　**B.** Unplugging the printer

　　○　**C.** Resetting the printer

　　○　**D.** Turning off the printer

48. You are troubleshooting a coworker's computer. When you ping the loopback address, you receive no response. Which of the following is the most likely cause of this problem?

　　○　**A.** The LAN is unresponsive.

　　○　**B.** The DHCP server is down.

　　○　**C.** The Ethernet cable needs to be replaced.

　　○　**D.** The TCP/IP protocol is not functioning.

49. Which of the following steps should be performed when troubleshooting a Bluetooth connection that is malfunctioning? (Select the two best answers.)

　　❏　**A.** Verify that WLAN is enabled.

　　❏　**B.** Check whether you are in range.

　　❏　**C.** Unpair the devices.

　　❏　**D.** Turn Bluetooth off and on.

50. A customer brings in a computer that doesn't display anything when it is turned on. You verify that the computer and monitor are receiving power and that the monitor is securely connected to the computer's only video port. Which of the following is the most likely cause of this problem? (Select all that apply.)

　　❏　**A.** Motherboard

　　❏　**B.** RAM

　　❏　**C.** Hard drive

　　❏　**D.** DVD-ROM

　　❏　**E.** CPU

　　❏　**F.** Power supply

　　❏　**G.** Video card

　　❏　**H.** SATA data cable

51. While troubleshooting a network problem, you discover that one set of LED lights on a switch is blinking rapidly even when all other nodes are disconnected. Which of the following is the most likely cause of this problem? (Select the two best answers.)

- ❑ **A.** A switch that is not plugged into a server
- ❑ **B.** A defective hard drive in the computer
- ❑ **C.** A defective network card in the computer
- ❑ **D.** An unplugged server
- ❑ **E.** A defective port on the network switch

52. A user with an Android phone is attempting to get email to work properly. The user can send email but cannot receive it. The user is required to connect to a secure IMAP server, as well as an SMTP server that uses SSL. To fix the problem, which port should you configure?

- ○ **A.** 25
- ○ **B.** 110
- ○ **C.** 143
- ○ **D.** 443
- ○ **E.** 993

53. You are called to a school lab to fix a computer. The computer supposedly worked fine the day before, but now it does not power on. The computer is plugged into a power strip with another computer. The other computer works fine. Which of the following is the most likely cause of this problem? (Select the two best answers.)

- ❑ **A.** The power cable is unplugged from the computer.
- ❑ **B.** The power strip is overloaded.
- ❑ **C.** The monitor is unplugged.
- ❑ **D.** The voltage switch on the power supply is set incorrectly.
- ❑ **E.** The power strip is unplugged.

54. Tracy cannot connect to the network and asks you to help. Which of the following steps should be performed first?

- ○ **A.** Replace the NIC.
- ○ **B.** Reconfigure TCP/IP.
- ○ **C.** Check for a link light on the NIC.
- ○ **D.** Install the latest NIC drivers.

55. You have been tasked with setting up a Wi-Fi thermostat for a customer. The customer has concerns about IoT devices getting hacked and possibly acting as a gateway to other devices and computers on the network. Which are the *best* ways to address the customer's concern? (Select the two best answers.)

- ❏ **A.** Upgrade the customer's router to the latest firmware version.

- ❏ **B.** Disable wireless access to the thermostat to make it unhackable.

- ❏ **C.** Upgrade the customer's wireless network to WPA.

- ❏ **D.** Separate the IoT thermostat by placing it in a DMZ.

- ❏ **E.** Use the latest encryption standard on the wireless network and set a strong password.

- ❏ **F.** Enable two-factor authentication for the IoT device's cloud account.

56. Your coworker's iPad is having trouble connecting to email. Which of the following steps should be performed to troubleshoot this problem? (Select the three best answers.)

- ❏ **A.** Verify Internet access.

- ❏ **B.** Check for Bluetooth connectivity.

- ❏ **C.** Check port numbers.

- ❏ **D.** Make sure that GPS is enabled.

- ❏ **E.** Verify username/password.

57. You just installed Microsoft Windows to a computer with three internal SATA hard drives and one external USB hard drive. SATA hard drive 1 contains the operating system. SATA hard drive 2 contains the user profiles. SATA hard drive 3 and the external USB flash drive are empty. Where should you place the page file to maximize performance?

- ○ **A.** External USB flash drive

- ○ **B.** Internal SATA hard drive 1

- ○ **C.** Internal SATA hard drive 2

- ○ **D.** Internal SATA hard drive 3

58. One of your customers is having difficulty with two network connections in the accounting office. The accounting office is adjacent to the building's mechanical room. Network cables run from the accounting office, through the drop ceiling of the mechanical room, and into the server room next door. Which of the following solutions should be recommended to the customer?

○ **A.** UTP

○ **B.** Plenum-rated cable

○ **C.** T568B

○ **D.** Fiber optic

59. A customer reports that a computer is very loud and occasionally turns itself off. The computer is located under a desk directly on top of the carpet. Which of the following steps should be performed to remedy this situation? (Select the two best answers.)

❏ **A.** Remove the computer from the floor.

❏ **B.** Install a new hard drive.

❏ **C.** Replace the power cord.

❏ **D.** Wipe down the computer with a cloth.

❏ **E.** Clean the inside of the computer.

60. Michelle's laptop powers on only when the AC adapter is connected to it. Which of the following is the most likely cause of this problem?

○ **A.** Bad transformer

○ **B.** Bad AC port on the laptop

○ **C.** Bad battery

○ **D.** Bad CMOS battery

61. A user reports that a laser printer is printing poorly. You observe that the pages have wrinkles and random patterns of missing print. Which of the following is the most likely cause of this problem?

○ **A.** The fuser needs to be replaced.

○ **B.** The toner cartridge is defective.

○ **C.** The corona wire is frayed.

○ **D.** There is high humidity in the room.

62. A user asks you to explain a message that comes up on the computer display before the operating system boots. The message states that the UEFI/BIOS logged a chassis intrusion. Which of the following would be your explanation to the user?

Quick Answer: **102**
Detailed Answer: **118**

○ **A.** The optical drive tray is open.

○ **B.** The CPU is loose.

○ **C.** A malicious individual has hacked the system.

○ **D.** The computer case has been opened.

63. Jim attempts to plug a scanner into the front USB port of a Windows computer, but the scanner does not power on. Which of the following solutions should be recommended to Jim?

Quick Answer: **102**
Detailed Answer: **118**

○ **A.** Use a different USB cable.

○ **B.** Run Windows Update on the computer.

○ **C.** Upgrade the computer's drivers.

○ **D.** Use the onboard USB ports.

64. One of your coworkers just installed a newer, more powerful video card in a customer's computer. The computer powers down before it completes the boot process. Before the installation, the computer worked normally. Which of the following is the most likely cause of this problem?

Quick Answer: **102**
Detailed Answer: **119**

○ **A.** The video card is not compatible with the CPU.

○ **B.** The monitor cannot display the higher resolution of the new video card.

○ **C.** The computer's RAM needs to be upgraded.

○ **D.** The power supply is not providing enough wattage for the new video card.

65. One of the users at your organization will be attending several day-long conferences and wants to make sure a mobile device will have enough power for the events. There will be a lack of AC outlet availability, and the user needs to continuously use the mobile device throughout the event. The user also needs to access the mobile device's USB port to access flash drives and access the Internet to get updates. What should you recommend to the user?

Quick Answer: **102**
Detailed Answer: **119**

○ **A.** Purchase a built-in battery case.

○ **B.** Use a wireless charging pad.

○ **C.** Bring extra charging cords.

○ **D.** Put the mobile device into airplane mode.

66. You want your computer to boot off the network and have the capability to be brought out of sleep mode over the network. Which two technologies should be implemented in the BIOS?

- ○ **A.** WAP and WPA2
- ○ **B.** WDS and Magic Packet
- ○ **C.** PXE and WOL
- ○ **D.** Symantec Ghost and Unattend.xml

67. A customer tells you that a networked printer is not printing documents. You successfully ping the printer's IP address. Which of the following is the most likely cause of this problem? (Select the two best answers.)

- ❏ **A.** The printer is low on toner.
- ❏ **B.** The network cable is unplugged.
- ❏ **C.** The printer is out of paper.
- ❏ **D.** The gateway address on the printer is incorrect.
- ❏ **E.** The spooler is not functioning.

68. A customer has a home office. Which of the following technologies would benefit from the use of QoS?

- ○ **A.** SSID
- ○ **B.** Instant messaging
- ○ **C.** Email
- ○ **D.** VoIP

69. A PC's monitor has no display after a power failure. The LED light on the monitor is on. Which of the following steps should be performed first?

- ○ **A.** Power cycle the PC.
- ○ **B.** Power cycle the peripherals.
- ○ **C.** Power cycle the UPS.
- ○ **D.** Power cycle the breaker switches.

70. Which of the following should be checked when a laptop fails to turn on? (Select the four best answers.)

- ❑ **A.** Power LED
- ❑ **B.** Sound port
- ❑ **C.** AC adapter
- ❑ **D.** Inverter
- ❑ **E.** Hibernate mode
- ❑ **F.** Function key
- ❑ **G.** Power button

71. A computer just had a memory upgrade installed. After the computer is booted, it does not recognize the new memory, even though it is listed as being compatible on the manufacturer's website. Which of the following steps should be performed to resolve the issue?

- ○ **A.** UEFI/BIOS update
- ○ **B.** Adjust jumper settings
- ○ **C.** OS Update
- ○ **D.** New CMOS battery

72. A computer has a RAID 1 array. SATA Drive 0 failed, and now the computer will not boot. Which of the following steps would most likely fix the problem by allowing the computer to boot again?

- ○ **A.** Replace SATA Drive 1.
- ○ **B.** Mark SATA Drive 1 as active.
- ○ **C.** Replace SATA Drive 0.
- ○ **D.** Replace the array's controller.

73. You are troubleshooting what you believe to be a power issue. Which of the following should be tested first?

- ○ **A.** Power supply
- ○ **B.** 24-pin power connector
- ○ **C.** IEC cable
- ○ **D.** AC outlet
- ○ **E.** Circuit breaker

74. A CAD/CAM workstation running AutoCAD is displaying rotating 3D images very slowly. The customer needs the images to rotate quickly and smoothly. Which of the following should be upgraded on the computer? (Select the best answer.)

- ○ **A.** CPU
- ○ **B.** RAM
- ○ **C.** Video card
- ○ **D.** Hard drive

75. Which of the following devices is used to implement network security for an IT environment?

- ○ **A.** Managed switch
- ○ **B.** Repeater
- ○ **C.** Gateway
- ○ **D.** Firewall

76. Your end users work with a web-based calendar app. Which of the following cloud-based technologies are they using?

- ○ **A.** SaaS
- ○ **B.** IaaS
- ○ **C.** PaaS
- ○ **D.** DaaS

77. You are now a manager of a technical services team. One of your technicians notices that a printer is jamming just above the printer tray. Which of the following steps should the technician first perform to resolve the issue?

- ○ **A.** Clean the feeder rollers.
- ○ **B.** Clean the pickup rollers.
- ○ **C.** Replace the fuser.
- ○ **D.** Replace the drum.

78. You configured a customer's router to automatically assign only five IP addresses in an attempt to make the network more secure. Now you notice that the wireless printer is intermittently losing connections when there are multiple users on the wireless network. Which of the following steps represents the best solution?

- ○ **A.** Increasing the wireless router IP lease times
- ○ **B.** Installing another access point
- ○ **C.** Configuring the printer to use a static IP address
- ○ **D.** Configuring the printer for DHCP

79. Which of the following steps can be performed to ensure that all external traffic to your website is directed through a firewall to the right computer?

Quick Answer: **102**
Detailed Answer: **123**

  ○ **A.** Configure port forwarding.

  ○ **B.** List in the exceptions the IP address of the local website.

  ○ **C.** Configure NAT.

  ○ **D.** Configure all interior traffic appropriately.

80. You are troubleshooting an Internet connectivity issue. Several laptop users cannot connect to any websites. Users with PCs do not have any trouble. Which of the following devices is most likely causing the problem?

Quick Answer: **102**
Detailed Answer: **124**

  ○ **A.** Router

  ○ **B.** Cable modem

  ○ **C.** WAP

  ○ **D.** Encryption mismatch

  ○ **E.** Firewall

  ○ **F.** UTM

Quick-Check Answer Key

1. B	28. B	55. D, E
2. B	29. B	56. A, C, E
3. D	30. C	57. D
4. A, E	31. A, D	58. D
5. C	32. B	59. A, E
6. D	33. C	60. C
7. C, D	34. D	61. A
8. C	35. B	62. D
9. C	36. D	63. D
10. A	37. A	64. D
11. D	38. C	65. B
12. A	39. A, C, E	66. C
13. C	40. A, C	67. C, E
14. D	41. A, C	68. D
15. B	42. C	69. A
16. C	43. B	70. A, C, E, G
17. C	44. C, D	71. A
18. B	45. C	72. B
19. C	46. A	73. C
20. C	47. A	74. C
21. C	48. D	75. D
22. B	49. B, D	76. A
23. C	50. A, B, E, G	77. B
24. A, D	51. C, E	78. C
25. A, E	52. E	79. A
26. C	53. A, D	80. C
27. A	54. C	

Answers and Explanations

1. Answer: B

Explanation: Print a test page after doing preventative maintenance to a laser printer.

Incorrect answers: Normally, when you maintain a laser printer, you power it down and unplug it before any work begins. So, you do not need to restart the printer; when you finish, you simply start it. You also do not need to restore a printer to factory settings unless it fails. Your preventative maintenance will hopefully stave off that dark day. The paper trays probably still have paper in them, and regardless, part of preventative maintenance is to fill the trays. Printing the test page should be last.

2. Answer: B

Explanation: Most likely, repetitive flashing lights on a keyboard indicate the presence of a hardware error, probably internal to the computer. If nothing comes up on the display, and all you have to go by are flashing lights on the keyboard, you can probably ascertain that the POST has failed and that the problem lies within the big four (as I like to call them): CPU, RAM, video, or motherboard.

Incorrect answers: Software errors can't occur until the operating system attempts to boot, and without the POST finishing successfully, that won't happen. Passwords are required when you see a repetitive flashing light on the screen, not on the keyboard—and even then, only if you are attempting to access the BIOS (or UEFI) or if someone configured a user password in the BIOS. External peripherals don't need to post properly for the computer to boot to the OS. Even the keyboard isn't necessary. The POST is more interested in the guts of the computer, especially the big four and the hard drive.

3. Answer: D

Explanation: The port numbers 21, 22, 25, 53, 443, and 3389 correspond to the protocols FTP, SSH, SMTP, DNS, HTTPS, and RDP.

Incorrect answers: The Telnet protocol uses port 23. Telnet is deprecated, insecure, and outdated; plus, it isn't even installed or enabled on newer versions of operating systems. Use SSH in its place for a more secure connection. HTTP uses port 80. POP3 uses port 110. Know your port numbers!

4. Answers: A and E

Explanation: Of the listed answers, continuity and resistance are the settings that you should use when there is no electrical flow through the part being tested, and you want to be sure that there is no electrical flow when doing these tests. Examples of continuity or resistance tests include testing a fuse's impedance (measured in ohms) and testing a network cable for continuity. In each example, you don't want any electricity flowing through the device or line. It would give erratic results and could possibly cause damage to your testing equipment and even you.

Incorrect answers: When testing for watts, volts, and amps, you need to have electricity flowing through the item you want to test.

5. **Answer: C**

   Explanation: The power-on self-test (POST) checks the CPU, memory, video card, and so on when the computer first boots and displays any error messages if any errors occur.

   Incorrect answers: BIOS setup (or UEFI setup) is the program you can access to configure the system. The BIOS itself is more than just the setup program that you can access, and the POST is a part of that BIOS. The CMOS chip retains settings that the BIOS records during the POST. The bootstrap loader is within the ROM chip as well. When the computer is turned on, it automatically reads the hard drive boot sector to continue the process of booting the operating system.

6. **Answer: D**

   Explanation: A docking station meets the needs of all the requirements including security (often with a Kensington security lock), charging, accessing the LAN, and connecting hardware.

   Incorrect answers: A port replicator is similar to a docking station, but it doesn't have as much functionality; it is generally used to connect peripherals such as keyboard, mouse, and monitor. Thunderbolt is an expansion bus and external port used for data transfer and displays. A USB hub allows for connecting removable hardware but doesn't meet the other needs. A cable lock is a good idea for securing laptops, but it meets only one of the requirements—security.

7. **Answers: C and D**

   Explanation: The first thing you should do is put on your antistatic strap. The last thing you should do is test the motherboard. Always remember to test!

   Incorrect answers: You already selected the motherboard. Technically, installing the CPU isn't really part of the motherboard installation process, but you can't really test the motherboard without it. Either way, the CPU would be installed before testing. Cables need to be connected during the installation and prior to testing. But anything that deals with power or circuit boards should not be touched unless you are wearing an antistatic strap.

8. **Answer: C**

   Explanation: Use a power supply unit (PSU) tester to determine why a computer fails to boot. One of the culprits could be a faulty power supply.

   Incorrect answers: A cable tester checks network cables only to see if they are wired correctly and have continuity. Loopback plugs are used to test network cards and serial ports. The tone and probe kit is used to test phone lines and network connections for continuity. So, the rest of the answers are all tools that are used externally from the computer, whereas the PSU tester is the only one used inside the computer.

9. **Answer: C**

   Explanation: L3 cache is shared by all of the cores of the CPU.

   Incorrect answers: L1 cache is built into the CPU. L2 cache is built onto the CPU; it is also known as *on-die*. DRAM is the memory modules you install into the slots in the motherboard. DRAM is not cache memory. Some people consider DRAM to be L4 cache, but there is an actual CPU cache known as L4 used by Xeon and other high-end processors.

10. **Answer: A**

    Explanation: Hyper-threading (for example, Intel HT) calculates two independent sets of instructions simultaneously, simulating two CPUs.

    Incorrect answers: HyperTransport is a high-speed link between various devices such as the CPU and northbridge on AMD systems. Turbo Boost is a basic form of overclocking that Intel allows with many of its processors. Multi-core is the technology in which a CPU physically contains two or more processor cores. Many CPU designs combine multi-core technology with hyper-threading to allow for even more processing.

11. **Answer: D**

    Explanation: The tone and probe kit allows you to find the network drop in the wiring closet. Here's how this works: you take the tone generator portion of the tone and probe kit and connect it via RJ45 to the network port in the user's cubicle. Then you switch it on so that it creates tone. Then you go to the wiring closet (or network room or server room) and use the probe (an inductive amplifier) to find the tone. You do this by pressing the probe against each of the cables. This is an excellent method when there are dozens, or hundreds, of cables in the wiring closet. When you find the right cable, plug it into the patch panel or directly to a network switch. When you return to the user's cubicle, the RJ45 jack should be hot, meaning it can be used to send and receive data.

    Incorrect answers: A PSU tester tests the power supply of a computer. A multimeter can test any wire's voltage or AC outlets. *Cable tester* is somewhat of a vague term, but it usually means either a network patch cable tester or a LAN tester, which checks the individual wires of longer network cable runs.

12. **Answer: A**

    Explanation: SATA power connections have 3.3, 5, and 12 volt wires.

    Incorrect answers: There are no negative voltage wires on SATA power connections. Molex power connections use 5 V and 12 V only, but SATA includes the 3.3 volt line. In this scenario, you should test the SATA power connector and the main power connector from the power supply with your trusty PSU tester. (Most PSU testers have an SATA power port in addition to the main 24-pin power port.)

13. **Answer: C**

    Explanation: Amperage can be defined as electric current or the movement of electric charge. It is measured in amps (A). You should know your circuits in your office. The more you know, the less chance of overloading them. For example, a standard 15 amp circuit might be able to handle three or four computers and monitors. But a 20 amp circuit can handle a computer or two more than that. Circuit breakers, electrical cable, and outlets all must comply with a certain number of amps. If you connect a power strip or surge protector, make sure that it is specified to work with your circuit's amp rating.

    Incorrect answers: Voltage is a representation of potential energy, measured in volts (V). Wattage is electric power, the rate of electric energy in a circuit, measured in watts (W). Impedance is the amount of resistance to electricity, measured in ohms (Ω).

14. **Answer: D**

    Explanation: Use a simple moist cloth, not too wet; you don't want to get any liquid inside the printer.

    Incorrect answers: Soap and water can be used to clean the outside of a computer case. WD-40 can cause damage in the long run. Alcohol is too strong.

15. **Answer: B**

    Explanation: Chances are that the inverter has failed and needs to be replaced. Most of today's laptops do not have this problem because they are LED-backlit, instead of using a CCFL, and therefore don't need an inverter. You can guess that this is an older laptop because it is running Windows 7 (which consequently should be updated). Because you can see the image with a flashlight, you know that the video card is working and that the display is okay. It's just that the backlight is not receiving any power from the inverter, which is used to convert DC voltage inside the laptop to AC voltage for use by the backlight.

    Incorrect answers: Chances are the laptop does not use a digitizer (or touchscreen) because of its age. Regardless, the failure of a digitizer would simply stop touchscreen functionality; it wouldn't affect the brightness of the display. On a laptop such as this, there is a high probability that the video card is embedded, and not user-replaceable—unless the whole motherboard was replaced, and at that point you might as well replace the entire laptop. As mentioned, you know the LCD display works because the image can be seen dimly when shining a flashlight on it. (You could also turn off the lights and look carefully at the display to verify whether or not it is working.)

16. **Answer: C**

    Explanation: In DHCP, set a reservation by MAC address. In this scenario, the clients are most likely connecting to the printer by IP address. The Internet Printing Protocol (IPP) can be used in this manner. By default, the moment the new printer is connected to the network, it acquires an IP address from the DHCP server—a new IP address, different from the one used by the old printer. This causes the clients to fail when attempting to connect, and print, to the new printer. To prevent this problem, you go to the router (or other DHCP device) and configure a MAC address reservation. The MAC address of the printer (which might be on a label or can be accessed from the onscreen display) can be plugged into the DHCP server and reserved to a specific IP address. Of course, a better option would be to simply configure the printer to use a static IP address.

    Incorrect answers: Renaming the printer with the old name doesn't help because the client computers are most likely connecting by IP, not by name. Printing the configuration page is great and might help you to figure out what the problem could be, but it doesn't actually solve the problem!

17. **Answer: C**

Explanation: Hypertext Transfer Protocol Secure (HTTPS) is used to make secure connections to websites. It uses the Secure Socket Layer (SSL) or Transport Layer Security (TLS) protocols to encrypt the connection and make it safe for logins, purchases, and so on. HTTPS relies on port 443.

Incorrect answers: SSH stands for Secure Shell; it is used to make secure remote connections between computers for the purposes of command execution and remote control, and it replaces the deprecated Telnet protocol. It uses port 22. SFTP is the SSH File Transfer Protocol, a more secure version of FTP that is built on SSH. Kerberos is a network authentication protocol used by various systems, including Microsoft domains. It uses port 88.

18. **Answer: B**

Explanation: The Simple Network Management Protocol (SNMP) can be used to monitor remote computers and printers. This requires the installation of SNMP on the appropriate hosts.

Incorrect answers: SMTP is the Simple Mail Transfer Protocol, which deals with the sending of email. TCP/IP is the entire suite of protocols that you use when you connect to an IP network. IPP is the Internet Printing Protocol, which allows hosts to print documents to a remote printer without the need for UNC paths. DNS is the Domain Name System, which resolves domain names to their corresponding IP addresses.

19. **Answer: C**

Explanation: An indication of a power supply issue is frequent failure of hard drives. If the power supply fails to provide clean power to the 3.3 V, 5 V, and 12 V lines to the hard drives, they will fail frequently. These are often the first devices to fail when a power supply starts having intermittent problems. You should test this with a power supply tester or multimeter.

Incorrect answers: If the power supply fails, the CPU would not overclock—quite the reverse, it might lose power and turn off the computer altogether. Overclocking is controlled in the BIOS, and there are thresholds in place to stop the CPU from overclocking too far. The wireless adapter would either work or not work. Reduced range could be due to obstruction or distance from the wireless access point (WAP). If the CD burner takes longer to write data than usual, the reason could be that the system is busy doing other tasks, or perhaps the burn rate setting was lowered.

20. **Answer: C**

Explanation: Virtualization workstations require powerful CPUs with multiple cores—as many cores as possible, as well as maximized RAM. This allows the system to run virtualization software that can house multiple virtual machines (VMs), each with its own OS that can run simultaneously. While it is helpful for any computer to have a powerful CPU, such as a gaming PC or a design PC, the virtualization workstation requires it the most—in addition to as much RAM as possible.

Incorrect answers: The other custom PCs are not as reliant on CPUs. Graphic design workstations are more reliant on high-end video, RAM, and SSDs. Audio/video editing workstations rely most on specialized audio and video cards, dual monitors, and fast hard drives. Network-attached storage (NAS) devices rely on RAID arrays, a good network adapter, and sometimes increased RAM.

21. **Answer: C**

    Explanation: You should select a barcode reader. This tool reads barcodes such as UPC barcodes that have groupings of parallel lines of varying widths.

    Incorrect answers: A biometric scanner authenticates individuals by scanning physical characteristics such as fingerprints. There are many types of image scanners; multifunction printers have these and allow you to scan in photos or make copies of documents. The touchpad is a device that takes the place of a mouse. It is often used in laptops but can be purchased as an external peripheral for PCs as well.

22. **Answer: B**

    Explanation: The best answer is two PCI Express (PCIe) version 3 slots (that is, version 3 minimum). For SLI to work properly, you need two identical PCIe slots. SLI is an NVIDIA technology; AMD CrossFire (CF) is a similar technology.

    Incorrect answers: Version 2 PCIe slots are probably too slow for the type of video cards that are installed in an SLI configuration—unless it is an older motherboard—so version 3 PCIe (or higher) becomes necessary. The technology cannot span different expansion slots. Video cards are normally placed into x16 slots only, not x1 slots. USB is not an expansion slot at all; it is a port, as mentioned, and does not work together with PCIe in an SLI configuration.

23. **Answer: C**

    Explanation: RAID 5 is fault tolerant and allows for striping with parity (given you have three drives minimum to dedicate to the array). It's the parity information that makes it fault tolerant.

    Incorrect answers: RAID 0 is simply striping of data. It is not fault tolerant, meaning that it cannot re-create data after a failure or continue to function after a failure. RAID 1 is mirroring; it requires two drives and is fault tolerant. (An advanced version of RAID 1 is called disk duplexing, when each hard drive in the mirror is connected to its own hard drive controller.) RAID 10 is a stripe of mirrors. It requires four drives and is fault tolerant. It stripes the mirrors but does not stripe with parity.

24. **Answers: A and D**

    Explanation: The mouse can move erratically due to an incorrect driver or an uneven surface. Remember to visit the website for the manufacturer of the device to get the latest and greatest driver. That should fix the problem. But optical mice are very sensitive and need to be on an even, flat surface. Also, it helps if that surface is nonreflective.

    Incorrect answers: Optical mice don't have a trackball. Older ball mice had these, and they had to be cleaned to fix this problem. The mouse should not conflict with the keyboard. Every USB device gets its own resources; this is taken care of by the USB controller. Finally, if the mouse needs to be charged or needs new batteries, it should simply stop working.

25. **Answers: A and E**

   Explanation: Two ways to conserve power on a laptop are to disable cellular and Bluetooth. Some laptops might have cellular adapters, which can be quite a drain on the device. In fact, any wireless connections, including Wi-Fi, can use a lot of power. Don't forget to use airplane mode to shut off all wireless connections when they are not necessary. Other ways to save battery power include reducing the brightness of the display, setting the display to turn off after a short period of inactivity, disabling GPS, and disabling any other power-hungry apps. The list goes on!

   Incorrect answers: Playing music or sounds at high volume for long periods of time could drain the battery, but that is unlikely. For the average laptop user, video uses more power than audio. The orientation of the screen is unlikely to change enough to significantly affect the battery. The touchpad is a low-power device; it is designed that way on purpose because it is built into the laptop. A fingerprint reader is used only when a person logs in to the system. Because of that infrequent use, it doesn't affect the battery much. However, excessive USB-based devices can put a strain on the battery, so be ready to disable or remove them.

26. **Answer: C**

   Explanation: You should check the wall outlet first if you are dealing with a power issue. Because power comes from the AC outlet, it should be foremost on your mind.

   Incorrect answers: If you already deduced that the wall outlet is not causing a problem, check the power supply next. Input devices don't often cause a power issue unless they are active devices, meaning they plug into an AC outlet. But once again, you should unplug them and check the AC outlet where they are plugged in. Phone and network cabling can carry power surges and spikes, especially if they are not installed or grounded properly. However, it is less likely that the power issue emanates from a networking or telecommunications cable. After checking the wall outlet and power supply, unplug them from the computer when troubleshooting power issues.

27. **Answer: A**

   Explanation: If a computer is attempting to obtain an IP address automatically and it receives the IP address 169.254.127.1, or any other IP address starting with 169.254, DHCP has failed either at the client or the server. When this happens, Windows automatically assigns an APIPA address. The computer will be able to communicate only with other computers on the 169.254 network, which is pretty worthless if that is not your main network number. What went wrong? The problem could be one of several things. Perhaps the DHCP client service on the client computer needs to be restarted. Or maybe the computer is not connected to the right network. It could even be a problem with the server: lack of IP addresses, the DHCP service failed, the DHCP server is down, and so on. Get your problem-solving hat on and start troubleshooting!

   Incorrect answers: DNS deals with resolving domain names to IP addresses; it doesn't affect DHCP address assignment. The Windows Internet Name Service (WINS) is an older Microsoft service that resolves NetBIOS names to IP addresses; like DNS, it doesn't affect DHCP. Both DNS and WINS could fail and a computer could still obtain an IP address from a DHCP server. If APIPA failed, the computer wouldn't be able to get an address on the 169.254 network. If DHCP and APIPA were both to fail, the client computer would effectively have an IP address of 0.0.0.0. (or nothing would be listed in the ipconfig screen), placing the computer in the Twilight Zone.

> **NOTE**
>
> If you do not understand any of the acronyms used in that explanation, or you are having trouble with any of the concepts listed (besides the Twilight Zone), it is a strong indicator that you need to study more.

28. Answer: B

Explanation: Remove the CMOS battery from the motherboard. Normally, this trick resets any variable settings in the UEFI/BIOS, such as the password and time/date. Some older systems also have a BIOS configuration jumper that must be moved to another position in addition to removing the battery.

Incorrect answers: Removing the RAM doesn't do anything. When the computer is turned off, RAM contents are emptied. Today's motherboards usually don't have RAM jumpers. Removing the main power connection from the motherboard will have no effect if the computer was already turned off and unplugged. By the way, RAM and power connections should not be removed unless the power has been shut off and the AC cable has been unplugged.

29. Answer: B

Explanation: One hard drive can fail in a RAID 5 array, and the array can rebuild that drive's data from the remaining drives. However, if a second drive fails, the array is toast. The reason is that the array requires the parity information from all the other drives.

Incorrect answers: If you had a RAID 6 array (which includes another parity stripe), you could lose as many as two drives and still continue to function. Regardless, be sure to have a backup plan in place.

30. Answer: C

Explanation: Remove the hard drive before releasing a computer to a third party. There could very well be confidential company data on the drive. Store the drive in a locking cabinet. Don't worry; the manufacturer of the laptop has plenty of hard drives it can use to test the laptop!

Incorrect answers: You don't need to remove the LCD or WLAN card because they do not contain confidential information. Also, if the laptop is under warranty, you should not remove the display yourself; instead, send it to the manufacturer for repair and set up a temporary laptop for the user in question. Finally, you could clean it if you want, but do you really have time for that?

31. Answers: A and D

Explanation: Intel CPU virtualization is named VT-x. AMD CPU virtualization is named AMD-V. However, on newer systems within the UEFI/BIOS, it might simply be called "Virtualization."

Incorrect answers: AMD-Vi is the name for AMD chipset virtualization. VT-d is the name for Intel chipset virtualization.

32. **Answer: B**

    Explanation: At 16x speed, 576 Mb/s is the answer. The default 1x speed of Blu-ray allows a data rate of 36 Mb/s (4.5 MB/s).

    Incorrect answers: The maximum storage capacity of a standard size dual-layer Blu-ray disc is 50 GB. The 1x data rate of a CD-ROM drive is 150 KB/s.

33. **Answer: C**

    Explanation: DVI-I accepts analog and digital video signals. All DVI ports are video only; they do not support audio.

    Incorrect answers: DVI-D is digital only, as you may guess from the *D*, and DVI-A is analog only. HDMI can accept video *and* audio signals. HDMI type B is known as double bandwidth; it supports higher resolutions than type A.

34. **Answer: D**

    Explanation: A mobile hotspot, when enabled, allows a mobile device to share its Internet connection with other Wi-Fi–capable devices. This might also be referred to as "Wi-Fi tethering."

    Incorrect answers: In USB tethering, a mobile device shares its Internet connection with a PC or laptop via USB. The term *Wi-Fi sharing* is not typically used. For Internet passthrough, a mobile device connects to a PC via USB, making use of the PC's Internet connection—basically the reverse of USB tethering.

35. **Answer: B**

    Explanation: Three-dimensional (3D) printers use filaments (often made of plastic) to build three-dimensional objects.

    Incorrect answers: Laser printers use toner cartridges. Inkjet printers use ink cartridges. Thermal printers use specially coated paper that is super-heated.

36. **Answer: D**

    Explanation: Add memory to the printer. Large documents, especially ones with graphics, require more memory to print. A printer's memory can be upgraded in a similar manner to a PC's.

    Incorrect answers: The paper doesn't have an effect on large documents, but it could be an issue if the entry rollers are grabbing more than one piece of paper at a time; that would indicate that the pound size of the paper is too thin. If the communications cable were faulty, no pages would print at all; you would probably get a message on the printer's display warning of a bad connection. If a toner cartridge began to fail, you would see white lines, smearing, or faded ink.

37. **Answer: A**

    Explanation: A ghosted image or one that seems to repeat usually means the drum (or the entire toner cartridge including the drum) needs to be replaced.

    Incorrect answers: If the printer is offline, you cannot print to the printer. An incorrect driver often results in a garbage printout (garbled characters) that is quite unreadable (unless you know garbage printout language). A dirty primary corona wire often results in lines or smearing.

38. Answer: C

Explanation: You should first attempt reseating the laptop in the docking station; the laptop probably doesn't have a sturdy connection, resulting in a blinking battery light telling you that the laptop is not charging properly (or at all).

Incorrect answers: Do this before you attempt to reseat or replace the battery. This is a hardware issue; the operating system does not have an effect on the blinking battery light.

39. Answers: A, C, and E

Explanation: You can try power cycling the device, checking if the SSID was correct, and forgetting the network and then reconnecting to it. You should also check whether the device is within range of the wireless access point, whether the device supports the necessary encryption, and whether Internet passthrough or other Internet sharing technologies are conflicting. Furthermore, you can power cycle the Wi-Fi program, check if any Wi-Fi sleep is enabled, and try enabling best Wi-Fi performance if the device offers it.

Incorrect answers: Using the cellular GPRS connection is not a valid option when troubleshooting the Wi-Fi connection. Setting up a static IP on a mobile device is usually not a good idea and not necessary; in fact, this is one of the things you should check in the Advanced settings of the device. A static IP applied to the Wi-Fi adapter could prevent the device from connecting to all wireless networks except the one that uses that IP network number.

40. Answers: A and C

Explanation: To connect a Bluetooth headset to a smartphone, you must pair the device to the phone; then, if necessary, you enter a passcode into the phone to use the device.

Incorrect answers: Drivers are usually not necessary; most mobile devices have Bluetooth installed and usually recognize devices automatically. If not, you might have to update Bluetooth on the device or update the device's OS. Disabling Wi-Fi is not necessary; however, Wi-Fi and Bluetooth have been known to have conflicts, and sometimes one must be disabled to use the other.

41. Answers: A and C

Explanation: You should make sure that the heat sink is secure and that the fan is connected. Either of these issues could cause the CPU to overheat. Also, make sure that thermal compound was applied to the heat sink. If you didn't log in writing somewhere that you did this, you will have to take the heat sink off and inspect it. It's a good idea to log when you apply thermal compound because if you remove the heat sink, you will need to reapply thermal compound before reinstalling it.

Incorrect answers: The BIOS temperature threshold is what tripped, causing the system to shut down. You could increase the threshold, which would fix the problem temporarily but could cause permanent damage to the CPU. The threshold is there to protect the CPU; therefore, "Check the BIOS temperature threshold" is not the best answer. If the RAM needed to be reseated, you might get one of several errors or beeps, but the system should not automatically shut down.

42. **Answer: C**

   Explanation: The power supply is the most likely source of a burning smell. If it is a very slight smell, the power supply could be brand new. New power supplies have a "burn-in" period of 24–48 working hours. However, you should be very careful with this. If the power supply is about to fail, or if it does fail, it could burn up the motor that drives the fan. This situation could be an electrical and/or fire hazard. So, to be safe, you should remove the power supply and test it in your lab, or call the manufacturer for a replacement.

   Incorrect answers: It is possible but unlikely that the thermal compound would cause a burning smell; however, if this were to occur, it would be much less noticeable and more chemical in nature. The keyboard should not present a burning smell no matter how fast you type on it. The AC outlet could possibly be the cause of a burning smell, and that would be very bad news. In that case, disconnect devices from that outlet, turn off the circuit breaker immediately, and call an electrician. However, the AC outlet is not part of the computer.

43. **Answer: B**

   Explanation: The laptop is probably connecting to a different wireless network, either in the home next door or an adjacent business—one without encryption, it would seem. Based on the speed—54 Mbps—you could safely assume that the connection being made is to either an 802.11g or an 802.11a network. The best course of action is to verify the SSID name of the 802.11ac router, forget the current wireless network, and connect to the new network. You might find that in some cases a laptop connects at a slower speed (such as 802.11g), even though faster speeds (such as 802.11n and 802.11ac) are available. The reason could be due to the configuration of the WAP or the wireless adapter on the laptop. That's not one of the listed answers and is not the case here because of the poor signal strength mentioned in the scenario.

   Incorrect answers: The cable modem isn't a part of the equation in this scenario. You are only interested in connecting to the wireless network to start. A router (wireless access point) doesn't have a wireless card such as the ones in a PC or laptop. Also, you don't know whether the device is faulty yet because the laptop never connected to it. The same goes for the wireless antennas.

44. **Answer: C and D**

   Explanation: RAID 1 (mirroring) provides fault tolerance by copying information to two drives. RAID 5 (striping with parity) provides fault tolerance by keeping a compressed copy of the data (in the form of parity) on each of the disks other than where the original data is stored.

   Incorrect answers: RAID 0 is striping only, and a spanned volume is one that stores data on two or more drives, but as whole files, not as stripes of data.

45. **Answer: C**

   Explanation: The best of the listed answers is 3 TB HDD, meaning a 3 terabyte magnetic-based hard disk drive. It can be installed internally to the computer, is relatively inexpensive, and offers a good storage size that probably won't be exceeded in the next 6 months (although anything can happen!).

   Incorrect answers: A 500 TB storage-area network (SAN) is an entire network of storage devices that exists outside the desktop computer. Also, for a typical PC, it is way bigger than you need. A 50 GB network-attached storage (NAS) device also exists outside the desktop computer. In addition, the storage size is quite limited. A 512 GB SSD is a possibility, but it doesn't have as much space as the 3 TB HDD, and it will be more expensive per megabyte. A good rule of thumb is to use SSDs for the OS, apps, and working projects. Then use an HDD for backup and long-term storage. Keep in mind that this does not take into account any fault tolerance.

46. **Answer: A**

   Explanation: The F connector (also known as F-type) is commonly used to terminate coaxial cable that is used for television or cable Internet. Generally, it is used to terminate RG-6 cable but might also be seen with RG-59 cable, which has a thinner conductor and therefore isn't used as much. Note: RG-59 cable may also be terminated with BNC connectors for professional video applications.

   Incorrect answers: The DB-9 connector (more accurately named the DE-9) is used for serial connections between computers. RJ11 plugs are used with telephone lines. RJ45 plugs are commonly found as the terminators of patch cables in twisted-pair networks.

47. **Answer: A**

   Explanation: Clear the printer spooler. You do this by stopping the Print Spooler service in Computer Management (or in the Command Prompt by entering **net stop spooler**) and then deleting the files in the path C:\Windows\System32\Spool\Printers.

   Incorrect answers: Try not to turn off or unplug the printer unless absolutely necessary. Resetting the printer is somewhat vague but would most likely result in a need for printer reconfiguration.

48. **Answer: D**

   Explanation: Pinging the loopback address should return results even if you are not physically connected to the network. This trick deals with the computer internally and doesn't even need a LAN. You can ping the local computer with the commands **ping loopback** and **ping localhost**; however, the best option is to ping the actual IPv4 loopback IP address by typing **ping 127.0.0.1** (or **ping ::1** for IPv6). This removes any possible name resolution that might occur in Windows. Note that name resolution happens whenever you connect to a system by name (such as computerA, workstationB, and so on); the name must ultimately be translated to its corresponding IP address. So, to avoid any name resolution issues, we computer techs like to go right to the source and ping the IP address directly. This way, we can troubleshoot whether or not the TCP/IP protocol suite is functioning properly, without being concerned with any other services and name resolution getting in the way. It's a good general practice for connecting to systems directly.

Incorrect answers: Pinging the loopback address doesn't make use of the network, so the LAN, DHCP servers, and the Ethernet cable do not play into the scenario.

49. **Answers: B and D**

    Explanation: Check if you are within range; the range of Bluetooth devices is limited; for example, Class 2 devices are limited to 10 meters. Also try power cycling the Bluetooth program by turning Bluetooth off and on. In addition to those correct answers, you can try charging the device, restarting the device, working with a known good Bluetooth device, attempting to forget the device, and reconnecting it.

    Incorrect answers: WLAN is a separate wireless technology from Bluetooth, so it should not have any bearing on how Bluetooth functions. If devices are paired within Bluetooth, they should work; unpairing and re-pairing should not have any effect.

50. **Answers: A, B, E, and G**

    Explanation: If the computer is receiving power, everything is hooked up properly, and there is no display, you need to consider the big four: motherboard, CPU, video card, and RAM. These are the four components of the computer that could cause a no-display issue. The most common is the video card. Check whether it is seated properly into the expansion slot. You should also check whether that card works in one of your test systems. Next, check whether the RAM and then the CPU are properly installed and compatible. Finally, check the motherboard, if necessary. Of course, at the beginning of this process, you should inquire of the customer when this computer failed and if anything was recently modified on the system. Doing so might help you troubleshoot the problem. You would question the user during step 1 of the CompTIA A+ troubleshooting process: Identify the problem.

    Incorrect answers: The hard drive won't even be accessed if the system's RAM, motherboard, or CPU fails because the system won't even POST. There will be little to no activity on the hard drive LED. If the video card failed, the system might still boot, but without video, and you would see some hard drive LED activity. However, some systems will not boot; lack of video will cause the system to stop at POST. The DVD-ROM drive won't cause a no-display issue because it is a secondary device. The power supply is not the cause of the problem in this case. The scenario said that the computer was receiving power. If the power supply failed, nothing would happen when you press the computer's power-on button. If the SATA data cable were disconnected (and that was the only problem), you would get video; the system would POST (and most likely record a hard drive error); and then when the system attempted to boot to the hard drive, you would get a "missing OS" error or a similar message.

51. **Answers: C and E**

    Explanation: If only one computer is connected to the switch, there shouldn't be much activity. Rapidly blinking LED lights might lead you to believe that the computer's network card (NIC) or the port on the switch is faulty. The problem could be that the person is sending a lot of data to himself while you are testing the network, but that would be strange and rare.

    Incorrect answers: Switches are not plugged into servers; however, they facilitate network connections between many computers. A defective hard drive would cause some kind of boot failure. The server doesn't have anything to do with this scenario.

52. **Answer: E**

Explanation: What should have been port 993 was probably configured incorrectly if the person can send but not receive email. To securely send email over Internet Message Access Protocol (IMAP), use port 993.

Incorrect answers: The Simple Mail Transfer Protocol (SMTP) uses port 25 by default to send mail but will use port 587 (or 465) if SSL or TLS security is implemented. Port 110 is the POP3 email port. POP3 also is used to receive email, but not in this question's scenario. IMAP can receive email on port 143, but it is not considered secure. Port 443 is commonly used by HTTPS. Configuring email on mobile devices such as Android phones can be a little more difficult, as compared to PCs. Be sure to work with mobile devices and go through the steps of setting up email on both Android and iOS.

53. **Answers: A and D**

Explanation: Check the basics first! Make sure the power cable isn't disconnected from the computer, and verify that the voltage switch on the power supply is in the correct position (if the PSU is not auto-switching). Kids like to play tricks on lab computers!

Incorrect answers: A standard power strip should not overload with just two computers connected to it, but if it does, press the reset switch on the power strip. The monitor being unplugged could be a separate problem, but it won't prevent the computer from powering on. If the second computer works fine, that tells you the power strip is plugged in.

54. **Answer: C**

Explanation: Start with the physical! Check for a link light on the NIC first. This light tells you whether there is physical connectivity.

Incorrect answers: Then, if necessary, you can, in order, test the patch cable, reconfigure TCP/IP, install drivers (from the manufacturer's website, mind you), and, finally, replace the NIC.

55. **Answers: D and E**

Explanation: Start securing the IoT device by separating it (and other IoT devices). Do this by moving it to a DMZ or a guest network (or both). Also, use the latest encryption standards for the wireless network—meaning WPA2 or higher and AES.

Incorrect answers: You should definitely upgrade the router to the latest firmware, but that is not the best answer listed because it does not directly affect the IoT device. More importantly, update the IoT device's firmware—often! Disabling wireless access would render the thermostat nonfunctional. Upgrading to WPA is not enough. Newer versions of WPA are available. Two-factor authentication (if it is even available) would be good security, but that is something that concerns the account that accesses the thermostat. And that is only if the thermostat can be controlled over the cloud. You don't know that based on the information in the scenario. If this feature does exist, you should secure the login as much as possible, but the device itself can still be accessed via Wi-Fi.

56. **Answers: A, C, and E**

    Explanation: First, make sure that the iPad has a connection to the Internet. Then check that the email settings, including port numbers, server names, username/password, and any security settings, were entered properly.

    Incorrect answers: Bluetooth can be off while email is being used. GPS tracks where a mobile device is located, and it too can be turned off when accessing email.

57. **Answer: D**

    Explanation: Use Internal SATA hard drive 3 for the page file. By separating the page file from the operating system and the user profiles, you maximize performance of the system.

    Incorrect answers: If the page file were on either of the other SATA drives, the constant accessing of the page file would slow down the OS performance or would slow down the access of user files. SATA hard drive 3 is a better option than the external USB flash drive for a variety of reasons: it is probably faster; it has less latency; and in general, internal drives perform more efficiently than external drives.

58. **Answer: D**

    Explanation: Of the listed answers, you should recommend fiber-optic cables. Another option would be shielded twisted pair (STP). Furthermore, you could rerun the cables through a metal conduit or reroute the cables around the mechanical room. Chances are, in this scenario, the mechanical room's contents are causing interference on the network cables. Electromagnetic interference (EMI) can be prevented with STP or fiber-optic cables.

    Incorrect answers: UTP is unshielded twisted pair, and because it is the most common, it is probably what the customer is using currently. Plenum-rated cable is used in areas where sprinklers cannot get to. It has a coating that makes it burn much more slowly. T568B is the most common network cabling wiring standard.

59. **Answers: A and E**

    Explanation: First, remove the computer from the floor. Second, take the computer outside, clean it by removing the biggest dust bunnies (which you will undoubtedly find), and use compressed air and an antistatic vacuum. That should fix the noise problem; there is probably a lot of dust and dirt in one or more of the fans. Also, remember to wear a dust mask when dealing with dusty computers. In addition, a clogged CPU fan can cause the CPU to overheat, resulting in the computer turning itself off.

    Incorrect answers: A new hard drive isn't necessary unless you find that it is malfunctioning. The power cord most likely isn't the problem here, but you could always swap it with another one to be sure. Wiping down the outside of a computer with a cloth won't do much to fix the situation, and you wouldn't wipe down the inside of the computer. On a slightly different topic, static electricity could be generated when a person touches the power button of the computer. Combine this with the computer lying on a carpet, and it could cause the computer to short out and shut down. So, it's best to keep the computer off the floor for a variety of reasons.

60. **Answer: C**

    Explanation: If the laptop gets power when plugged in but doesn't work when disconnected from AC power, the battery must be dead or defective.

    Incorrect answers: A bad transformer means that the AC adapter would need to be replaced. That and a bad AC port would cause the laptop to fail when plugged into the AC adapter, but it should work fine on battery power (until the battery fully discharges, that is). A bad CMOS battery causes the time, date, and passwords to be reset in the BIOS.

61. **Answer: A**

    Explanation: The wrinkled pages are the number-one indicator that the fuser needs to be replaced. Random patterns of missing print further indicate that the fuser is not working properly. If you note that toner is not being fused to the paper, that is the last clue. The fuser usually needs to be replaced every 200,000 pages or so on a laser printer.

    Incorrect answers: If the toner cartridge were defective, either you would get blank printouts or you would see lines or smears, but there wouldn't be page wrinkles. If the transfer corona wire were defective, it might result in blank paper. Damage to the primary corona wire can also result in black lines or smearing. High humidity could cause the separation pads or rollers to fail.

62. **Answer: D**

    Explanation: A chassis intrusion means that the computer case has been opened. Some UEFI/BIOS programs have the capability to detect this. This is a security feature that informs the user of a possible breach. As a PC technician, you should check the computer inside and out for any possible tampering.

    Incorrect answers: The UEFI/BIOS program will not detect if the optical drive is open. If the CPU were loose, the computer would not boot, and there would be nothing to display. It is possible that a malicious individual has hacked, or attempted to hack, the system. However, this is not necessarily the case, although you should check just to make sure.

63. **Answer: D**

    Explanation: Tell the customer to use the onboard ports. This means the ports that are integrated directly to the motherboard on the back of the computer. This tip is a quick, temporary fix, but it should work because they are hardwired to the board. The front USB plugs are part of the computer case; they probably were never connected to the motherboard properly. You should also check whether the USB scanner needs to be plugged into an AC outlet.

    Incorrect answers: If the *back* USB ports don't work, you could try a different USB cable. Software shouldn't affect the USB device getting power. If it has a proper USB connection, it should power up. But, after that, if Windows doesn't recognize it, try updating drivers and Windows.

64. Answer: D

Explanation: Today's video cards can be very powerful and might require a more powerful power supply than is in the computer currently.

Incorrect answers: Video cards need to be compatible with the motherboard, not necessarily with the CPU. If the monitor could not display the higher resolution, the operating system would still boot, but you would probably see garbled information on the screen. Because a video card comes with its own RAM, the computer's RAM usually does not need to be upgraded.

65. Answer: B

Explanation: Of the listed answers, the best option is to use a wireless charging pad for the mobile device. It can be charged before each event and can work as a good portable solution.

Incorrect answers: A built-in battery case usually has to connect to the device's USB port (or Lightning port), which—if there is no passthrough capability—might stop the user from working with flash drives. (It's also better to *use* something that is already available as opposed to *purchasing* something new—from a monetary standpoint.) It doesn't matter how many charging cords you have. If AC wall outlets are not accessible, you will have to charge during the event in another way. Putting the device into airplane mode would stop it from accessing the Internet, which is a requirement.

66. Answer: C

Explanation: To configure the BIOS to boot off the network, you have to enable the Preboot Execution Environment (PXE) network adapter. To allow the computer to be brought out of sleep mode by another system on the network, you need to configure Wake-on-LAN (WOL) in the BIOS.

Incorrect answers: WAP stands for wireless access point; WPA2 is the Wi-Fi Protected Access version 2 encryption used on a WAP. WDS stands for Windows Deployment Services and is used on Windows Server to deploy installations of Windows to remote computers. A Magic Packet is a special packet sent to a computer to wake it up, but it is configured in Windows. Symantec Ghost is used to create or install images of operating systems. Unattend.xml is the answer file created for unattended installations of Windows over the network.

67. Answers: C and E

Explanation: The printer could simply be out of paper, or the spooler could be malfunctioning. If the printer is out of paper, fill all trays and suggest that the user check the trays every couple of days or so. If the spooler is not functioning, you should restart the spooler service in the Services console window or in the Command Prompt with the **net stop spooler** and **net start spooler** commands.

Incorrect answers: If the printer were low on toner, you would get weak print or completely blank pages. If the network cable were unplugged, you wouldn't be able to ping the printer. Printers don't always use gateway addresses, but if this one did, it wouldn't affect your ability to connect to it (as long as it was on the LAN). The gateway address is used so that the printer can communicate with computers beyond the LAN.

68. Answer: D

Explanation: Voice over IP (VoIP) is a streaming telephony application. Streaming applications such as VoIP and online games can benefit from QoS. QoS stands for quality of service, which is the capability to provide different priorities to different applications (or computers). It guarantees network bandwidth for real-time streaming of the media applications such as VoIP.

Incorrect answers: The SSID is the name or identifier of a wireless network. Instant messaging and email are not streaming applications; therefore, they would not benefit from the use of QoS.

69. Answer: A

Explanation: If a power failure occurs, try power cycling the PC. In this scenario it could be that power went out for five minutes. When power returned, the monitor was still on (thus, the LED) but the computer remained off (thus, nothing on the display). Really, in this case, you are just turning *on* the computer.

Incorrect answers: Peripherals should have no bearing on this scenario unless they also plug in. If you power cycle the PC and there is still nothing on the display, try disconnecting the peripherals from the PC, disconnecting the AC power (if the PC has that), and rebooting the PC. If the monitor has an LED light, you know it is getting power, so the UPS does not need to be power cycled. However, if there was a five-minute power loss and the UPS didn't keep the PC running, you should check the UPS battery. Turning the breaker switches for the circuit on and off is always fun but would simply cut power to the AC outlets temporarily.

70. Answers: A, C, E, and G

Explanation: Check the power LED on the laptop first and see what it is doing. It could be that the user simply wasn't pressing the power button. If it blinks slowly once in a while, the laptop might be in a sleep state. Then check the power light on the AC adapter. Make sure the AC adapter is getting power; if it is, check whether it is the right adapter. Check whether the system is in hibernate mode by pressing and holding the power button. Finally, the power button might be faulty, so make sure it isn't loose. If no AC adapter is available, you should also check whether the battery is connected properly and charged. Make sure the user keeps the AC adapter on hand at all times.

Incorrect answers: Audio, the inverter, and the function keys usually do not cause booting failure. They should not affect whether you can turn on the laptop.

71. Answer: A

Explanation: You should update the UEFI/BIOS. If it hasn't been updated in a while, it probably won't recognize newer memory modules.

Incorrect answers: Most of today's motherboards don't have jumper settings for RAM. In fact, the only jumper you often find is the BIOS configuration jumper, which needs to be configured only if a person forgot a password. The BIOS will have a problem recognizing the RAM far before the OS starts up; no OS updates are required to make RAM recognizable to the system. If the computer needed a new CMOS battery, you would know because the time in the BIOS would reset to an earlier date.

72. **Answer: B**

    Explanation: You would mark SATA Drive 1 as active. If you cannot access Disk Management, you would have to do it by booting the system with WinRE (System Recovery Options); accessing the Command Prompt; executing the **diskpart** command; and typing the commands **select disk 1**, **select partition 1**, and **active**. A RAID 1 array is a mirroring array with two drives. The second drive keeps an exact copy of the first drive in real time. If Drive 1 doesn't take over automatically when Drive 0 fails, you will have to set it to active. Remember that a partition with an operating system must be set to active; otherwise, the computer will not be able to boot to the partition.

    Incorrect answers: Replacing Drive 1 is not necessary because it did not fail. Replacing Drive 0 is inevitable if you want to re-create the mirror but not necessary if you just want to get the system to boot for now. Replacing the array's controller is most likely not necessary. You should try replacing the drive first. It is possible (though unlikely) that the drive and the controller failed at the same time, but always start with the most likely culprit (and never change out more than one device at a time).

73. **Answer: C**

    Explanation: Check the IEC cable first if you sense that there is a power issue. That is the power cable for the computer; make sure it is connected to the computer and to the AC outlet.

    Incorrect answers: Afterward, if the cable is not the issue, you could check the AC wall outlet. Use a receptacle tester or your trusty multimeter to make sure the AC outlet is wired properly and supplying the correct voltage. If that is fine, you can check the power supply and the 24-pin power connector. Check the circuit breaker only if the power has been cut to an area of the building and only if you have access to the electrical panels.

74. **Answer: C**

    Explanation: The video card should be your first stop on the upgrade express train. Images that do not display properly are usually due to a subpar video card. CAD/CAM workstations require a powerful video card.

    Incorrect answers: Though not as much, the CPU will also play into this, especially when rendering images, so that is the second thing you should check. Use third-party benchmarking tools, or view the Windows Experience Index (Windows 7) or WinSAT (Windows 8 and higher) details to find out what has the lowest score and go from there. The video card is most likely the lowest. See the following note for more information about WinSAT. CAD/CAM workstations often require video cards that can cost a thousand dollars or more. Always read the directions carefully and set up proper ESD prevention techniques prior to installing a card this expensive. RAM is important, but not as important to the CAD/CAM workstation as the video card (especially based on the question's scenario). Generally, as long as the computer has enough RAM to run Windows and the AutoCAD software, it should be okay. The hard drive doesn't play much of a factor while the CAD software is running, but for storing and accessing files, an SSD (or M.2) drive is recommended.

> **NOTE**
>
> To run WinSAT on Windows 8 or higher, open the PowerShell (as an admin) and run the command **winsat prepop**. Warning! It's best to run this with no other applications open; be ready for the test to take several minutes. You can watch what is being tested in real time, but to see the actual results, you must type **Get-WmiObject -Class Win32_WinSAT**. That will pull data from an XML file—created during the previous procedure—and display those results. Following is an example of the results after running this test on a Core i5 laptop with an SSD and upgraded RAM. Note that the GraphicsScore is the lowest, which is common with laptops, though the DiskScore could be low as well if the laptop uses a magnetic-based drive.
>
> ```
> CPUScore:       8.6
> D3DScore:       9.9
> DiskScore:      8.2
> GraphicsScore:  6.5
> MemoryScore:    8.6
> ```
>
> That just scratches the surface of the **WinSAT** command. Be sure to update PowerShell for best results.

75. Answer: D

Explanation: A firewall is used to implement security for the computer network—for example, access control lists (ACLs) that allow or deny incoming and outgoing traffic.

Incorrect answers: A managed switch connects computers and servers on the network and can be configured from a remote workstation (usually by logging in to the switch via a browser). A repeater is a physical device that amplifies a network signal so that it can travel farther. The gateway device is usually a router; it acts as the doorway to the Internet or other networks for the computer on the LAN.

76. Answer: A

Explanation: This is an example of software as a service (SaaS). Google, Microsoft, Apple, and other companies offer this service to end users and business users.

Incorrect answers: Infrastructure as a service (IaaS) offers computer networking, storage, load balancing, routing, and VM hosting. Platform as a service (PaaS) provides various software solutions to organizations, especially the capability to develop and test applications. DaaS can stand for either data as a service or desktop as a service. Data as a service is similar to SaaS in that products are provided on demand, but it is more data-oriented as opposed to app-oriented. In desktop as a service, a cloud provider hosts the back end of a virtual desktop, also known as virtual desktop infrastructure (VDI).

77. **Answer: B**

Explanation: The technician should clean the pickup rollers. If they are dirty or oily, they could cause a paper jam directly behind or above the paper tray.

Incorrect answers: The feeder rollers would cause a jam further in the printer. A fuser issue would cause a jam up toward the end of the printing path. The drum (or toner cartridge) will usually not cause a paper jam, but in the rare case, simply replace the toner cartridge.

78. **Answer: C**

Explanation: If the wireless printer is losing connections when multiple users are on the network, the reason is probably that there aren't enough automatically assigned IP addresses to go around. You should configure the printer to use a static IP address instead of receiving one dynamically from the router. This address will be permanent and should fix the problem. Often, companies insist that printers (as well as routers, switches, and servers) always get a static address to avoid problems of this sort.

Incorrect answers: Increasing the IP lease times might work; it might not. When multiple users attempt to get on the wireless network, someone is going to lose out; it might be a person at a laptop, or it might be the printer or other device. Therefore, this is not a permanent solution. Another access point might increase your wireless coverage, but it will do nothing for your IP issue. The whole problem here is that the printer was configured for DHCP; it was obtaining its IP address automatically from the DHCP server within the router. When it is changed to static, it doesn't have to compete for the five dynamically assigned IPs.

79. **Answer: A**

Explanation: In this scenario, your organization is running a web server on the LAN. Your job is to make sure that all clients outside your network on the Internet that are attempting to access the web server can do so. You must configure port forwarding for this to work. The HTTPS requests, or whatever port the clients use to access the web server (perhaps 443, but not necessarily), should be forwarded to the IP address and port of the web server on your network.

Incorrect answers: Exceptions are meant to allow certain computers access in or out of the firewall, but this would give the external clients too much access. You should streamline this configuration so that the external traffic is all directed to your web server, and port forwarding is the best way to do this. NAT, which stands for Network Address Translation, is used to match up the private IP address numbers of your internal computers to the external public IPs they attempt to connect to; it protects the private IP identity of the internal computers. However, it's actually not the interior traffic you are concerned with. Instead, you are concerned with the external traffic trying to get into your network and visit your web server, and the web server *only*.

80. **Answer: C**

    Explanation: The wireless access point is most likely the problem. Perhaps it was turned off or disabled or lost its connection to the network. This WAP failure causes the laptops to fail when attempting to connect to websites, and furthermore, the laptops won't have any Internet connection whatsoever. There are a lot of possibilities for why a client computer cannot connect to a WAP, but if several wireless clients cannot make the connection, you can usually assume that the problem is not at the client side and instead is at the central connecting device, in this case the WAP. Laptops often connect wirelessly because they are mobile devices, whereas PCs often connect in a wired fashion because they are stationary and don't necessarily need a wireless connection.

    Incorrect answers: If the PCs can connect to the Internet fine (as the question states), you can probably rule out the router, cable modem, firewall, and UTM device. That is, unless of course, one of the devices was configured with some kind of rule stating that the laptops can't connect to websites. This is unlikely but is a possibility if the network has a firewall or UTM. UTM stands for unified threat management; UTM devices combine the functionality of firewalls, intrusion detection systems (IDS), and proxy servers, among other things. UTMs and next-generation firewalls (NGFWs) are designed to integrate a variety of threat defenses into one device. An encryption mismatch is always possible when it comes to wireless connections. Perhaps the WAP is configured for WPA2 and AES, but a laptop is configured with WPA or TKIP, or both. That mismatch would cause the laptop to fail to connect to the wireless network, and ultimately, the Internet. However, for *several* laptops to fail due to encryption mismatches, they would all have to be configured improperly, which again is unlikely, and at which point someone would be held accountable for the mistake. Don't let this happen to you! Verify your configurations after you have made them; always test! Testing and troubleshooting are huge parts of the real IT world and the A+ exams, so be sure you study them and practice them intensely.

CHAPTER FIVE

Review of the Core (220-1001)

Phew! That was a lot of questions. But if you're reading this, you survived. Great work!

Now that you have completed the practice exams, let's do a little review of the 220-1001 domains, talk about your next steps, and look at some test-taking tips.

Review of the Domains

Remember that the 220-1001 exam is divided into five domains, as shown in Table 5.1.

TABLE 5.1   Core 1 (220-1001) Domains

Domain	Percentage of Exam
1.0 Mobile Devices	14
2.0 Networking	20
3.0 Hardware	27
4.0 Virtualization and Cloud Computing	12
5.0 Hardware and Network Troubleshooting	27
Total	100

Hardware and troubleshooting make up the majority of questions on the exam, but let's not forget about networking, mobile devices, and virtualization and cloud computing. Remember to practice all of the domains and objectives in a hands-on manner while you study the theory behind the concepts.

Many technicians are great with PC hardware, mobile devices, and networking. But if a tech is weak in the troubleshooting area, the final exam score could be in jeopardy. Study all the concepts in each of the domains. Pay strict attention to troubleshooting concepts; this is where many techs are lacking in knowledge and experience.

Everyone who takes the exam gets a different group of questions. Because the exam is randomized, one person may see more questions on, say, printers than the next person. Or one person might see more questions on laptops. The exam differs from person to person. To reduce your risk of failing, be ready for any question from any domain, and study all of the objectives.

In general, this exam deals with installation, configuration, and especially troubleshooting methods, and it is hardware-based for the most part. The bulk of the software side of things is reserved for the 220-1002 exam, as is security.

Review What You Know

At this point, you should be pretty well versed when it comes to the 220-1001 exam. I still recommend going back through all of the questions and making sure there are no questions, answers, concepts, or explanations you are unclear about. If there are, additional study is probably necessary. If something really just doesn't make sense, is ambiguous or vague, or doesn't appear to be technically correct, feel free to contact me at my website (https://dprocomputer.com), and I will do my best to clarify.

Here are a couple great ways to study further:

▶ **Take the exams in flash card mode**—Use a piece of paper to cover up the potential answers as you take the exams. This approach helps make you think a bit harder and aids in committing everything to memory. There are also free flash card applications that you can download to your computer to help you organize your studies.

▶ **Download the A+ 220-1001 objectives**—You can get these from https://certification.comptia.org/ or from my website. Go through the objectives one by one, and check each item that you are confident in. If you are unsure about any items in the objectives, study them hard. That's where the test will trip you up. There are approximately 20 pages of objectives, so going through them will take a while. But this approach really helps close any gaps in your knowledge and gives that extra boost for the exam.

► **Study the 220-1002 questions, and then return to the 220-1001 practice exams**—This might sound a bit crazy, but I have found that if an A+ candidate has a strong grasp of *all* A+ topics, he or she is more likely to pass either one of the exams. My recommendation is for you to go through the 220-1002 practice exams, return to the 220-1001 exams for a review, and then take the actual CompTIA A+ 220-1001 exam. It's a big extra step, but it has proven very effective with my students and readers.

► **Check out my website for addition materials**—My A+ Study Page is designed to help you get ready for the exam. You never know what you might find there!

► **Consider my other A+ products**—For example, consider the main A+ Exam Cram guide or my A+ Complete Video Course. You can find more information about these on my A+ Study Page, which you can find at https://dprocomputer.com/blog/?p=3030.

More Test-Taking Tips

The CompTIA A+ exams contain two types of questions—multiple choice and performance-based. The majority of them are multiple-choice questions where you are asked to select one or more correct answers to a question. The performance-based questions are scenario-oriented questions that test your knowledge by asking you to click on items, click and drag or navigate through a system, and type commands. This is why knowing the theory is not enough; you have to actually prove your technical ability in a hands-on way.

The majority of multiple-choice questions have four multiple-choice answers, but some have more. These answers are usually connected within the same concept. For example, a question about video connectors might provide four answers—DVI, HDMI, DisplayPort, and VGA—all of which are video ports. Some of the questions are not as synergistic; they might have a group of answers that seem at odds with each other. For example, a question about computer networking protocols might provide four answers: DHCP, DNS, Cat 6, and T568B. While DHCP and DNS are protocols within the TCP/IP suite, Cat 6 and T568B are cabling standards. Likewise, a question might ask about hard drive technologies and list SATA, magnetic disk, DVD-ROM, and solid-state. While SATA and magnetic disk are definitely hard drive technologies, DVD-ROM is not, and solid-state is a type of long-term memory storage that *might* be used as a hard drive technology. This will be true on the real exam as well.

Regardless of the type of question, there is often one answer that is just totally wrong. Learn to identify it; once you have, you will automatically improve to at least a 33% chance of getting the answer right, even if you have to guess.

No single question is more important than another. Approach each question with the same dedication, even if you are not interested in the topic or don't like how the question is worded. Remember that the CompTIA exams are designed and double-checked by an entire panel of experts. However, keep in mind that you can mark questions, skip them, and return to them later. If a question doesn't make any sense at all to you, try using that technique.

When you take the exam, remember to slowly read through the questions and each of the answers. Don't rush through. Let's look at some more smart methods you can use when presented with difficult questions:

▶ Use the process of elimination.

▶ Be logical in the face of adversity.

▶ Use your gut instinct.

▶ Don't let one question beat you.

▶ If all else fails, guess.

I expand on these points in the final chapter. If you finish the exam early, use the time allotted to you to review all of your answers. Chances are you will have time left over at the end, so use it wisely. Make sure that everything you have marked has a proper answer that makes sense to you. But try not to overthink! Give it your best shot, and be confident in your answers.

Taking the Real Exam

Do not register until you are fully prepared. When you are ready, schedule the exam to commence within a day or two so that you don't forget what you have learned. Registration can be done online. Register at Pearson VUE (https://home.pearsonvue.com/). The site accepts payment by major credit card for the exam fee. First-timers need to create an account with Pearson VUE.

Here are some good general practices for taking the real exams:

▶ Pick a good time for the exam.

▶ Don't overstudy the day before the exam.

▶ Get a good night's rest.

- ▶ Eat a decent breakfast.
- ▶ Show up early.
- ▶ Bring earplugs.
- ▶ Brainstorm before starting the exam.
- ▶ Take small breaks while taking the exam.
- ▶ Be confident.

I embellish on these concepts in the final chapter.

Well, that's it for the 220-1001 portion of this book. Good luck on your exam!

CHAPTER SIX

Introduction to the 220-1002 Exam

The CompTIA A+ Core 2 (220-1002) exam covers operating systems such as Windows, Linux, and macOS; computer and network security; mobile device operating systems such as Android and iOS; software troubleshooting; and operational procedures. The largest percentage of the exam focuses on operating systems—mainly, the installation, configuration, and troubleshooting of Windows—but you will also see many questions on the other topics.

In this chapter, I briefly discuss how the exam is categorized, give you some test-taking tips, and then prepare you to take the three 220-1002 practice exams that follow.

Exam Breakdown

The CompTIA A+ 220-1002 exam is divided by domain. Each domain makes up a certain percentage of the test. The four domains of the A+ 220-1002 exam and their respective percentages are listed in Table 6.1.

TABLE 6.1   220-1002 Domains

Domain	Percentage of Exam
1.0 Operating Systems	27
2.0 Security	24
3.0 Software Troubleshooting	26
4.0 Operational Procedures	23
Total	100

Chances are, when you take the real CompTIA exam, the questions will be based on these percentages. But you never know. The questions are chosen at random, so you have to be prepared for anything and study all of the objectives. As with the 220-1001 exam, troubleshooting plays a huge role. Remember: Without good troubleshooting skills and experience, you have very diminished hopes of passing the exam.

Each domain has several objectives. There are far too many to list in this book, but I recommend you download a copy of the objectives for yourself. You can get them from CompTIA's A+ web page, and I link to them at my website as well: https://dprocomputer.com.

Let's talk about each domain briefly.

Domain 1.0: Operating Systems (27%)

We've hardly talked about Windows up until this point. But now that we're here, you'll see lots of questions on Windows—I guarantee it. Domain 1.0 deals with Windows 10, Windows 8 and 8.1, and Windows 7.

This domain covers how the operating systems can be installed, how they are configured, and how they are utilized. It covers the Windows Control Panel (and Windows 10 Settings) and a plethora of Windows tools. You'll have to be ready to network Windows computers together too; be ready to set up workgroups, domains, networking connections, and plenty more. In addition, this domain gets into commands such as ipconfig, netstat, shutdown, and robo-copy, which are issued in the Command Prompt. Then there's maintenance and backup of Windows; and this is not a finite list. However, it's not only Windows—Linux, macOS, iOS, Android, and Chrome OS are covered in this domain as well. So, the objectives are in depth. There's a lot of information to cram into one domain, but remember that this domain does not cover Windows troubleshooting; that topic is left for Domain 3.0.

Domain 2.0: Security (24%)

Security takes on a bigger role every year in the IT world. The CompTIA A+ 220-1002 exam reflects this growth. This domain deals with common security threats, physical and digital prevention methods, how to secure the various operating systems listed in the first domain, how to dispose of hard drives properly, and how to secure a small office or home office (SOHO) network. Basically, careful consideration for security should be applied to anything technology-oriented.

> **NOTE**
>
> Many test-takers have the most difficulty with this domain and the troubleshooting domain. Be ready.

Domain 3.0 Software Troubleshooting (26%)

Here it is: troubleshooting. It's the troubleshooting methodologies that make the ultimate computer tech. And it's those skills that will make or break you on this exam. Whenever you encounter a technical problem, try to approach it in a logical manner. The best way to do this is to use some kind of troubleshooting theory.

Remember the CompTIA six-step troubleshooting methodology from the 220-1001 exam? I'd like you to try to incorporate this six-step process into your line of thinking as you read through the practice exams and whenever you troubleshoot a PC, mobile device, networking, or security issue:

Step 1. Identify the problem.

Step 2. Establish a theory of probable cause. (Question the obvious.)

Step 3. Test the theory to determine cause.

Step 4. Establish a plan of action to resolve the problem and implement the solution.

Step 5. Verify full system functionality and, if applicable, implement preventive measures.

Step 6. Document findings, actions, and outcomes.

This section could be considered the most difficult and, unfortunately in the IT field, the most insidious. Issues can look or act like one thing yet be another. Stay really focused when dealing with troubleshooting questions. You'll know them when you see them; they include real-world scenarios and often end in a question such as "What should you do to fix the problem," or "How can this be resolved," and so on.

Master this domain, and you will be well on your way to passing the A+ 220-1002 exam, attaining your A+ certificate, and becoming a true expert at troubleshooting.

Domain 4.0: Operational Procedures (23%)

The fourth domain of the 220-1002 exam deals with safety procedures, environmental concerns, incident response, prohibited content, communication, professionalism, basic scripting, and remote access. Many of these are the "intangibles" of the A+ exam, and although this domain is the smallest—coming in at 23 percent of the exam—they could be considered some of the most important topics for the real world. This last domain helps develop a well-rounded technician. Apply the concepts in this domain to everything else you do.

Test-Taking Tips

Just like with the 220-1001 practice exams, I recommend you take it slow through these practice exams. Carefully read through each question. Read through *all* of the answers. Look at each answer and think to yourself whether it is right or wrong. And if an answer is wrong, define why it is wrong. This approach will help you eliminate wrong answers in the search for the correct answer. When you select an answer, be confident in your decision.

Be ready for longer questions. The length of these questions is due to the complexity of some of the scenarios. You need to imagine yourself within the situation and think how you would approach the problem step by step. Be prepared to write things down as you look at a question. Doing so can help you organize your thoughts. It's allowed on the real exam as well.

> **NOTE**
>
> In fact, the testing center is required to give you something to write on. Be sure that you receive it before you start your exam.

Finally, don't get stuck on any one question. You can always mark it and return to it later. I provide more tips as you progress through the book, and I summarize all test-taking tips at the end of this book.

Getting Ready for the Practice Tests

The practice tests in the following three chapters are based on the 220-1002 exam. Each exam is followed by in-depth explanations. Be sure to read them carefully. Don't move on to another exam until you have mastered the first one by scoring 90 percent or higher. Be positive that you understand the concepts before moving on to another exam. This will make you an efficient test-taker and allow you to benefit the most from this book.

Consider timing yourself. Give yourself 90 minutes to complete each exam. Write down your answers on a piece of paper. When you are finished, if you still have time left, review your answers for accuracy.

Each exam gets progressively more difficult. Don't get overconfident if you do well on the first exam because your skills will be tested more thoroughly as you progress. And don't get too concerned if you don't score 90 percent on the first try. That just means you need to study more and try the test again later. Keep studying and practicing!

After each exam is an answer key, followed by the in-depth answers/explanations. Don't skip the explanations, even if you think you know the concept. I often add my two cents, which can add insight to the nature of the question, as well as help you answer other similar questions correctly.

Ready yourself: prepare the mind, and then go ahead and begin the first 220-1002 exam!

CHAPTER SEVEN

220-1002 Practice Exam A

Welcome to the first 220-1002 practice exam. This is the easiest of the 220-1002 exams. The subsequent exams will get progressively harder.

Take this first exam slowly. The goal is to make sure you understand all of the concepts before moving on to the next test.

Write down your answers and check them against the Quick-Check Answer Key, which immediately follows the exam. After the answer key, you will find the explanations for all of the answers. Good luck!

Practice Questions

1. Which of the following are Microsoft operating systems? (Select all correct answers.)

   ☐ **A.** Windows 8.1
   ☐ **B.** iOS
   ☐ **C.** 10 version 1803
   ☐ **D.** Android
   ☐ **E.** Linux
   ☐ **F.** Windows 7

   Quick Answer: **154**
   Detailed Answer: **155**

2. Which of the following is the default file system used by Windows?

   ○ **A.** FAT32
   ○ **B.** CDFS
   ○ **C.** NTFS
   ○ **D.** exFAT

   Quick Answer: **154**
   Detailed Answer: **155**

3. Where is the Notification Area located in Windows?

- ○ **A.** In the System Properties dialog box
- ○ **B.** In the System32 folder
- ○ **C.** On the taskbar
- ○ **D.** Within the Start menu

Quick Answer: **154**
Detailed Answer: **155**

4. Which of the following is the minimum amount of RAM needed to install a 64-bit version of Windows 10?

- ○ **A.** 512 MB
- ○ **B.** 1 GB
- ○ **C.** 2 GB
- ○ **D.** 4 GB

Quick Answer: **154**
Detailed Answer: **155**

5. In Windows, an MMC is blank by default. Which of the following should be added to the MMC to populate it with programs?

- ○ **A.** Applets
- ○ **B.** Files
- ○ **C.** Directories
- ○ **D.** Snap-ins

Quick Answer: **154**
Detailed Answer: **155**

6. Which of the following files is the boot loader in Windows?

- ○ **A.** Winload.exe
- ○ **B.** BCD
- ○ **C.** Setup.exe
- ○ **D.** Ntoskrnl.exe

Quick Answer: **154**
Detailed Answer: **156**

7. Which specific tool enables you to create a partition in Windows?

- ○ **A.** Disk Management
- ○ **B.** Format command
- ○ **C.** Computer Management
- ○ **D.** Disk Cleanup

Quick Answer: **154**
Detailed Answer: **156**

8. Which type of partition should an operating system be installed to?

- ○ **A.** Primary
- ○ **B.** Extended
- ○ **C.** Dynamic
- ○ **D.** Logical drive

Quick Answer: **154**
Detailed Answer: **156**

9. Which of the following tools enables you to find out how much memory a particular application is using?

Quick Answer: **154**
Detailed Answer: **156**

   ○ **A.** Msconfig

   ○ **B.** Task Manager

   ○ **C.** Chkdsk

   ○ **D.** System Information

10. Which of the following features is used to both start and stop services? (Select the two best answers.)

Quick Answer: **154**
Detailed Answer: **157**

   ❑ **A.** Computer Management

   ❑ **B.** Task Manager

   ❑ **C.** Performance Monitor

   ❑ **D.** MMC

   ❑ **E.** Msconfig

11. Which of the following user account permissions are needed to install device drivers on Windows?

Quick Answer: **154**
Detailed Answer: **157**

   ○ **A.** Standard user

   ○ **B.** Guest

   ○ **C.** Administrator

   ○ **D.** Power users

12. Which of the following commands creates a new directory in the Windows Command Prompt?

Quick Answer: **154**
Detailed Answer: **157**

   ○ **A.** CD

   ○ **B.** MD

   ○ **C.** RD

   ○ **D.** SD

13. Which of the following commands is entered at the Command Prompt to learn more about the dir command? (Select the two best answers.)

Quick Answer: **154**
Detailed Answer: **157**

   ❑ **A.** dir help

   ❑ **B.** help dir

   ❑ **C.** dir /?

   ❑ **D.** dir man

14. Which interface is used to launch the `ipconfig` command?

Quick Answer: **154**
Detailed Answer: **157**

- ○ **A.** Command Prompt
- ○ **B.** Control Panel
- ○ **C.** MMC
- ○ **D.** Task Manager

15. A customer's computer is using FAT32. Which file system can you upgrade it to when using the `convert` command?

Quick Answer: **154**
Detailed Answer: **158**

- ○ **A.** NTFS
- ○ **B.** ext4
- ○ **C.** exFAT
- ○ **D.** NFS

16. Which of the following can be used to keep hard drives free of errors and ensure that Windows runs efficiently? (Select the two best answers.)

Quick Answer: **154**
Detailed Answer: **158**

- ❏ **A.** Disk Management
- ❏ **B.** Disk Defragmenter
- ❏ **C.** Check Disk
- ❏ **D.** System Restore
- ❏ **E.** Task Scheduler

17. What is Windows Recovery Environment known as? (Select the two best answers.)

Quick Answer: **154**
Detailed Answer: **158**

- ❏ **A.** WinRE
- ❏ **B.** Recovery Console
- ❏ **C.** Advanced Boot Options
- ❏ **D.** System Recovery Options

18. Which log file contains information about Windows setup errors?

Quick Answer: **154**
Detailed Answer: **158**

- ○ **A.** setupact.log
- ○ **B.** setuperr.log
- ○ **C.** unattend.xml
- ○ **D.** diskmgmt.msc

19. Which of the following represents the RAM limitation of Windows 8.1 Pro 64-bit?

Quick Answer: **154**
Detailed Answer: **158**

- ○ **A.** 4 GB
- ○ **B.** 128 GB
- ○ **C.** 512 GB
- ○ **D.** 2 TB

20. A customer's Device Manager shows an arrow pointing down over one of the devices. What does this tell you?

Quick Answer: **154**
Detailed Answer: **159**

- ○ **A.** The device's driver has not been installed.
- ○ **B.** The device is not recognized.
- ○ **C.** The device is disabled.
- ○ **D.** The device is in queue to be deleted.

21. Which of the following is *not* an advantage of NTFS over FAT32?

Quick Answer: **154**
Detailed Answer: **159**

- ○ **A.** NTFS supports file encryption.
- ○ **B.** NTFS supports larger file sizes.
- ○ **C.** NTFS supports larger volumes.
- ○ **D.** NTFS supports more file formats.

22. A coworker just installed a second hard drive in his Windows computer. However, he does not see the drive in Explorer. What did he forget to do? (Select the three best answers.)

Quick Answer: **154**
Detailed Answer: **159**

- ❏ **A.** Format the drive
- ❏ **B.** Partition the drive
- ❏ **C.** Run FDISK
- ❏ **D.** Initialize the drive
- ❏ **E.** Set up the drive in the UEFI/BIOS

23. How would you create a restore point in Windows?

Quick Answer: **154**
Detailed Answer: **159**

- ○ **A.** Run Disk Defragmenter from the MMC.
- ○ **B.** Run Backup and Restore from the Control Panel.
- ○ **C.** Run the System Restore program from System Properties.
- ○ **D.** Run the Disk Cleanup program from System Properties.

24. Which of the following tasks *cannot* be performed from the Printer Properties screen?

Quick Answer: **154**
Detailed Answer: **159**

- ○ **A.** Modifying spool settings
- ○ **B.** Adding ports
- ○ **C.** Pausing printing
- ○ **D.** Enabling sharing

25. You are setting up auditing on a Windows computer. If it's set up properly, which of the following logs should contain entries?

Quick Answer: **154**
Detailed Answer: **160**

- ○ **A.** Application log
- ○ **B.** System log
- ○ **C.** Security log
- ○ **D.** Maintenance log

26. Which type of virus propagates itself by tunneling through the Internet and networks?

Quick Answer: **154**
Detailed Answer: **160**

- ○ **A.** Macro
- ○ **B.** Phishing
- ○ **C.** Trojan
- ○ **D.** Worm

27. Which component of Windows enables users to perform common tasks as nonadministrators and, when necessary, as administrators without having to switch users, log off, or use Run As?

Quick Answer: **154**
Detailed Answer: **160**

- ○ **A.** USMT
- ○ **B.** UAC
- ○ **C.** USB
- ○ **D.** VNC

28. Which of the following tasks can be performed to secure your WAP/router? (Select all that apply.)

Quick Answer: **154**
Detailed Answer: **160**

- ❑ **A.** Changing the default SSID name
- ❑ **B.** Turning off SSID broadcasting
- ❑ **C.** Enabling DHCP
- ❑ **D.** Disabling DHCP

29. When you connect to a website to make a purchase by credit card, you want to make sure the website is secure. Which of the following statements best describes how to determine whether a site is secure? (Select the two best answers.)

Quick Answer: **154**
Detailed Answer: **161**

- ❏ **A.** You should look for the padlock (in the locked position) toward the top or bottom of the screen.

- ❏ **B.** You should look for the padlock (in the unlocked position) toward the top or bottom of the screen.

- ❏ **C.** You should look for the protocol HTTP in the address or URL bar.

- ❏ **D.** You should look for the protocol HTTPS in the address or URL bar.

30. Which type of software helps protect against viruses that are attached to email?

Quick Answer: **154**
Detailed Answer: **161**

- ○ **A.** Firewall software
- ○ **B.** Antivirus software
- ○ **C.** Internet Explorer
- ○ **D.** Hardware firewall

31. Which of the following is an example of social engineering?

Quick Answer: **154**
Detailed Answer: **161**

- ○ **A.** Asking for a username and password over the phone
- ○ **B.** Using someone else's unsecured wireless network
- ○ **C.** Hacking into a router
- ○ **D.** A virus

32. Where are software-based firewalls most commonly implemented?

Quick Answer: **154**
Detailed Answer: **161**

- ○ **A.** On routers
- ○ **B.** On servers
- ○ **C.** On clients
- ○ **D.** On switches

33. Making data appear as if it is coming from somewhere other than its original source is known as which of the following terms?

Quick Answer: **154**
Detailed Answer: **162**

- ○ **A.** Impersonation
- ○ **B.** Phishing
- ○ **C.** Zero-day
- ○ **D.** Spoofing

34. A fingerprint reader is known as which type of security technology?

- ○ **A.** Biometrics
- ○ **B.** Smart card
- ○ **C.** Barcode reader
- ○ **D.** SSID

Quick Answer: **154**
Detailed Answer: **162**

35. Which of the following is the most secure password?

- ○ **A.** marquisdesod
- ○ **B.** Marqu1sDeS0d
- ○ **C.** MarquisDeSod
- ○ **D.** Marqu1s_De_S0d_ver_2

Quick Answer: **154**
Detailed Answer: **162**

36. Which shortcut key combination immediately locks Windows?

- ○ **A.** Ctrl+Alt+Del
- ○ **B.** Windows+R
- ○ **C.** Windows+M
- ○ **D.** Windows+L

Quick Answer: **154**
Detailed Answer: **162**

37. Which of the following is the most secure file system in Windows?

- ○ **A.** ext4
- ○ **B.** exFAT
- ○ **C.** NTFS
- ○ **D.** FAT32

Quick Answer: **154**
Detailed Answer: **163**

38. Which of the following is the most secure for your wireless network?

- ○ **A.** WEP
- ○ **B.** WPA2
- ○ **C.** TKIP
- ○ **D.** WPA

Quick Answer: **154**
Detailed Answer: **163**

39. Which of the following terms refers to when people are manipulated into giving access to network resources?

- ○ **A.** Shoulder surfing
- ○ **B.** Social engineering
- ○ **C.** Phishing
- ○ **D.** Spear phishing

Quick Answer: **154**
Detailed Answer: **163**

40. A customer's Windows computer needs a new larger, faster hard drive. Another technician in your company installs the new drive and then formats the old drive before delivering it to you for disposal. How secure is the customer's data?

- ○ **A.** Confidential
- ○ **B.** Very insecure
- ○ **C.** Secure
- ○ **D.** Completely secured

Quick Answer: **154**
Detailed Answer: **163**

41. Which of the following offers hardware-based authentication?

- ○ **A.** NTFS
- ○ **B.** Smart card
- ○ **C.** Strong passwords
- ○ **D.** Encrypted passwords

Quick Answer: **154**
Detailed Answer: **164**

42. Which protocol encrypts transactions through a website?

- ○ **A.** HTTP
- ○ **B.** SSL
- ○ **C.** PuTTY
- ○ **D.** Kerberos

Quick Answer: **154**
Detailed Answer: **164**

43. Which of the following is a common local security policy?

- ○ **A.** Use of RAID
- ○ **B.** Password length
- ○ **C.** Router passwords
- ○ **D.** Use of a password to log in

Quick Answer: **154**
Detailed Answer: **164**

44. A coworker downloads a game that ends up stealing information from the computer system. What is this known as?

- ○ **A.** Worm
- ○ **B.** Spam
- ○ **C.** Trojan
- ○ **D.** Spyware

Quick Answer: **154**
Detailed Answer: **164**

45. Which of the following is an open-source operating system?

- ○ **A.** Android
- ○ **B.** iOS
- ○ **C.** Windows 8.1
- ○ **D.** macOS

Quick Answer: **154**
Detailed Answer: **164**

46. Where can you obtain applications for mobile devices? (Select the three best answers.)

    ❑ **A.** Spotlight

    ❑ **B.** App Store

    ❑ **C.** Google Play

    ❑ **D.** iTunes

Quick Answer: **154**
Detailed Answer: **165**

47. You need to locate a mobile device that was stolen. Which technology can aid in this?

    ○ **A.** GPS

    ○ **B.** Screen orientation

    ○ **C.** Passcode locks

    ○ **D.** Gmail

Quick Answer: **154**
Detailed Answer: **165**

48. Which kinds of data are typically synchronized on a smartphone? (Select the two best answers.)

    ❑ **A.** Contacts

    ❑ **B.** PHP pages

    ❑ **C.** Email

    ❑ **D.** SQL databases

Quick Answer: **154**
Detailed Answer: **165**

49. Which of the following is the second step of the A+ troubleshooting theory?

    ○ **A.** Identify the problem.

    ○ **B.** Establish a probable cause.

    ○ **C.** Test the theory.

    ○ **D.** Document.

Quick Answer: **154**
Detailed Answer: **165**

50. You successfully modified the Registry on a customer's PC. Now the customer's system gets onto the Internet normally. Which of the following steps should be performed next?

    ○ **A.** Bill the customer.

    ○ **B.** Move on to the next computer.

    ○ **C.** Document your solution.

    ○ **D.** Run Disk Defrag.

Quick Answer: **154**
Detailed Answer: **165**

51. Buzz gets an error that says "Error log full." Where should you go to clear his error log?

- ○ **A.** Device Manager
- ○ **B.** System Information
- ○ **C.** Recovery Console
- ○ **D.** Event Viewer

52. Which of the following tools checks protected system files?

- ○ **A.** Chkdsk
- ○ **B.** Dism
- ○ **C.** Scandisk
- ○ **D.** SFC

53. After installing a new hard drive on a Windows computer, Len tries to format the drive. Windows does not show the format option in Disk Management. What did Len forget to do first?

- ○ **A.** Run chkdsk.
- ○ **B.** Partition the drive.
- ○ **C.** Defragment the drive.
- ○ **D.** Copy system files.

54. Which Windows System Recovery Option attempts to automatically fix problems?

- ○ **A.** System Restore
- ○ **B.** Startup Repair
- ○ **C.** File History
- ○ **D.** Reset Your PC

55. Which utility enables you to troubleshoot an error with a file such as ntoskrnl.exe?

- ○ **A.** Registry
- ○ **B.** Event Viewer
- ○ **C.** REGSVR32
- ○ **D.** Terminal

56. A blue screen is most often caused by _____.

- ○ **A.** Driver failure
- ○ **B.** Memory failure
- ○ **C.** Hard drive failure
- ○ **D.** CD-ROM failure

57. A technician is installing a program on a Windows computer and the installation fails. Which of the following statements describes the next best step?

- ○ **A.** Run the installer as an administrator.
- ○ **B.** Contact the program's manufacturer.
- ○ **C.** Reinstall Windows on the computer.
- ○ **D.** Upgrade to the latest version of Windows.

58. Which of the following statements best describes how to apply spray cleaner to a monitor?

- ○ **A.** Spray the cleaner directly on the monitor screen.
- ○ **B.** Spray the cleaner on the top of the monitor and wipe down.
- ○ **C.** Spray evenly on the monitor.
- ○ **D.** Spray the cleaner on a clean, lint-free cloth first.

59. You and a coworker are running network cables above the drop ceiling. The coworker accidentally touches a live AC power line and is thrown off the ladder and onto the ground. He is dazed and can't stand. He is no longer near the AC power line. Which of the following statements best describes the first step you should take?

- ○ **A.** Cut the power at the breaker.
- ○ **B.** Move the coworker farther down the hall.
- ○ **C.** Apply CPR.
- ○ **D.** Call 911.

60. A computer you are working on has a lot of dust inside it. Which of the following statements best describes how to clean this?

- ○ **A.** Disassemble the power supply and remove the dust.
- ○ **B.** Use a household vacuum to clean up the dust.
- ○ **C.** Use a surface dust cleaning solution.
- ○ **D.** Use compressed air to remove the dust.

61. You are working on a very old printer and it begins to smoke. Which of the following statements best describes the first step you should take?

Quick Answer: **154**
Detailed Answer: **168**

- ○ **A.** Turn off the printer.
- ○ **B.** Call 911.
- ○ **C.** Unplug the printer.
- ○ **D.** Call maintenance.
- ○ **E.** Tell the printer it is bad to smoke.

62. Which of the following statements best describes the recommended method for handling an empty toner cartridge?

Quick Answer: **154**
Detailed Answer: **168**

- ○ **A.** Throw it away.
- ○ **B.** Incinerate it.
- ○ **C.** Refill it.
- ○ **D.** Recycle it.

63. One of your technicians is on a service call and is dealing with a furious customer who has been shouting loudly. The technician tries but cannot calm down the customer. Which of the following statements best describes the next step the technician should take?

Quick Answer: **154**
Detailed Answer: **168**

- ○ **A.** He should let the customer continue to shout; sooner or later the customer will get tired and calm down.
- ○ **B.** He should call the supervisor and complain.
- ○ **C.** He should leave the customer site and document the incident.
- ○ **D.** He should shout back at the customer in an attempt to regain control of the situation.

64. While you are working at a customer site, a friend calls you on your cell phone. Which of the following statements best describes the recommended course of action?

Quick Answer: **154**
Detailed Answer: **168**

- ○ **A.** Ignore the call for now.
- ○ **B.** Go outside and take the call.
- ○ **C.** Answer the phone as quietly as possible.
- ○ **D.** Text your friend.

65. Which of the following tools is used when setting the computer to boot with the Selective Startup feature?

    ○ **A.** Task Manager

    ○ **B.** Windows RE

    ○ **C.** Safe Mode

    ○ **D.** `Msconfig`

Quick Answer: **154**
Detailed Answer: **168**

66. Which of the following file extensions is used when saving PowerShell scripts?

    ○ **A.** .js

    ○ **B.** .vbs

    ○ **C.** .ps1

    ○ **D.** .py

Quick Answer: **154**
Detailed Answer: **169**

67 You have been given the task of installing a new hard drive on a server for a customer. The customer will be supervising your work. Which of the following questions should you ask the customer first?

    ○ **A.** "What is the administrator password?"

    ○ **B.** "Are there any current backups?"

    ○ **C.** "Do you want me to shut down the server?"

    ○ **D.** "Which version of Windows Server is this?"

Quick Answer: **154**
Detailed Answer: **169**

68. You just upgraded the president's computer's video driver. Now, the Windows 10 system will not boot. Which of the following steps should be taken first?

    ○ **A.** Access the Windows RE Command Prompt.

    ○ **B.** Boot into Safe Mode and roll back the driver.

    ○ **C.** Reinstall the operating system.

    ○ **D.** Boot into Directory Services Restore mode.

Quick Answer: **154**
Detailed Answer: **169**

69. Which tool is used to analyze and diagnose a video card, including its DirectX version?

    ○ **A.** Device Manager

    ○ **B.** DxDiag

    ○ **C.** Services.msc

    ○ **D.** USMT

Quick Answer: **154**
Detailed Answer: **169**

70. Which of the following statements best describes a common risk when installing Windows drivers that are unsigned?

- ○ **A.** System stability may be compromised.
- ○ **B.** Files might be cross-linked.
- ○ **C.** The drive might become fragmented.
- ○ **D.** Physical damage to devices might occur.

71. Which of the following settings must be established when you want to make a secure wireless connection? (Select all that apply.)

- ❏ **A.** The brand of access point
- ❏ **B.** The wireless standard used
- ❏ **C.** The encryption standard used
- ❏ **D.** The SSID of the access point

72. Which Windows utility is used to prepare a drive image for duplication across the network?

- ○ **A.** Robocopy
- ○ **B.** Sysprep
- ○ **C.** Ghost
- ○ **D.** Image Clone

73. In Windows, when will a computer dump the physical memory?

- ○ **A.** When the wrong processor is installed
- ○ **B.** When a device is missing drivers
- ○ **C.** When the computer is shut down improperly
- ○ **D.** When the computer detects a condition from which it cannot recover

74. When a person takes control of a session between a server and a client, it is known as which type of attack?

- ○ **A.** DDoS
- ○ **B.** Brute force
- ○ **C.** Session hijacking
- ○ **D.** Malicious software

75. The message "The Windows Boot Configuration Data File Is Missing Required Information" appears on the screen. Which command can repair this issue?

Quick Answer: **154**
Detailed Answer: **171**

- ○ **A.** `bootrec /fixboot`
- ○ **B.** `bootrec /fixmbr`
- ○ **C.** `bootrec /rebuildbcd`
- ○ **D.** `boot\bcd`

76. Which of the following should be performed during a hard drive replacement to best maintain data privacy?

Quick Answer: **154**
Detailed Answer: **171**

- ○ **A.** Completely erase the old drive prior to disposal.
- ○ **B.** Format the new hard drive twice prior to installation.
- ○ **C.** Use only FAT32 file systems when formatting the new drives.
- ○ **D.** Install antivirus software on the computer before removing the old hard drive.

77. Which tool is used to back up data on the C: drive in Windows 10?

Quick Answer: **154**
Detailed Answer: **171**

- ○ **A.** Backup and Restore
- ○ **B.** BitLocker
- ○ **C.** Time Machine
- ○ **D.** File History

78. Which of the following is the minimum processor requirement for Windows 10?

Quick Answer: **154**
Detailed Answer: **171**

- ○ **A.** 32 GB
- ○ **B.** 1 GHz
- ○ **C.** 2 GHz
- ○ **D.** 2 GB

79. You create an answer file to aid in installing Windows. Which type of installation are you performing? (Select the best answer.)

Quick Answer: **154**
Detailed Answer: **171**

- ○ **A.** Drive image installation
- ○ **B.** USB installation
- ○ **C.** Multiboot installation
- ○ **D.** Unattended installation

80. Which of the following utilities can be used to view the startup programs?

    ○   **A.** Ipconfig

    ○   **B.** Ping

    ○   **C.** Regedit

    ○   **D.** DxDiag

Quick-Check Answer Key

1. A, C, F	28. A, B, D	55. B
2. C	29. A, D	56. A
3. C	30. B	57. A
4. C	31. A	58. D
5. D	32. C	59. D
6. A	33. D	60. D
7. A	34. A	61. C
8. A	35. D	62. D
9. B	36. D	63. C
10. A, B	37. C	64. A
11. C	38. B	65. D
12. B	39. B	66. C
13. B, C	40. B	67. B
14. A	41. B	68. B
15. A	42. B	69. B
16. B, C	43. B	70. A
17. A, D	44. C	71. C, D
18. B	45. A	72. B
19. C	46. B, C, D	73. D
20. C	47. A	74. C
21. D	48. A, C	75. C
22. A, B, D	49. B	76. A
23. C	50. C	77. D
24. C	51. D	78. B
25. C	52. D	79. D
26. D	53. B	80. C
27. B	54. B	

Answers and Explanations

1. **Answers: A, C, and F**

   Explanation: Windows 8.1, Windows 10 (version 1803), and Windows 7 are all Microsoft operating systems that you should know for the exam.

   Incorrect Answers: iOS is the operating system Apple uses on its mobile devices. Android is the competitor of iOS and is an open-source operating system used on many other manufacturers' mobile devices. Android is developed from Linux. The original Linux was made for PCs with the goal of being a freely accessible, open-source platform; today it is more commonly found in server form. Okay, that was an easy one...moving on!

2. **Answer: C**

   Explanation: The New Technology File System (NTFS) is the default file system that Windows uses.

   Incorrect Answers: FAT32 is an older, less desirable file system that offers less function-ality and less security and accesses smaller partition sizes. Compact Disc File System (CDFS) is the file system used by an optical disc. exFAT is another file system supported by Windows that works best with flash-based drives (such as USB thumb drives).

3. **Answer: C**

   Explanation: The Notification Area is the area toward the bottom right of your screen within the taskbar. It contains the time and any applications (shown as icons) currently running in memory. The System Properties dialog box contains configuration tabs for the computer name and network, hardware, system restore, and more. You can access any of the tabs in that dialog box quickly by going to Run and typing `systemprop-ertiescomputername.exe`, `systempropertiesadvanced.exe`, and so on.

   Incorrect Answers: The System32 folder resides within the Windows folder; it contains the critical Windows system files such as ntoskrnl.exe as well as applications such as cmd.exe. The Start menu gives access to most programs and configurations in Windows.

4. **Answer: C**

   Explanation: Windows 10 64-bit requires a minimum of 2 GB of RAM.

   Incorrect Answers: The 32-bit version requires 1 GB. The same goes for Windows 8.1. A minimum requirement for older versions of Windows was 512 MB. No doubt, 4 GB will be the minimum for some Windows versions at some point.

5. **Answer: D**

   Explanation: The MMC (Microsoft Management Console) is a blank shell until you add snap-ins (such as Computer Management or the Performance Monitor) for functionality.

   Incorrect Answers: Some people refer to each program in the Control Panel as an *applet*; the term was made famous by Apple. You don't add actual files or directories (folders) to the MMC; you add other programs within Windows. The MMC acts as an index for your programs and remembers the last place you were working (if you save it).

6. **Answer: A**

   Explanation: Winload.exe is the Windows boot loader program for Windows 10, 8, and 7. It is located in %systemroot%\System32 (which is usually C:\Windows\System32). It works in conjunction with the Bootmgr file (Windows Boot Manager). Bootmgr is the first file to load in Windows. It reads the BCD and displays an OS menu (if there is more than one OS).

   Incorrect Answers: The BCD is the Boot Configuration Data store; it is the successor to boot.ini. Setup.exe is the default name of the file that starts installations of Windows and many other programs. Ntoskrnl.exe is the main system file of Windows; without it, the system would crash and the file would have to be replaced or repaired.

7. **Answer: A**

   Explanation: Disk Management is a tool found in Computer Management and allows for the creation, deletion, and formatting of partitions and logical drives. To view this application, use the Search tool (and search for Disk Management), utilize the Start menu, or go to Run and type `diskmgmt.msc`.

   Incorrect Answers: The format command is a utility in the Windows Command Prompt that can be used to format partitions as NTFS or another file system type, but it does not *create* partitions. Disk Cleanup is a built-in Windows program that can remove temporary files and other data that you probably won't use.

8. **Answer: A**

   Explanation: Primary partitions are the first partitions created on a drive. An OS should always be installed to a primary partition, but before you install the OS, you should set the primary partition to active. If you are installing to a new hard drive, Windows will automatically set the partition to active for you. A Master Boot Record (MBR)-based hard drive can have four primary partitions maximum, each with its own drive letter.

   Incorrect Answers: If you need to subdivide the hard drive further, you can also use an extended partition, which is then broken up into logical drives. A GUID Partition Table (GPT)-based hard drive is not limited to this number; it can have up to 128 primary partitions. Dynamic refers to a dynamic drive; if you want to resize partitions, you have to convert the drive to dynamic in Disk Management. By the way, any drive in Windows that has a drive letter is known as a volume.

9. **Answer: B**

   Explanation: The Task Manager enables you, via a click of the Processes tab, to view all current running processes and see how much memory each is using. You can open the Task Manager by right-clicking the Taskbar and selecting it, by going to Run and typing `taskmgr`, by pressing Ctrl+Shift+Esc, or by pressing Ctrl+Alt+Del and selecting Task Manager.

   Incorrect Answers: `Msconfig` is a utility in Windows that allows you to enable and disable services and boot Windows in different modes. `Chkdsk` is a Command Prompt utility that searches for errors and fixes them (with the `/F` or `/R` switches). The System Information tool gives a summary of hardware resources, components, and the software environment; you can open it by going to Run and typing `msinfo32`.

10. **Answer: A and B**

    Explanation: You can start, stop, and restart services within Computer Management > Services and Applications > Services. From there, right-click the service in question and configure it as you wish. You can also open Services by going to the Run prompt and typing `services.msc`. The Task Manager can also be used to start and stop services, as well as to analyze the performance of the CPU, RAM, and the networking connections. You can also start and stop services with the `net start` / `net stop` and `sc start` / `sc stop` commands.

    Incorrect Answers: Performance Monitor analyzes the computer in much more depth than the Task Manager. The MMC is the Microsoft Management Console, which is the index that can store other console windows such as Computer Management. Among other things, `Msconfig` is used to enable/disable services, but not to *start* them.

11. **Answer: C**

    Explanation: The administrator is the only account level that can install device drivers.

    Incorrect Answers: Standard user, and especially guest, accounts cannot install drivers or programs. The Power Users group is an older group from the Windows XP days that was carried over to newer versions of Windows for application compatibility, but it has no real power in those operating systems.

12. **Answer: B**

    Explanation: MD is short for make directory and is the command to use when creating directories in the Command Prompt.

    Incorrect Answers: CD is change directory. RD is remove directory, and SD, which deals with memory cards, is not a valid command in the Command Prompt.

13. **Answers: B and C**

    Explanation: To learn more about any command in Windows, open the Command Prompt, type the command and then /?, or type `help dir`.

    Incorrect Answers: `dir help` would attempt to find the file named HELP within the current directory. `dir man` would most likely result in a "file not found" error. MAN pages are help pages used in Linux and macOS.

14. **Answer: A**

    Explanation: Use the Command Prompt to launch the command `ipconfig`. **ipconfig** is a networking command that displays the configuration of your network adapter. You can open the Command Prompt in a variety of ways. You can open the default Command Prompt by going to Run and typing `cmd.exe`. However, many commands require you to open the Command Prompt as an administrator (in elevated mode). To run it as an administrator, locate it in Windows, right-click it, and select Run as Administrator. Or, you could type `cmd` in the search field and then press Ctrl+Shift+Enter. You can also locate it in Windows 10 or 8.1 by right-clicking the Start button.

    Incorrect Answers: The other tools are used in the GUI and cannot run commands such as `ipconfig`. Use the Command Prompt or the PowerShell to run commands in Windows.

15. **Answer: A**

    Explanation: In Windows, the `convert` command is used to upgrade FAT and FAT32 volumes to NTFS without loss of data.

    Incorrect Answers: Ext4, or fourth extended file system, is a type of file system used by Linux-based systems. exFAT (FAT64) is especially designed for flash drives. NFS is the Network File System, something you might see in a storage area network.

16. **Answers: B and C**

    Explanation: Disk Defragmenter keeps Windows running more efficiently by making the files contiguous, lowering the amount of physical work the hard drive has to do. Check Disk or Error checking checks the hard drive for errors.

    Incorrect Answers: Disk Management is used to partition and format drives. System Restore allows you to take a snapshot of the OS, enabling you to revert to older settings if something goes wrong. The Task Scheduler (previously Scheduled Tasks), as the name implies, enables you to set what time you want particular tasks to run.

17. **Answers: A and D**

    Explanation: The Windows Recovery Environment (Windows RE or WinRE) is also known as System Recovery Options. From here, you can restore the system, fix file errors, and work in an unprotected Command Prompt.

    Incorrect Answers: The Recovery Console is the predecessor of WinRE, in the deprecated Windows XP. Advanced Boot Options is the menu that you can access by pressing F8. It is also referred to as ABOM, and in Windows 8/8.1/10 is known as Startup Settings.

> **NOTE**
>
> In Windows 10 and 8, you cannot access the Advanced Boot Options menu with the F8 key unless you have previously issued the following command:
> `bcdedit /set {DEFAULT} bootmenupolicy legacy`

18. **Answer: B**

    Explanation: Setuperr.log contains information about setup errors during the installation of Windows. Start with this log file when troubleshooting. A file size of 0 bytes indicates no errors during installation.

    Incorrect Answers: Setupact.log contains the events that occurred during the installation. Unattend.xml is the answer file used by Windows during unattended installations. Diskmgmt.msc is a command that can be run from the Run prompt or Command Prompt, which opens the Disk Management utility.

19. **Answer: C**

    Explanation: The physical memory limit of Windows 8.1 Pro is 512 GB on a 64-bit system. That is also the RAM limit for Windows 8.1 Enterprise; however, Windows 8.1 standard can access only 128 GB of RAM. Even though 64-bit CPUs can address a realistic maximum of 256 terabytes (TB), software is usually far more limited (as of the writing of this book in 2019).

Incorrect Answers: Windows 10 Home can access 128 GB. Windows 10 Pro and Education can access 2 TB of RAM. Windows 10 Enterprise can access 6 TB. The maximum that Windows 7 64-bit Professional, Ultimate, and Enterprise can access is 192 GB of RAM. Keep in mind that 32-bit versions of Windows 8.1 (and other versions of Windows) can access only a maximum of 4 GB of RAM, due to the limitations of 32-bit CPUs. See this link for memory limits of various Windows OSs: https://docs.microsoft.com/en-us/windows/desktop/Memory/memory-limits-for-windows-releases.

20. **Answer: C**

    Explanation: The arrow pointing down tells you that the device is disabled in Windows. In many cases, you can easily enable it by right-clicking and selecting Enable.

    Incorrect Answers: If the driver had not been installed, the device would most likely be sitting in a category called Unknown Devices. If the device is not even recognized by Windows, it will not show up on the list or will show up under Unknown Devices. There is no queue to be deleted.

21. **Answer: D**

    Explanation: NTFS and FAT32 support the same number of file formats. This is actually the only listed similarity between the two.

    Incorrect Answers: Otherwise, NTFS has the advantage: it supports file encryption in the form of Encrypting File System (EFS) and BitLocker, supports larger file sizes, and supports much larger volumes.

22. **Answers: A, B, and D**

    Explanation: For secondary drives, you must go to Disk Management and initialize, partition, and format them. *Explorer* in the question could mean File Explorer (Windows 10) or Windows Explorer (Windows 7).

    Incorrect Answers: FDISK is an older DOS command. Today's computers' UEFI/BIOS should see the drive automatically with no configuration needed. In special cases, a hard drive might require special drivers.

23. **Answer: C**

    Explanation: System Restore is the tool used to create restore points. In all versions of Windows, you can find it with the Search utility or by going to the **Control Panel > All Control Panel Icons > System**, and then clicking the **System Protection** link. (Or, go to Run and type `systempropertiesprotection.exe`.) In Windows 7, you can find it in **Start > All Programs > Accessories > System Tools** as well.

    Incorrect Answers: The Disk Defragmenter is used to fix hard drives that have become slow with fragmentation. Backup and Restore is the built-in backup program included with Windows 7. Disk Cleanup removes unwanted junk from the system, such as temporary files.

24. **Answer: C**

    Explanation: To pause printing in general and pause individual documents, double-click on the printer in question and make the modifications from the ensuing window.

    Incorrect Answers: All other tasks listed can be modified from the Printer Properties screen.

25. **Answer: C**

    Explanation: After Auditing is turned on and specific resources are configured for auditing, you need to check the Event Viewer's Security log for the entries. These could be successful logons or misfired attempts at deleting files; there are literally hundreds of options.

    Incorrect Answers: The Application log contains errors, warnings, and informational entries about applications. The System log deals with drivers and system files and so on. A system maintenance log can be used to record routine maintenance procedures; it is not included in Windows.

26. **Answer: D**

    Explanation: Worms travel through the Internet and through local-area networks (LANs). They are similar to viruses but differ in that they self-replicate.

    Incorrect Answers: Macros are viruses that attach to programs like Microsoft Word and Word files. Trojans are viruses that look like programs and often seek to gain back-door access to a system. Phishing is an attempt to fraudulently acquire information, often by email or phone.

27. **Answer: B**

    Explanation: With User Account Control (UAC) enabled, users perform common tasks as nonadministrators and, when necessary, as administrators without having to switch users, log off, or use Run As. If the user is logged in as an administrator, a pop-up window will appear verifying that the user has administrative privileges before action is taken; the user need only click Yes. If the user is not logged on as an administrator, clicking Yes will cause Windows to prompt the user for an administrative username and password.

    Incorrect Answers: USMT stands for User State Migration Tool, which is used to move files and user settings from one system (or systems) to another. USB is the universal serial bus and has little to do with this question except to serve to confuse the unwary with another acronym. VNC stands for Virtual Network Computing; it's a type of program that allows a person at a computer to remotely take control of another computer or device. Examples include RealVNC and TightVNC.

28. **Answers: A, B, and D**

    Explanation: A multifunction network device that acts as both a wireless access point (WAP) and a router may come with a standard, default SSID name (that everyone knows). It is a good idea to change it (if the router doesn't ask you to do so automatically). After PCs and laptops have been associated with the wireless network, turn off SSID broadcasting so that no one else can find your WAP (with normal means). Disabling DHCP and instead using static IP addresses removes one of the types of packets that are broadcast from the WAP, making it more difficult to hack, but of course less functional and useful. Other ways to secure the wireless access point include changing the password; incorporating strong encryption such as Wi-Fi Protected Access version 2 (WPA2) with Advanced Encryption Standard (AES); disabling WPS; and initiating MAC filtering, which only allows the computers with the MAC addresses you specify access to the wireless network.

    Incorrect Answers: Enabling DHCP will make it easier to connect to the SOHO router from clients but won't increase the security of the router.

29. Answers: A and D

Explanation: Although it could possibly be spoofed, the padlock in the locked position gives you a certain level of assurance and tells you that the website is using a secure certificate to protect your session. This padlock could be in different locations depending on the web browser used. Hypertext Transfer Protocol Secure (HTTPS) also defines that the session is using either the Secure Sockets Layer (SSL) protocol or the Transport Layer Security (TLS) protocol.

Incorrect Answers: HTTP by itself is enough for regular web sessions when you read documents and so on, but HTTPS is required when you log in to a site, purchase items, or do online banking. HTTPS opens a secure channel on port 443 as opposed to the default, insecure HTTP port 80. To be sure that you have a secure session, you can analyze the certificate and verify it against the certificate authority.

30. Answer: B

Explanation: Antivirus software (from vendors such as McAfee or Symantec) updates automatically to protect you against the latest viruses, whether they are attached to emails or are lying in wait on removable media. You might also choose to use Windows Defender on newer versions of Windows.

Incorrect Answers: Firewalls protect against intrusion but not viruses. They could be hardware-based, such as the ones found in most SOHO multifunction network devices, or software-based, such as the Windows Defender Firewall. Internet Explorer (and other web browsers) can be configured to make your system more secure (especially when dealing with web-based emails), but it is not the best answer listed.

31. Answer: A

Explanation: Social engineering is the practice of obtaining confidential information by manipulating people. Asking for a username and password over the phone is a type of phishing attack (known as vishing).

Incorrect Answers: Using someone else's network is just plain theft. Hacking into a router is just that, hacking. And a virus is a program that spreads through computers and networks (if executed by the user); it might or might not cause damage to files and applications.

32. Answer: C

Explanation: Software-based firewalls, such as the Windows Defender Firewall, normally run on client computers.

Incorrect Answers: It is possible that software-based firewalls will run on servers, especially if the server is acting as a network firewall, but the servers might rely on a hardware-based network firewall or an IDS/IPS solution. Hardware-based firewalls are also found in multifunction network devices. Some people might refer to these devices as *routers*, but the router functionality is really just one of the roles of the multifunction network device—separate from the firewall role. Plus, higher-end routers for larger networks are usually not combined with firewall functionality. Switches don't employ software firewalls, mainly because they don't use software (for the most part).

33. **Answer: D**

    Explanation: Spoofing is when a malicious user makes web pages, data, or email appear to be coming from somewhere else.

    Incorrect Answers: Impersonation is to present oneself as another person, imitating that other person's characteristics. It is often a key element in what is known as pretexting—the inventing of a scenario in the hopes that a key person will reveal confidential information. Phishing is when a person fraudulently attempts to gain confidential information from unsuspecting users. Zero-day attacks exploit vulnerabilities that haven't even been discovered yet or have been discovered but have not been disclosed through the proper channels so that security administrators can be aware of them.

34. **Answer: A**

    Explanation: Biometrics is the study of recognizing humans. A fingerprint reader falls into this category as a biometric device.

    Incorrect Answers: Smart cards are often the size of credit cards and store information that is transmitted to a reader. A barcode reader is a device that scans codes made up of different-width parallel lines, and SSID is a form of device identification that is broadcast from a wireless access point.

35. **Answer: D**

    Explanation: A password gets more secure as you increase its length and then add capital letters, numbers, and finally special characters. Note that Marqu1s_De_S0d_ ver_2 has a capital M, a 1 in the place of an *I*, underscores, a capital *D*, a capital *S*, and a zero. Plus, it is lengthy; it has 20 characters. Fifteen characters or more is an industry standard for highly secure passwords.

    Incorrect Answers: The rest of the passwords are either not as long or not as complex as the correct answer.

36. **Answer: D**

    Explanation: Windows+L automatically and immediately locks the computer. Only the person who locked it or an administrator can unlock it (unless, of course, another user knows your password).

    Incorrect Answers: Ctrl+Alt+Del brings up the Windows Security dialog box. From there, you can lock the computer, too, but with an extra step. Windows+R brings up the Run prompt, and Windows+M minimizes all open applications.

NOTE

Another fun shortcut is Windows+X, which brings up the Power User menu. You can also do this by right-clicking Start.

37. Answer: C

Explanation: NTFS is Windows' New Technology File System. It secures files and folders (and, in fact, the whole partition) much better than the older FAT32 system does. EFS, BitLocker, and NTFS permissions are just a few of the advantages of an NTFS partition.

Incorrect Answers: Ext4 (and ext3) is used by Linux-based systems. exFAT is another type of file system used often by USB thumb drives, SD cards, and other removable memory cards. FAT32 is the predecessor to NTFS and is not used often, but you might see it used with flash drives or older hard drives.

38. Answer: B

Explanation: WPA2 is superior to WPA and WEP and takes much longer to crack (if it is crackable at all). It works best with AES.

Incorrect Answers: Wired Equivalent Privacy (WEP) is deprecated (outdated) and is considered insecure. It should be avoided unless it is the only encryption option you have; even then, you should consider new hardware and software. TKIP stands for Temporal Key Integrity Protocol; it is a deprecated encryption protocol used with WEP and WPA. The replacement is either AES or (less commonly) CCMP.

39. Answer: B

Explanation: Social engineering is when fraudulent individuals try to get information from users through manipulation.

Incorrect Answers: Shoulder surfing is a form of social engineering where a person uses direct observation to find out a target's password, PIN, or other such authentication information. Phishing is a type of social engineering; it is implemented via email or over the phone (vishing). In spear phishing, specific individuals or groups of individuals are targeted with streamlined phishing attacks.

40. Answer: B

Explanation: The data is very insecure. Many tools can recover data from a drive after it is formatted. Some companies will "low-level" format the drive, or sanitize the drive (as opposed to a standard format in Windows, for example) and keep it in storage indefinitely. The organization might go further and use data wiping software; in fact, this might be a policy for the organization. Always check your organization's policies to be sure you are disposing of or recycling hard drives properly.

Incorrect Answers: *Confidential* is a term used to classify data. For example, personally identifiable information should be kept confidential (where only the appropriate personnel can access it). *Secure* is a relative term. Remember: nothing is ever *completely secured.*

41. **Answer: B**

    Explanation: Smart cards are actual physical cards that you use as authentication tools. They are sometimes referred to as *tokens* and have built-in processors. Examples of smart cards include the Personal Identity Verification (PIV) card used by U.S. government employees and the Common Access Card (CAC) used by Department of Defense personnel.

    Incorrect Answers: All of the other answers are software related and are logical in their implementations.

42. **Answer: B**

    Explanation: Secure Sockets Layer (SSL) and the newer Transport Layer Security (TLS) encrypt the transactions through the website. These SSL certificates are often accompanied by the protocol HTTPS.

    Incorrect Answers: HTTP by itself is not secure. PuTTY is a tool used for secure text-based connections to hosts and does not involve the website. Kerberos is the protocol used on a Microsoft domain to encrypt passwords.

43. **Answer: B**

    Explanation: Common local security policies include password length, duration, and complexity. Just the use of a password doesn't constitute a password policy. An example of a password policy would be when an organization mandates that passwords be 15 characters in length with at least 1 capital letter, 1 number, and 1 special character. In Windows you would access **Local Security Policy > Security Settings > Account Policies > Password Policy** to make changes to these things.

    Incorrect Answers: Simply having a RAID array is not a security policy, though security policies often define how the RAID array will be used. Again, just having passwords (such as router passwords or other passwords used to log in) does not establish policy. Modifying how passwords are selected and enforced is a security policy.

44. **Answer: C**

    Explanation: A Trojan is a disguised program that is used to gain access to a computer and either steal information or take control of the computer.

    Incorrect Answers: A worm is code that infects a system and self-replicates to other systems. Spam is the abuse of email and the bane of mankind. Spyware is software unwittingly downloaded from the Internet that tracks a user's actions while surfing the web.

45. **Answer: A**

    Explanation: Android is an open-source OS. It is freely downloadable and can be modified by manufacturers of mobile devices to suit their specific hardware.

    Incorrect Answers: Apple's iOS and macOS and Microsoft's OSs are closed source; a company would have to pay a fee for every license of the OS—that is, if it were even available to them.

46. **Answers: B, C, and D**

    Explanation: Android users download applications (apps) from Google Play. Apple users download apps from the App Store or from within iTunes.

    Incorrect Answers: The Spotlight tool is a utility in Apple's macOS that allows you to search the computer and the Internet by typing in search phrases.

47. **Answer: A**

    Explanation: The Global Positioning System (GPS) technology (or location services) can be instrumental in locating lost or stolen mobile devices. Many devices have this installed; others rely on geotracking or Wi-Fi hotspot locating techniques. (You are being watched!)

    Incorrect Answers: Screen orientation is how the screen is displayed depending on how you hold the device—vertical or horizontal (or upside down). It can be calibrated on Android devices with the G-Sensor calibration tool. Passcode locks are sets of numbers that are required to be entered when a mobile device is turned on or taken out of sleep mode. Gmail is a web-based email service by Google. It is incorporated into the Android operating system.

48. **Answers: A and C**

    Explanation: Some of the things you might synchronize on a smartphone include contacts, email, programs, pictures, music, and videos.

    Incorrect Answers: Mobile devices would not normally synchronize PHP web pages or Microsoft SQL databases. PHP is a commonly used programming language for websites and is often used either by itself or within HTML pages.

49. **Answer: B**

    Explanation: The second step is to establish a theory of probable cause. You are looking for the obvious or most probable cause for the problem.

    Incorrect Answers: Establishing a theory of probable cause comes after identifying the problem and before testing your theory. Documentation is last. While the troubleshooting process is listed in the 220-1001 objectives, it's still good practice—you'll always be using it, regardless of what technology you are working with. You never know what you might see on the exam!

50. **Answer: C**

    Explanation: Documentation is the final step in the troubleshooting theory. This helps you better understand and articulate exactly what the problem (and solution) was. If you see this problem in the future, you can consult your documentation for the solution. Plus, others on your team can do the same. In addition, it is common company policy to document all findings as part of a trouble ticket.

    Incorrect Answers: Generally, as a technician working for individual customers on the road, you would present a bill at the end of your technical visit (after everything else is complete). But for many technicians, billing is not a responsibility; someone else takes care of that task. Always document the solution before moving on to the next computer. Running programs such as Disk Defrag (Optimize Drives) is something you would do during an earlier phase of troubleshooting.

51. Answer: D

Explanation: The Event Viewer contains the error logs; they are finite in size. You could either clear the log or increase the size of the log.

Incorrect Answers: The other three applications do not contain error logs. The Recovery Console is a repair utility used in older versions of Windows; it is unlikely that you will see it.

52. Answer: D

Explanation: System File Checker (SFC) checks protected system files and replaces incorrect versions.

Incorrect Answers: None of the other options check system files. Chkdsk can check for and repair errors, but just regular files. Dism is a tool used to work with Windows images. Scandisk is an older command-line scanning tool that today's versions of Windows don't use. It was replaced by Chkdsk.

53. Answer: B

Explanation: You must partition the drive before formatting.

Incorrect Answers: You can copy files only after formatting is complete. Chkdsk has little value on an unformatted drive because it checks files for errors and integrity. Something else not mentioned here is that a second drive would have to be initialized in Windows before use.

54. Answer: B

Explanation: The best answer is Startup repair. Startup repair attempts to fix issues automatically. This is available in the Windows RE System Recovery Options.

Incorrect Answers: Although System Restore can "fix" problems, it only does this by resetting the computer to an earlier point in time, and as such, this is not the best answer. File History is the file backup program for Windows 10 and 8 but is not available within the system recovery environment. Reset Your PC is a Windows Recovery Environment. This might fix a problem, but it wipes settings and data in Windows 8, making it a possible solution, but only after you have tried other methods. (Instead of Reset Your PC, consider Refresh Your PC on Windows 8 systems first.) In Windows 10, Reset Your PC reinstalls but allows you to choose whether or not you want to wipe all data.

55. Answer: B

Explanation: The Event Viewer logs all errors that occur on a system. Particularly, the System log would contain the information useful in troubleshooting this error.

Incorrect Answers: The Windows Registry is a database that stores the settings for Windows. It contains hardware and software information, plus user settings. If you need to troubleshoot certain Dynamic-Link Libraries (DLLs) or ActiveX controls (for example, ones that work with Internet Explorer), you can manipulate them with the REGSVR32 command. macOS and Linux use a utility called Terminal that allows you to manipulate data and make configuration changes similar to the Command Prompt in Windows.

56. **Answer: A**

    Explanation: The most common reason for a BSOD (blue screen of death, otherwise known as a stop error) is driver failure.

    Incorrect Answers: Second on the list is memory/processor-related errors. Hard drives and optical drives themselves should not cause stop errors, but their drivers might.

57. **Answer: A**

    Explanation: Run the installer as an administrator. Programs cannot be installed by standard users or guests. You must have administrative rights to do so.

    Incorrect Answers: You should try to resolve the problem yourself before contacting the manufacturer, but in the end, the manufacturer might not be able to provide meaningful help. Be ready to solve problems on your own. Upgrading to a new version of Windows and reinstalling Windows are a bit extreme. Always remember to install as an admin and, if necessary, run older programs in compatibility mode.

58. **Answer: D**

    Explanation: Spray on a lint-free cloth first, and then wipe the display gently. A lot of companies sell products that are half isopropyl alcohol and half water. You could also make this cleaner yourself. Again, remember to put the solution on a lint-free cloth first.

    Incorrect Answers: Never spray any cleaner directly on a display. Try not to get any liquid in the cracks at the edge of the screen because it could get behind the display and possibly cause damage to circuitry (especially over time).

59. **Answer: D**

    Explanation: Because the immediate danger is gone, call 911 right away.

    Incorrect Answers: After calling 911, you would apply first aid and CPR as necessary. The next step would be to shut off the power at the electrical panel or call the building supervisor to have the power shut off. However, it is always important to be aware of and comply with company policies before taking certain actions. Be aware of company policies before accidents happen!

60. **Answer: D**

    Explanation: Compressed air is safe. However, you might want to do this outside and vacuum up the leftover residue. Or if you are working inside, use compressed air to blow dust out of the computer while using an antistatic vacuum to suck up the dust at the same time.

    Incorrect Answers: Never disassemble the power supply. It is called a field replaceable unit (FRU) for good reason. Do not use a household vacuum cleaner inside a computer; it could damage the components. Instead, use an antistatic computer vacuum, but be sure not to touch any of the components anyway. Do not spray any kind of solution inside the computer; this will damage the components.

61. **Answer: C**

    Explanation: Turning off the printer might not be enough. It might be seriously mal-functioning, so pull the plug.

    Incorrect Answers: Dialing 911 is not necessary unless a fire has started. Wait at least 15 minutes before opening the printer to see what caused the smoke. Printer power supplies can fail just like a PC's power supply can. In fact, a laser printer power supply does more work because it needs to convert for high voltages in the 600-V range. If you have a maintenance contract with a printer company, and the printer is under warranty or contained in the service contract, you could call the maintenance company to fix the problem. Be ready to give a detailed account of exactly what happened. You could tell the printer that it is bad to smoke, but that would be belligerent and would probably show that you have been working too hard. All kidding aside, be ready to disconnect power at a moment's notice.

62. **Answer: D**

    Explanation: Recycle toner cartridges according to your company's policies and proce-dures, or according to municipality rules and regulations.

    Incorrect Answers: Do not throw away or incinerate toner cartridges. Although it is possible to refill toner cartridges, this is not the recommended way to handle an empty cartridge because it is messy and time-consuming. Most companies simply purchase new toner cartridges.

63. **Answer: C**

    Explanation: The technician should leave the customer site and document the incident. In rare cases, there is no way to calm down the customer, and you might have to leave the site if there is no other alternative.

    Incorrect Answers: If the customer has been shouting for a while and the technician cannot calm down the customer, it's pointless to stay and wait. You don't want to call your supervisor and complain about the situation while you're at the customer's loca-tion; this will probably serve to infuriate the customer further. Wait until you have left the customer's premises. Never shout back at the customer; this is not a battle for power, and you should never take it personally. Be sure to document the incident in depth after leaving the customer's location. Definitely let your supervisor know what has happened—without complaining.

64. **Answer: A**

    Explanation: While you're on the job site, limit phone calls to only emergencies or calls from your employer about other customers.

    Incorrect Answers: Taking a personal phone call, texting, or using social media sites while working at a client site is considered unprofessional. Be professional when you're on the job.

65. **Answer: D**

    Explanation: `Msconfig` enables you to modify the startup selection. You can boot the computer in different modes with `Msconfig`. You can also enable and disable services.

Incorrect Answers: The Task Manager gives you a snapshot of your system's performance and allows you to shut down applications (tasks) or processes, even if the application is hanging or frozen. Windows RE is the Windows Recovery Environment, a special repair environment that is used to fix issues in the operating system. From here, you can fix system file issues and repair the boot sector, along with GPT and MBR-related issues. Safe Mode is one of the options in the Startup Settings/Advanced Boot Options menu. It starts the computer with a basic set of drivers so that you can troubleshoot why devices have failed. It is also instrumental when dealing with viruses.

66. **Answer: C**

Explanation: The .ps1 extension is used for PowerShell files and scripts.

Incorrect Answers: .js is JavaScript, .vbs is Visual Basic script, and .py is Python.

67. **Answer: B**

Explanation: Always check whether there are backups, and physically inspect and verify the backups before changing out any drives. Making sure that a backup is available is the first order of business.

Incorrect Answers: After the backup has been taken care of, you can have the customer give you the password to log in (or let the customer log in) and find out which version of Windows Server is running.

68. **Answer: B**

Explanation: By rolling back the driver (which is done in the Device Manager) while in Safe Mode, you can go back in time to the old working video driver.

Incorrect Answers: The Windows Recovery Environment might help (for example, if you used **Startup Settings > Safe Mode**, or System Restore), but the WinRE Command Prompt is not the best answer because it is a different tool. Reinstalling the OS would wipe the partition of the president's data (and probably wipe you of your job). Directory Services Restore mode (although listed in the Advanced Startup Options) is only for Windows Server domain controllers.

69. **Answer: B**

Explanation: The DxDiag utility is used to analyze a video card and its DirectX version and to check if drivers are digitally signed. You can access it by going to Run and typing `dxdiag`.

Incorrect Answers: The Device Manager is used to install drivers for devices— among other things—but is not used to view the DirectX version that is installed. Services.msc is the console window where you can start and stop and enable/disable services such as the Print Spooler. USMT stands for User State Migration Tool, a command-line tool used to migrate user files and settings from one or more computers.

70. **Answer: A**

    Explanation: By installing a driver that is not signed by Microsoft, you are risking instability of the operating system.

    Incorrect Answers: The driver has no effect on files or drive fragmentation. It is extremely uncommon for a driver to cause physical damage to a device. Note that Windows 8 and newer have driver signature enforcement enabled by default, so it becomes more difficult to install unsigned drivers.

71. **Answer: C and D**

    Explanation: To make a secure connection, you first need to know the Service Set Identifier (SSID) of the AP and then the encryption being used (for example, WPA or WPA2). The SSID takes care of the "connection" portion, and the encryption takes care of the "secure" portion. After all computers are connected, consider disabling the SSID for increased security.

    Incorrect Answers: Knowing the wireless standard being used can help you verify whether your computer is compatible (802.11ac, n, or g), but the brand of access point isn't really helpful.

72. **Answer: B**

    Explanation: Sysprep is one of the utilities built into Windows for image deployment over the network.

    Incorrect Answers: Ghost and Image Clone are third-party offerings. Robocopy copies entire directories (in the same physical order, too). Sysprep preps the system to be moved as an image file.

73. **Answer: D**

    Explanation: If the computer fails and cannot recover, you usually see some type of critical or stop error. At this point, you must restart the computer to get back into the operating system (unless it is configured to do so automatically, which is the default setting in Windows). The reason for the physical dump of memory is for later debugging. The physical dump writes the contents of memory (when the computer failed) to a file on the hard drive.

    Incorrect Answers: Missing drivers do not cause this error, but a failed driver might. If the wrong processor is installed, you can probably not get the system to boot at all. Shutting down the computer improperly just means that the computer recognizes this upon the next reboot and might attempt to automatically fix errors if any occurred.

74. **Answer: C**

    Explanation: Session hijacking occurs when an unwanted mediator takes control of the session between a client and a server (for example, an FTP or HTTP session). An example of this would be a man-in-the-middle (MITM) attack.

    Incorrect Answers: DDoS is a distributed denial-of-service attack, an attack perpetuated by hundreds or thousands of computers in an effort to take down a single server; the computers, individually known as zombies, are often unknowingly part of a botnet. A brute-force attack is an attempt to crack an encryption code or password. Malicious software is any compromising code or software that can damage a computer's files; examples include viruses, spyware, worms, rootkits, ransomware, and Trojans.

75. Answer: C

Explanation: `Bootrec /rebuildbcd` attempts to rebuild the boot configuration store.

Incorrect Answers: `Bootrec /fixboot` is one of the methods you can try to repair bootmgr.exe in Windows. `Bootrec /fixmbr` rewrites the master boot record in a Windows system that has an MBR-based hard drive (doesn't affect the more common GPT-based drive). `boot\bcd` is where the boot configuration store is located.

76. Answer: A

Explanation: The drive should be completely erased with bit-level erasure software. If it is to be disposed of or is to leave the building, it should also be shredded or degaussed (or both).

Incorrect Answers: Formatting is not enough because data remanence (residue) is left on the drive from which files can be reconstructed by smart people with some smart software. It is a waste of time to install AV software on a drive *before* removing it. However, AV software should be loaded up when the new drive is installed.

77. Answer: D

Explanation: The Windows 10 and 8 File History utility (accessible in the Control Panel) enables a user to back up files or the entire PC.

Incorrect Answers: The File History utility is the successor to Windows 7's Backup and Restore. BitLocker is Microsoft's full drive encryption software. Time Machine is the backup program that is built into macOS.

78. Answer: B

Explanation: Windows 10 (and Windows 8 and Windows 7) requires a *minimum* processor frequency of 1 GHz.

Incorrect Answers: Windows 10 64-bit requires 32 GB of hard drive space. As of the writing of this book, 2 GHz is not a valid answer for Windows. The minimum RAM requirement for 64-bit versions of Windows is 2 GB.

79. Answer: D

Explanation: An unattended installation of Windows requires an answer file. This file is normally named unattend.xml. Unattended installations can be done locally or as part of a network installation using Windows Deployment Services (WDS) in Server 2008 or higher.

Incorrect Answers: Drive image installations use third-party programs such as Ghost or work with a System Restore image created within Windows. Local installation from USB is possible if you copy the Windows .iso file to the USB flash drive (if the drive is big enough) and obtain the USB/DVD download tool from the Microsoft website. A multiboot installation means that more than one operating system is being installed to the same drive. One or both of these could possibly be unattended installations. Remember that with multiboot installs, each OS should inhabit its own primary partition.

80. Answer: C

Explanation: Regedit can be used to view startup programs. This is the executable that opens the Registry Editor. A common place to find some of the startup programs is the path HKEY_LOCAL_MACHINE\SOFTWARE\Microsoft\Windows\CurrentVersion\Ru. Several other subkeys, mostly within the CurrentVersion, also house startup program information.

Incorrect Answers: Ipconfig shows the network configuration of all network adapters. Ping is used to test whether other computers on the network can respond to TCP/IP packets of information, thus proving they are functional. DxDiag is used to analyze video cards and the version of DirectX that is running.

GREAT JOB SO FAR!

If you scored 90 percent or higher on this first 220-1002 practice exam, move on to the next one. If you did not, I strongly encourage you to study the material again and retake the practice exam until you get 90 percent or higher. Either way, you are doing excellent work so far — keep at it!

CHAPTER EIGHT

220-1002 Practice Exam B

The previous 220-1002 exam was the introduction. This next test takes the challenge to the next level and can be considered an intermediate practice test. I've blended in some more difficult questions this time.

The main goal of this practice exam is to make sure you understand all of the concepts before moving on to the next test. If you haven't taken a break already, I suggest taking one between exams. If you just completed the first exam, give yourself a half hour or so before you begin this one. If you didn't score 90 percent or higher on exam A, go back and study; then retake exam A until you pass with 90 percent or higher.

Write down your answers and check them against the answer key, which immediately follows the exam. After the answer key, you will find the explanations for all of the answers. Good luck!

Practice Questions

1. Which of the following statements best describes how to restart the Print Spooler service? (Select the two best answers.)

   ❏ **A.** Enter `net stop spooler` and then `net start spooler` on the command line.

   ❏ **B.** Enter `net stop print spooler` and then `net start print spooler` on the command line.

   ❏ **C.** Go to **Computer Management > Services** and restart the Print Spooler service.

   ❏ **D.** Go to **Computer Management > System Tools > Event Viewer** and restart the Print Spooler service.

Quick Answer: **192**
Detailed Answer: **193**

2. Where is Registry hive data stored?

- ○ **A.** \%systemroot%\Windows
- ○ **B.** \%systemroot%\Windows\System32\Config
- ○ **C.** \%systemroot%\System32
- ○ **D.** \%systemroot%\System32\Config

3. Clinton needs a more secure partition on his hard drive. Currently, the only partition on the drive (C:) is formatted as FAT32. He cannot lose the data on the drive but must have a higher level of security, so he is asking you to change the drive to NTFS. Which of the following is the proper syntax for this procedure?

- ○ **A.** `change C: /FS:NTFS`
- ○ **B.** `change C: NTFS /FS`
- ○ **C.** `convert C: /FS:NTFS`
- ○ **D.** `convert C: NTFS /FS`

4. Tom has a 200 GB hard drive partition (known as C:) on a Windows computer. He has 15 GB free space on the partition. Which of the following statements best describes how he can defrag the partition?

- ○ **A.** He can run the Disk Defragmenter in Computer Management.
- ○ **B.** He can run `defrag.exe` `-f` on the command line.
- ○ **C.** He can run `defrag.exe` `-v` on the command line.
- ○ **D.** He can run `defrag.exe` `-A` on the command line.

5. You are utilizing WSUS and are testing new updates on PCs. What is this an example of?

- ○ **A.** Host-based firewall
- ○ **B.** Application baselining
- ○ **C.** Patch management
- ○ **D.** Virtualization

6. Which versions of Windows 8 allow for joining domains? (Select the two best answers.)

- ❏ **A.** Standard
- ❏ **B.** Pro
- ❏ **C.** Ultimate
- ❏ **D.** Enterprise

7. One of your customers reports that there is a large amount of spam in her email inbox. Which of the following statements describes the best course of action to recommend to her?

Quick Answer: **192**
Detailed Answer: **194**

   ○ **A.** Advise her to create a new email account.

   ○ **B.** Advise her to add the senders to the junk email sender list.

   ○ **C.** Advise her to find a new ISP.

   ○ **D.** Advise her to reply to all spam and opt out of future emails.

8. In Windows, where can devices like the display and hard drives be configured to turn off after a certain amount of time?

Quick Answer: **192**
Detailed Answer: **194**

   ○ **A.** Power plans

   ○ **B.** Display Properties

   ○ **C.** Computer Management

   ○ **D.** Task Manager

9. Which of the following procedures best describes how to find out which type of connection the printer is using?

Quick Answer: **192**
Detailed Answer: **194**

   ○ **A.** Right-click the printer, select Properties, and click the Sharing tab.

   ○ **B.** Right-click the printer, select Properties, and click the Advanced tab.

   ○ **C.** Right-click the printer, select Properties, and click the Separator Page button.

   ○ **D.** Right-click the printer, select Properties, and click the Ports tab.

10. Your customer is having problems printing from an application. You attempt to send a test page to the printer. Which of the following statements best describes why a test page should be used to troubleshoot the issue?

Quick Answer: **192**
Detailed Answer: **195**

   ○ **A.** It allows you to see the quality of the printer output.

   ○ **B.** The output of the test page allows you to initiate diagnostic routines on the printer.

   ○ **C.** It verifies the connectivity and illuminates possible application problems.

   ○ **D.** It clears the print queue and resets the printer memory.

11. A user's hard drive seems very slow in its reaction time when opening applications. Which of the following statements best describes the most likely cause of this?

Quick Answer: **192**
Detailed Answer: **195**

- ○ **A.** The drive needs to be initialized.
- ○ **B.** The temporary files need to be deleted.
- ○ **C.** The drive is fragmented.
- ○ **D.** The drive's SATA data connector is loose.

12. Which of the following actions will *not* secure a functioning computer workstation?

Quick Answer: **192**
Detailed Answer: **195**

- ○ **A.** Setting a strong password
- ○ **B.** Changing default usernames
- ○ **C.** Disabling the guest account
- ○ **D.** Sanitizing the hard drive

13. Which utility enables you to implement auditing on a single Windows computer?

Quick Answer: **192**
Detailed Answer: **195**

- ○ **A.** Local Security Policy
- ○ **B.** Group Policy Editor
- ○ **C.** AD DS
- ○ **D.** Services.msc

14. Which of the following statements best describes the main function of a device driver?

Quick Answer: **192**
Detailed Answer: **196**

- ○ **A.** Modifies applications
- ○ **B.** Works with memory more efficiently
- ○ **C.** Improves device performance
- ○ **D.** Allows the OS to talk to the device

15. Where are restore points stored after they are created?

Quick Answer: **192**
Detailed Answer: **196**

- ○ **A.** The Recycler folder
- ○ **B.** The System32 folder
- ○ **C.** The %systemroot% folder
- ○ **D.** The System Volume Information folder

16. Which of the following is considered to be government-regulated data?

- ○ **A.** DRM
- ○ **B.** EULA
- ○ **C.** PII
- ○ **D.** DMCA

17. Which of the following are types of social engineering? (Select the two best answers.)

- ○ **A.** Malware
- ○ **B.** Shoulder surfing
- ○ **C.** Tailgating
- ○ **D.** Rootkits

18. Which of the following is the service that controls the printing of documents in a Windows computer?

- ○ **A.** Printer
- ○ **B.** Print server
- ○ **C.** Print pooling
- ○ **D.** Print Spooler

19. Which of the following is the best way to ensure that a hard drive is secure for disposal?

- ○ **A.** Magnetically erase the drive.
- ○ **B.** Format the drive.
- ○ **C.** Run `bootrec /fixmbr`.
- ○ **D.** Convert the drive to NTFS.

20. A month ago, you set up a wireless access point/router for a small business that is a customer of yours. Now, the customer calls and complains that Internet access is getting slower and slower. As you look at the WAP/router, you notice that it was reset at some point and is now set for open access. You then guess that neighboring companies are using the service connection. Which of the following statements best describes how you can restrict access to your customer's wireless connection? (Select the two best answers.)

- ○ **A.** Configure the wireless access point to use WPA2.
- ○ **B.** Configure MS-CHAPv2 on the WAP/router.
- ○ **C.** Disable SSID broadcasting.
- ○ **D.** Move the WAP/router to another corner of the office.

21. A first-level help desk support technician receives a call from a customer and works with the customer for several minutes to resolve the call, but the technician is unsuccessful. Which of the following steps should the technician perform next?

Quick Answer: **192**
Detailed Answer: **197**

○ **A.** The technician should explain to the customer that he will receive a callback when someone more qualified is available.

○ **B.** The technician should escalate the call to another technician.

○ **C.** The technician should explain to the customer that the problem cannot be resolved and end the call.

○ **D.** The technician should continue working with the customer until the problem is resolved.

22. A customer complains that there is nothing showing on the display of his laptop. Which of the following should you attempt first on the computer?

Quick Answer: **192**
Detailed Answer: **197**

○ **A.** You should replace the inverter.

○ **B.** You should reinstall the video drivers.

○ **C.** You should boot into Safe mode.

○ **D.** You should check whether the laptop is in Standby or Hibernate mode.

23. During an installation of Windows, you are given an opportunity to load alternative third-party drivers. Which device are you most likely loading drivers for?

Quick Answer: **192**
Detailed Answer: **198**

○ **A.** CD-ROM

○ **B.** SCSI drive

○ **C.** USB mouse

○ **D.** BIOS/UEFI

24. A Windows 10 computer in a Windows workgroup can have how many concurrent connections?

Quick Answer: **192**
Detailed Answer: **198**

○ **A.** 10 or fewer

○ **B.** 15 or fewer

○ **C.** 20 or fewer

○ **D.** 25 or fewer

25. Megan's laptop runs perfectly when she is at work, but when she takes it on the road, it cannot get on the Internet. Internally, the company uses static IP addresses for all computers. What should you do to fix the problem?

Quick Answer: **192**
Detailed Answer: **198**

  ○ **A.** Tell Megan to get a wireless cellular card and service.

  ○ **B.** Tell Megan to use DHCP.

  ○ **C.** Tell Megan to configure the alternate configuration tab of TCP/IP properties.

  ○ **D.** Configure a static IP address in the Alternate Configuration tab of the user's TCP/IP properties and enable DHCP in the General tab.

26. Which power-saving mode enables for the best power savings, while still allowing the session to be reactivated later?

Quick Answer: **192**
Detailed Answer: **198**

  ○ **A.** Standby

  ○ **B.** Suspend

  ○ **C.** Hibernate

  ○ **D.** Shutdown

27. John's computer has two hard drives, each 1 TB. The first is the system drive and is formatted as NTFS. The second is the data drive and is formatted as FAT32. Which of the following statements are true? (Select the two best answers.)

Quick Answer: **192**
Detailed Answer: **198**

  ○ **A.** Files on the system drive can be secured.

  ○ **B.** Larger logical drives can be made on the data drive.

  ○ **C.** The cluster size is larger, and storage is more efficient on the system drive.

  ○ **D.** The cluster size is smaller, and storage is more efficient on the system drive.

28. When using the command line, a switch _____.

Quick Answer: **192**
Detailed Answer: **199**

  ○ **A.** enables the command to work across any operating system

  ○ **B.** is used in application icons

  ○ **C.** changes the core behavior of a command, forcing the command to perform unrelated actions

  ○ **D.** alters the actions of a command, such as widening or narrowing the function of the command

29. You need to view any application errors that have occurred today. Which tool should be used?

- ○ **A.** Event Viewer
- ○ **B.** Local Security Policy
- ○ **C.** Msconfig
- ○ **D.** Sfc /scannow

Quick Answer: **192**
Detailed Answer: **199**

30. Which of the following commands can help you modify the startup environment?

- ○ **A.** Msconfig
- ○ **B.** Ipconfig
- ○ **C.** Boot Config Editor
- ○ **D.** Registry Editor

Quick Answer: **192**
Detailed Answer: **199**

31. Which of the following log files references third-party software error messages?

- ○ **A.** Security log
- ○ **B.** System log
- ○ **C.** Application log
- ○ **D.** Setuperr.log

Quick Answer: **192**
Detailed Answer: **199**

32. Which of the following provides the lowest level of wireless security protection?

- ○ **A.** Disable the SSID broadcast.
- ○ **B.** Use RADIUS.
- ○ **C.** Use WPA2.
- ○ **D.** Enable WEP on the wireless access point.

Quick Answer: **192**
Detailed Answer: **199**

33. A customer uses an unencrypted wireless network. One of the users has shared a folder for access by any computer. The customer complains that files sometimes appear and disappear from the shared folder. Which of the following statements best describes how to fix the problem? (Select the two best answers.)

- ○ **A.** Enable encryption on the router and the clients.
- ○ **B.** Encrypt the drive that has the share using EFS (Encrypting File System).
- ○ **C.** Increase the level of security on the NTFS folder by changing the permissions.
- ○ **D.** Change the share-level permissions on the shared folder.

Quick Answer: **192**
Detailed Answer: **200**

34. A customer is having difficulties with his hard drive, and the system won't boot. You discover that the operating system has to be reloaded. Which of the following statements best describes how to explain this to the customer?

Quick Answer: **192**
Detailed Answer: **200**

- ○ **A.** "I need to rebuild the computer."
- ○ **B.** "I need to format the hard drive and reload the software."
- ○ **C.** "I need to run a bootrec /fixmbr on the computer."
- ○ **D.** "I need to restore the system; data loss might occur."

35. Users in your accounting department are prompted to provide usernames and passwords to access the payroll system. Which type of authentication method is being requested in this scenario?

Quick Answer: **192**
Detailed Answer: **200**

- ○ **A.** MFA
- ○ **B.** Single-factor
- ○ **C.** TACACS+
- ○ **D.** RADIUS

36. Which of the following commands makes a duplicate of a file?

Quick Answer: **192**
Detailed Answer: **200**

- ○ **A.** Move
- ○ **B.** Copy
- ○ **C.** Dir
- ○ **D.** Ls

37. Which tool in Windows enables a user to easily see how much memory a particular process uses?

Quick Answer: **192**
Detailed Answer: **200**

- ○ **A.** System Information Tool
- ○ **B.** Registry
- ○ **C.** Task Manager
- ○ **D.** Performance Monitor

38. Windows was installed on a computer with two hard drives: a C: drive and a D: drive. Windows is installed to C:, and it works normally. The user of this computer complains that his applications are drive intensive and that they slow down the computer. Which of the following statements best describes how to resolve the problem?

Quick Answer: **192**
Detailed Answer: **201**

- ○ **A.** Move the paging file to the D: drive.
- ○ **B.** Reinstall Windows on the D: drive rather than on the C: drive.
- ○ **C.** Defrag the D: drive.
- ○ **D.** Decrease the paging file size.

39. Which of the following tools should be used to protect a computer from electrostatic discharge (ESD) while you are working inside it?

Quick Answer: **192**
Detailed Answer: **201**

- ○ **A.** Multimeter
- ○ **B.** Crimper
- ○ **C.** Antistatic wrist strap
- ○ **D.** PSU tester

40. You are running some cable from an office to a computer located in a warehouse. As you are working in the warehouse, a 55-gallon drum falls from a pallet and spills what smells like ammonia. Which of the following statements best describes the first step you should take in your efforts to resolve this problem?

Quick Answer: **192**
Detailed Answer: **201**

- ○ **A.** Call 911.
- ○ **B.** Call the building supervisor.
- ○ **C.** Get out of the area.
- ○ **D.** Save the computer.

41. While you are upgrading a customer's server hard drives, you notice looped network cables lying all over the server room floor. Which of the following statements best describes how to resolve this issue?

Quick Answer: **192**
Detailed Answer: **201**

- ○ **A.** Ignore the problem.
- ○ **B.** Tell the customer about safer alternatives.
- ○ **C.** Call the building supervisor.
- ○ **D.** Notify the administrator.

42. Which of the following statements best describes the recommended solution for a lithium-ion battery that won't hold a charge any longer?

Quick Answer: **192**
Detailed Answer: **202**

- ○ **A.** Throw it in the trash.
- ○ **B.** Return it to the battery manufacturer.
- ○ **C.** Contact the local municipality and inquire as to their disposal methods.
- ○ **D.** Open the battery and remove the deposits.

43. Which of the following statements is *not* assertive communication?

Quick Answer: **192**
Detailed Answer: **202**

- ○ **A.** "I certainly know how you feel; losing data is a terrible thing."
- ○ **B.** "Could you explain again exactly what you would like done?"
- ○ **C.** "Do your employees always cause issues on computers like these?"
- ○ **D.** "What can I do to help you?"

44. A customer has a malfunctioning PC, and as you are about to begin repairing it, the customer proceeds to tell you about the problems with the server. Which of the following statements best describes how to respond to the customer?

Quick Answer: **192**
Detailed Answer: **202**

- ○ **A.** "Wait until I finish with the PC."
- ○ **B.** "I'm sorry, but I don't know how to fix servers."
- ○ **C.** "Is the server problem related to the PC problem?"
- ○ **D.** "I have to call my supervisor."

45. Which of the following could be described as the chronological paper trail of evidence?

Quick Answer: **192**
Detailed Answer: **202**

- ○ **A.** First response
- ○ **B.** Chain of custody
- ○ **C.** Setting and meeting expectations
- ○ **D.** Data preservation

46. Which of the following statements best describes what *not* to do when moving servers and server racks?

Quick Answer: **192**
Detailed Answer: **202**

- ○ **A.** Remove jewelry.
- ○ **B.** Move a 70-pound wire rack by yourself.
- ○ **C.** Disconnect power to the servers before moving them.
- ○ **D.** Bend at the knees and lift with your legs.

47. Active communication includes which of the following?

Quick Answer: **192**
Detailed Answer: **203**

- ○ **A.** Filtering out unnecessary information
- ○ **B.** Declaring that the customer doesn't know what he or she is doing
- ○ **C.** Clarifying the customer's statements
- ○ **D.** Mouthing off

48. You are troubleshooting a tablet PC that has a frozen application. You have attempted to end the underlying task of the application but have not succeeded. Which of the following statements best describes the next recommended course of action?

Quick Answer: **192**
Detailed Answer: **203**

- ○ **A.** Hard reset
- ○ **B.** Force quit the app
- ○ **C.** Soft reset
- ○ **D.** Bring the tablet to an authorized service center

49. Which of the following statements best describes the first course of action to removing malware?

Quick Answer: **192**
Detailed Answer: **203**

- ○ **A.** Identify malware symptoms.
- ○ **B.** Quarantine infected systems.
- ○ **C.** Disable System Restore.
- ○ **D.** Remediate infected systems.
- ○ **E.** Schedule scans and run updates.
- ○ **F.** Enable System Restore.
- ○ **G.** Educate the end user.

50. You are working on a Windows computer that is performing slowly. Which of the following commands should you use to resolve the problem? (Select the two best answers.)

Quick Answer: **192**
Detailed Answer: **203**

- ❏ **A.** Format
- ❏ **B.** Dism
- ❏ **C.** Ipconfig
- ❏ **D.** Chkdsk
- ❏ **E.** Dir
- ❏ **F.** Diskpart

51. A customer reports that an optical drive in a PC is no longer responding. Which of the following statements best describes the first question you should ask the customer?

Quick Answer: **192**
Detailed Answer: **203**

- ○ **A.** "What has changed since the optical drive worked properly?"
- ○ **B.** "Did you log in with your administrator account?"
- ○ **C.** "What did you modify since the optical drive worked?"
- ○ **D.** "Have you been to any inappropriate websites?"

52. A coworker is traveling to Europe and is bringing her desktop computer. She asks you what concerns there might be. Which of the following statements best describes how to respond to the customer? (Select the two best answers.)

Quick Answer: **192**
Detailed Answer: **204**

- ❏ **A.** Advise her that the computer is not usable in other countries.
- ❏ **B.** Advise her to check for a compatible power adapter for that country.
- ❏ **C.** Advise her to use a line conditioner for the correct voltage.
- ❏ **D.** Advise her to check the voltage selector on the power supply.

53. After you remove malware/spyware from a customer's PC for the third time, which of the following steps should be taken next?

Quick Answer: **192**
Detailed Answer: **204**

- ○ **A.** Tell him you can't fix the system again.
- ○ **B.** Do nothing; the customer pays every time.
- ○ **C.** Show him how to avoid the problem.
- ○ **D.** Change his user permissions.

54. You are asked to fix a problem with a customer's Active Directory Domain Services domain controller that is outside the scope of your knowledge. Which of the following statements best describes the recommended course of action?

Quick Answer: **192**
Detailed Answer: **204**

- ○ **A.** Learn on the job by trying to fix the problem.
- ○ **B.** Tell the customer that the problem should be reported to another technician.
- ○ **C.** Assure the customer that the problem will be fixed very soon.
- ○ **D.** Help the customer find the appropriate channels to fix the problem.

55. When you are working on a computer, which of the following should be disconnected to prevent electrical shock? (Select the two best answers.)

Quick Answer: **192**
Detailed Answer: **204**

- ❑ **A.** Printer
- ❑ **B.** Mouse
- ❑ **C.** Telephone cord
- ❑ **D.** Power cord

56. You are troubleshooting a Windows Server computer that you have little knowledge about. The message on the screen says that there is a "DHCP partner down" error. No other technicians are available to help you, and your manager wants the server fixed ASAP or you are fired. Which of the following statements best describes the recommended course of action? (Select the two best answers.)

Quick Answer: **192**
Detailed Answer: **205**

- ❑ **A.** Identify the problem.
- ❑ **B.** Escalate the problem.
- ❑ **C.** Establish a plan of action.
- ❑ **D.** Call tech support.
- ❑ **E.** Verify full system functionality.
- ❑ **F.** Test the theory to determine cause.

57. Which of the following protects confidential information from being disclosed publicly?

Quick Answer: **192**
Detailed Answer: **205**

- ○ **A.** Classification
- ○ **B.** Social engineering
- ○ **C.** HTTP
- ○ **D.** Hard drive wipe

58. Programs that run when Windows starts are stored in which of the following registry hives?

Quick Answer: **192**
Detailed Answer: **206**

- ○ **A.** HKEY_CURRENT_CONFIG
- ○ **B.** HKEY_USERS
- ○ **C.** HKEY_LOCAL_MACHINE
- ○ **D.** HKEY_CLASSES_ROOT

59. Typically, which of the following Windows tools enables you to *configure* a SOHO router?

Quick Answer: **192**
Detailed Answer: **206**

- ○ **A.** Web Browser
- ○ **B.** Device Manager
- ○ **C.** Msconfig
- ○ **D.** File Explorer

60. Which of the following steps is performed first when running a clean install of Windows on a brand new SAS hard drive?

Quick Answer: **192**
Detailed Answer: **206**

- ○ **A.** Format the partition.
- ○ **B.** Partition the drive.
- ○ **C.** Configure Windows settings.
- ○ **D.** Load RAID drivers.

61. A coworker maps a network drive for a user, but after rebooting, the drive is not seen within Explorer. Which of the following steps should be taken first to ensure that the drive remains mapped?

Quick Answer: **192**
Detailed Answer: **206**

- ○ **A.** Check Reconnect at sign-in when mapping the drive.
- ○ **B.** Select the drive letter needed to connect each time the coworker logs on.
- ○ **C.** Check the Folder connection when mapping the drive.
- ○ **D.** Use the net use command instead.

62. Based on the physical hardware address of the client's network device, which of the following is commonly used to restrict access to a network?

Quick Answer: **192**
Detailed Answer: **206**

- ○ **A.** WPA key
- ○ **B.** DHCP settings
- ○ **C.** MAC filtering
- ○ **D.** SSID broadcast

63. A print job fails to leave the print queue. Which of the following services may need to be restarted?

Quick Answer: **192**
Detailed Answer: **207**

- ○ **A.** Print driver
- ○ **B.** Print Spooler
- ○ **C.** Network adapter
- ○ **D.** Printer

64. After installing a network application on a computer running Windows 10, the application does not communicate with the server. Which of the following actions should be taken first?

Quick Answer: **192**
Detailed Answer: **207**

- ○ **A.** Uninstall the latest service pack.
- ○ **B.** Reinstall the latest security update.
- ○ **C.** Add the port number and name of the service to the Exceptions list of Windows Defender Firewall.
- ○ **D.** Add the port number to the network firewall.

65. A customer reports a problem with a PC located in the same room as cement testing equipment. The room appears to have adequate cooling. The PC will boot up but locks up after 5–10 minutes of use. After a lockup, it will not reboot immediately. Which the following statements best describes the most likely problem?

Quick Answer: **192**
Detailed Answer: **207**

- ○ **A.** The PC has a virus.
- ○ **B.** The PC air intakes are clogged with cement dust.
- ○ **C.** The CPU heat sink is underrated for the CPU.
- ○ **D.** The power supply is underrated for the electrical load of the PC.

66. One of your Windows users is trying to install a local printer and is unsuccessful based on the permissions for the user account. Which of the following types best describes this user account?

- ○ **A.** Power user
- ○ **B.** Administrator
- ○ **C.** Guest
- ○ **D.** Domain Admin

67. When accessing an NTFS shared resource, which of the following are required? (Select the two best answers.)

- ❏ **A.** An active certificate
- ❏ **B.** Correct user permissions
- ❏ **C.** Local user access
- ❏ **D.** Correct share permissions

68. You are contracted to recover data from a laptop. In which two locations might you find irreplaceable, valuable data? (Select the two best answers.)

- ❏ **A.** Ntoskrnl.exe
- ❏ **B.** Windows folder
- ❏ **C.** Pictures
- ❏ **D.** Email
- ❏ **E.** System32 folder

69. Which utility enables auditing at the local level?

- ○ **A.** OU Group Policy
- ○ **B.** Local Security Policy
- ○ **C.** Active Directory Policy
- ○ **D.** Site Policy

70. A customer has forgotten his password. He can no longer access his company email address. Which of the following statements best describes the recommended course of action?

- ○ **A.** Tell him to remember his password.
- ○ **B.** Ask him for information confirming his identity.
- ○ **C.** Tell him that the password will be reset in several minutes.
- ○ **D.** Tell him that he shouldn't forget his password.

71. Which of the following can help locate a lost or stolen mobile device?

    ○ **A.** Passcode

    ○ **B.** Auto-erase

    ○ **C.** GPS

    ○ **D.** Encryption

72. Which of the following can be disabled to help prevent access to a wireless network?

    ○ **A.** MAC filtering

    ○ **B.** SSID broadcast

    ○ **C.** WPA2 passphrase

    ○ **D.** WPA key

73. Which of the following commands sets the time on a workstation?

    ○ **A.** Time

    ○ **B.** Net time

    ○ **C.** Net timer

    ○ **D.** Net time set

74. In Windows, which utility enables you to select and copy characters from any font?

    ○ **A.** Language bar

    ○ **B.** Sticky keys

    ○ **C.** Control Panel > Fonts

    ○ **D.** Character map

75. Which of the following can be described as removing the limitations of Apple iOS?

    ○ **A.** Rooting

    ○ **B.** Jailbreaking

    ○ **C.** VirusBarrier

    ○ **D.** Super-admin powers

76. In Windows, which of the following built-in applets should be used by a technician to enable and manage offline files, view conflicts and partnerships, and ensure locally stored files match those stored on an external device or server?

- ○ **A.** File History
- ○ **B.** USMT
- ○ **C.** Robust file copy
- ○ **D.** Sync Center

77. Which language support for representing characters is built into Windows?

- ○ **A.** Unicode
- ○ **B.** EBCDIC
- ○ **C.** ASCII
- ○ **D.** ITU-T
- ○ **E.** .PS1

78. Which of the following is the best source of information about malicious software detected on a computer?

- ○ **A.** Operating system documentation
- ○ **B.** Anti-spyware software website
- ○ **C.** Readme.txt file included with the anti-spyware software installation
- ○ **D.** The user of a previously infected computer

79. You are working for a company as a roaming PC tech and have been assigned work by a network administrator. The admin notifies you that the company is experiencing a DDoS attack. Half a dozen internal Windows PCs are the source of the traffic. The admin gives you the Windows computer names and tells you that they must be scanned and cleaned immediately. Which of the following effects to the PCs should you as a PC technician focus on fixing? (Select the two best answers.)

- ❑ **A.** Zombies
- ❑ **B.** Spyware
- ❑ **C.** Ransomware
- ❑ **D.** Worm
- ❑ **E.** Virus
- ❑ **F.** Botnet

80. You are troubleshooting a networking problem with Windows, and you can't seem to fix it using the typical Windows GUI-based troubleshooting tools or with the Command Prompt. You have identified the problem and established a theory of probable cause. (In fact, you are on your fourth theory.) Which tool should be used to troubleshoot the problem, and in what stage of the troubleshooting process should you do so?

    ○ **A.** Regsvr32; Conduct external or internal research based on symptoms.

    ○ **B.** GPUpdate; Perform backups before making any changes.

    ○ **C.** USMT; Verify full system functionality.

    ○ **D.** Regedit; Test the theory to determine cause.

    ○ **E.** Boot Camp; Document findings, actions, and outcomes.

Quick-Check Answer Key

1. A, D	28. D	57. A
2. D	29. A	58. C
3. C	30. A	59. A
4. B	31. C	60. D
5. C	32. A	61. A
6. B, D	33. A, C	62. C
7. B	34. D	63. B
8. A	35. B	64. C
9. D	36. B	65. B
10. C	37. C	66. C
11. C	38. A	67. B, D
12. D	39. C	68. C, D
13. A	40. C	69. B
14. D	41. B	70. B
15. D	42. C	71. C
16. C	43. C	72. B
17. B, C	44. C	73. A
18. D	45. B	74. D
19. A	46. B	75. B
20. A, C	47. C	76. D
21. B	48. C	77. A
22. D	49. A	78. B
23. B	50. B, D	79. A, D
24. C	51. A	80. D
25. D	52. B, D	
26. C	53. C	
27. A, D	54. D	
	55. C, D	
	56. A, D	

Answers and Explanations

1. **Answer: A and D**

   Explanation: In the command line, this service is simply known as Spooler. Type `net stop spooler` and `net start spooler` to restart the service. In Computer Management, the Print Spooler service is found in **Services and Applications > Services**. Or you could open the Run prompt and type `services.msc`. From there, you can start, stop, pause, resume, or restart services and also set their Startup type to Automatic, Manual, or Disabled.

   Incorrect answers: When stopping a service in the Command Prompt (or PowerShell), remember to use the command-line name, not the name used in the GUI. In this case, the command-line name is spooler, whereas the GUI-based name is Print Spooler. The Event Viewer is used to view and analyze log files.

2. **Answer: D**

   Explanation: Remember that %systemroot% is a variable. It takes the place of whatever folder contains the operating system. This is usually Windows. For example, if you were to run a default installation of Windows, the path to the Registry hives would be C:\Windows\System32\Config. The main hives are SAM, SECURITY, SOFTWARE, SYSTEM, and DEFAULT. You can access and configure them by opening the Registry Editor (**Run > regedit.exe**) and opening the HKEY_LOCAL_MACHINE subtree. Other hive information is stored in the user profile folders.

   Incorrect answers: The other locations are incorrect. The Windows folder is the %systemroot%, so the paths that include \%systemroot%\Windows don't make any sense. The System32 folder houses all of the 64-bit protected system files (and many applications) for Windows.

3. **Answer: C**

   Explanation: The `convert` command turns a FAT32 drive into an NTFS drive without data loss, allowing for a higher level of data security. The proper syntax is `convert volume /FS:NTFS`.

   Incorrect answers: There is no change command; however, there is a change directory (`CD`) command, which can allow you to navigate from one folder to another in the command line. The syntax `convert C: NTFS /FS` is not valid; it would result in the error "Invalid Parameter – NTFS."

4. **Answer: B**

   Explanation: Use `defrag.exe -f`. You need to have 15 percent free space on your partition to defrag it in the Disk Defragmenter GUI-based utility. In the scenario, Tom would need 30 GB free on the 200 GB drive. However, you can force a defrag on a partition even if you don't have enough free space by using the `-f` switch in the command line. (`-f` may not be necessary in some versions of Windows.)

   Incorrect answers: Because there is only 15 GB of free space on the 200 GB drive (7.5 percent free), the defrag probably won't work properly from within the Disk Defragmenter utility. The `-v` switch gives you verbose (or wordy) output. The `-a` switch gives analysis only and does not perform defragmentation.

5. **Answer: C**

   Explanation: Patch management is the patching of many systems from a central location. It includes the planning, testing, implementing, and auditing stages. There are various software packages you can use to perform patch management. Windows Server Update Services (WSUS) is an example of Microsoft patch management software. Other Microsoft examples include the System Center Configuration Manager (SCCM) and its predecessor Systems Management Center (SMS), but there are plenty of third-party offerings as well.

   Incorrect answers: A host-based firewall is a software firewall that is loaded on a computer to stop attackers from intruding on a network. Application baselining is the performance measurements of an application over time. Virtualization occurs when an operating system is installed to a single file on a computer. Often, it runs virtually on top of another OS.

6. **Answers: B and D**

   Explanation: Windows 8 Pro and Enterprise allow for the joining of domains.

   Incorrect answers: Windows 8 standard does not. Ultimate is the name used with the most powerful edition of Windows 7. In Windows 10, the Pro, Enterprise, and Education editions can join domains, but Home cannot.

7. **Answer: B**

   Explanation: You should recommend that the user add the senders to the junk email sender list. This blocks those senders' email addresses (or the entire domain can be blocked). However, this option could take a lot of time; another option is to increase the level of security on the spam filter within the email program. Any further spam can then be sent to the junk email sender list.

   Incorrect answers: Users need their email accounts, and creating a new one can result in a lot of work for the user. Finding a new ISP is overreacting a bit; plus, the user has no idea if one ISP will be better at stopping spam than another. Never tell a user to reply to spam. Spam emails should be sent to the spam folder and never replied to—unless you want 10 times the amount of spam.

8. **Answer: A**

   Explanation: To turn off devices after a specified period of time in Windows, access Control Panel > Power Options. Then click Change Plan Settings for the appropriate power plan.

   Incorrect answers: Display Properties allows you to modify things such as screen resolution. Computer Management is a commonly used console window in Windows; it includes the Event Viewer, Disk Management, and Services. The Task Manager is used to analyze system resources and end tasks (among other things).

9. **Answer: D**

   Explanation: On the Ports tab, you can find how the printer is connected to the computer. This can be a USB, COM, LPT, or TCP/IP port. You might get to this tab by selecting Properties or Printer Properties, depending on the printer.

Incorrect answers: The Sharing tab allows you to share a locally connected (or remotely controlled) printer on the network. The Advanced tab has options such as print spooling and printer pooling. The Separator page button allows you to configure a page that is inserted after every print job.

10. **Answer: C**

    Explanation: The test page verifies connectivity and gives you insight as to possible application problems at the computer that is attempting to print.

    Incorrect answers: In this case, you aren't worried about the quality of the printer output; it is the computer and the application that you are troubleshooting. You use test pages to make sure the computer can print properly to the printer, not to initiate diagnostic routines. Those would be initiated from the built-in display and menu on the printer, or in Windows by right-clicking the printer, selecting Printer properties, and then selecting Print Test Page. Printing a test page does not clear the print queue or reset printer memory. You would have to do this at the printer and/or at the computer controlling the printer.

11. **Answer: C**

    Explanation: The drive is fragmented. This is why it is very slow in its reaction time. It's also possible that the OS is infected with a virus. You should analyze and defragment the drive and run an AV sweep of the system.

    Incorrect answers: If a drive is not seen by Windows, it might have to be initialized; this can happen when you add a second drive to a system that already has Windows installed. Surplus temporary files might slow down the login process but shouldn't slow the hard drive when opening applications. You can remove them with the Disk Cleanup program or with third-party applications. If the hard drive's SATA data connector were loose, the drive should not be able to access applications. In fact, you would probably get a message that says "Missing OS" or something to that effect.

12. **Answer: D**

    Explanation: Sanitizing the hard drive does not secure a computer workstation. It does, however, prevent anyone from accessing data on the drive, but it also ensures the computer workstation won't be functional anymore. A data sanitization method is the specific way in which a data destruction program or file shredder overwrites the data on a hard drive or other storage device.

    Incorrect answers: Setting strong passwords, changing default usernames, and disabling the guest account are all ways of securing a computer workstation.

13. **Answer: A**

    Explanation: Because there is only one computer, you can implement auditing only locally. This is done with the *Local* Security Policy. (This policy is not available in all editions of Windows.)

    Incorrect answers: The Group Policy Editor and Active Directory Domain Services (AD DS) are used by Windows Servers in a domain environment. Some versions of Windows have the *Local* Group Policy Editor, where auditing can also be turned on. If you type `services.msc` at the Run prompt, services.msc will open the Services console window; you can turn services on and off and modify their startup type from here.

14. **Answer: D**

    Explanation: Device drivers are the connection between the operating system and the device itself. It is a program that makes the interaction between the two run efficiently. It simplifies programming by using high-level application code. The best device drivers come from the manufacturer of the device. They are the ones who developed the device, so it stands to reason that their code would be the most thoroughly tested and debugged.

    Incorrect answers: A device driver does not modify applications, but an updated driver could indirectly affect how an application behaves. Some device drivers use memory better than others; it all depends on how well they are coded. A device driver may or may not improve device performance; that will depend on several factors including whether or not it is an update and how the update is designed to change how the device functions.

15. **Answer: D**

    Explanation: After a restore point is made, it is stored in the System Volume Information folder. To view this folder, you must log on as an administrator, show hidden files and folders, and then assign permissions to the account that wants to view that folder. It is located in the root of the volume that the restore point was created for.

    Incorrect answers: The Recycler folder is the place where deleted information is stored temporarily (until the Recycle Bin is emptied). The System32 folder houses many of the 64-bit system files for the operating system. The %systemroot% folder is, by default, C:\Windows.

16. **Answer: C**

    Explanation: PII stands for personally identifiable information. It is regulated by many laws such as the Privacy Act of 1974 and several others, including GDPR and PCI-DSS.

    Incorrect answers: DRM stands for Digital Rights Management, which is a way of protecting data from illegal copying and distribution. EULA stands for end-user licensing agreement, which is an agreement seen in software such as Windows and Office. DMCA stands for the Digital Millennium Copyright Act, which provides laws dealing with digital information and ownership.

17. **Answers: B and C**

    Explanation: Shoulder surfing and tailgating are both types of social engineering. A shoulder surfer is someone who attempts to view information on a person's desk or display without the person's knowledge.

    Incorrect answers: Tailgating is when a person attempts to gain access to a secure area by following closely on the heels of another employee, usually without his knowledge. A rootkit is a program that is designed to gain administrator-level access to a computer. It is a type of malicious software abbreviated as malware.

18. **Answer: D**

    Explanation: The Print Spooler controls the queue and the printing of documents.

    Incorrect answers: The printer is the physical printing device; Microsoft also refers to the print driver software as the printer. A print server is a device that controls one or more printers; it is usually connected to the network. Print pooling is when two or more printers are grouped together so that a user's document will print faster: if one printer is occupied, the other takes over.

19. **Answer: A**

    Explanation: Magnetically erase the drive; for example, degauss the drive. Degaussing a drive is an excellent way to remove all traces of data, but only if the drive is elec-tromagnetic! Of course, physical destruction is better (shredding, pulverizing); and degaussing might be used on top of physical destruction.

    Incorrect answers: Formatting the drive is not enough due to the data residue that is left behind. Running `bootrec /fixmbr` rewrites the master boot record of the hard drive (not applicable if a GPT drive), but the data remains. Converting the drive from FAT32 to NTFS (with the `convert` command) keeps the data intact.

20. **Answers: A and C**

    Explanation: If the WAP/router was reset, any security settings that you originally set up are most likely gone. If you backed up the settings previously, you could restore them. Either way, some type of encryption protocol (preferably WPA2) is necessary. The passphrase or network key generated by the WAP/router needs to be installed on each client before it can be recognized on the network. This passphrase/key should be kept secret, of course. After all the clients have been associated with the WAP/router, disable SSID broadcasting so that no one else can "see" the router (without more advanced software).

    Incorrect answers: MS-CHAPv2 is used with remote connections such as VPN. Moving the WAP/router probably won't work if this is a small business. Today's SOHO routers have powerful radios with a lot of range. Chances are that moving the router to one corner of the office won't have any effect.

21. **Answer: B**

    Explanation: The tech should escalate the call to another technician. This is exactly why help desks are configured in groups: Level 1, Level 2, the masters (Level 3), and possibly beyond. Don't try to be a superhuman. In technology, there is almost always someone who knows more than you about a specific subject. First, route the call to the next-level tech, and then let the customer know that you are doing so.

    Incorrect answers: Good help desks are set up in such a way so that someone is always available. Every problem can be resolved. Finding the solution is just a matter of knowledge and persistence. (Remember that when you take the real exams.) Don't try to fix the problem regardless of the time necessary. Your time—and the customer's time—is very valuable. Escalate so that you, your organization, and the customer can approach and solve the problem efficiently.

22. **Answer: D**

    Explanation: The computer might need a special keystroke, a press of the power but-ton, or just a little more time to come out of Hibernation mode. Remember, check the simple, quick solutions first because they are usually the culprits.

    Incorrect answers: Booting into Safe Mode, reinstalling video drivers, and replacing the inverter are all quite time-consuming but, if necessary, should be attempted in that order—after checking the power state.

23. **Answer: B**

   Explanation: The SCSI hard drive is the most likely answer. SCSI hard drives (such as SAS SCSI) and RAID controllers need special drivers during the Windows installation process if they are not recognized automatically. Click the option for loading third-party drivers when the installation begins.

   Incorrect answers: Optical drives and USB devices do not require third-party drivers. The BIOS/UEFI doesn't use a driver; it is firmware.

24. **Answer: C**

   Explanation: A Windows 10 computer in a Windows workgroup can have 20 maximum concurrent connections to it over the network.

   Incorrect answers: If you need more than 20 concurrent Windows workgroup connections over the network, you should consider a Microsoft Domain.

25. **Answer: D**

   Explanation: The issue is that Megan needs to obtain an IP address through DHCP when on the road. But setting the network adapter to obtain an IP address automatically is not enough. To connect to the internal company network, the Alternate Configuration tab must be configured as a "User Configured" static IP address. This solution enables Megan to connect to networks while on the road by obtaining IP addresses automatically and allows her to connect to the internal company network with the static IP address.

   Incorrect answers: Megan shouldn't do anything. As a technician, you should fix the problem, so the other options where Megan is doing her own troubleshooting are incorrect.

26. **Answer: C**

   Explanation: Hibernate mode saves all the contents of RAM (as hiberfil.sys in the root of C:) and then shuts down the system so that it is using virtually no power. To reactivate the system, you must press the power button. At that point, the entire session is loaded from RAM, and you can continue on with the session.

   Incorrect answers: Standby (Sleep in Windows) and suspend modes turn off the hard drive and display and throttle down the CPU and RAM, but they still use power. Although these power modes use less power than the computer being powered on, altogether they end up using much more power than Hibernate mode does. Shutdown is great for power savings, but the session is lost when the computer is shut down.

27. **Answers: A and D**

   Explanation: NTFS can use NTFS file-level security, whereas FAT32 cannot. NTFS cluster sizes are smaller than FAT32 clusters. NTFS partitions are therefore more efficient (when installed correctly) than FAT32 partitions.

   Incorrect answers: NTFS can create larger partitions (or logical drives) than FAT32 in general, so larger logical drives would exist on an NTFS partition, not a FAT32 partition. Also, logical drives are based on the older MBR partitioning scheme and are not necessary on most of today's computers that use a GPT partitioning scheme.

28. **Answer: D**

    Explanation: A switch (aka option) alters the action of the command but not by forcing it to perform unrelated actions.

    Incorrect answers: The switch works only at the current time within the operating system you are currently using, so "work across any operating system" doesn't make sense in this scenario. Switches are not used in application icons. They are used within commands—for example, `dir /p`, which would display directory contents by the page.

29. **Answer: A**

    Explanation: The Event Viewer contains the log files of all the errors that occur on the machine. In this case, you would go to the Application log. Another common log is the System log, which shows errors concerning the OS and drivers.

    Incorrect answers: In the Local Security Policy, you can set up auditing and create password policies for the computer. `Msconfig` enables you to boot the computer in different modes and enable or disable services and applications. `Sfc /scannow` is a command run in the Command Prompt (as an administrator only) that scans the integrity of the protected system files and repairs them if possible.

30. **Answer: A**

    Explanation: The `msconfig` utility enables you to modify the startup environment via the General, Boot, and Startup tabs (in Windows 7), and the General and Boot tabs (in Windows 8 and Windows 10).

    Incorrect answers: `Ipconfig` displays all network adapters' settings. The Boot Config Editor is BCDEdit; it is used to modify the Boot Configuration Data (BCD) store. You might need to modify this if you are trying to dual-boot a computer. The Registry Editor allows you to make changes to Windows by accessing various hives of information and individual entries. Although the BCDEdit and Registry Editor utilities might be able to modify some startup features, they are not "commands" and are used for more advanced and less frequently used modifications than `msconfig`.

31. **Answer: C**

    Explanation: The Application log in the Event Viewer displays errors concerning Windows applications as well as third-party applications.

    Incorrect answers: The Security log shows auditing events. The System log shows events concerning system files, drivers, and operating system functionality. Setuperr. log is a log file that is created during the installation of Windows. If it is created, it is stored in %windir%\Panther and is not within the Event Viewer.

32. **Answer: A**

    Explanation: Disabling the SSID broadcast is a security precaution, but it only keeps out the average user. Any attacker with two bits of knowledge can scan for other things the wireless access point broadcasts.

    Incorrect answers: Using WEP is more secure than not using any encryption and disabling the SSID. RADIUS is an external method of authenticating users; it often requires a Windows Server. WPA2 is very secure; if you had one security option you could enable, make it WPA2.

33. Answers: A and C

Explanation: Use WPA or WPA2 on the router (and clients) to deny wardrivers and other stragglers access to the customer's network and, ultimately, any shared folders on the network. Increase the level of NTFS security by changing the permissions in the Security tab of the shared folder.

Incorrect answers: EFS isn't necessary if you set up WPA2 on the wireless access point, but if you are dealing in seriously confidential information, you might consider using it as well. Here's the deal: Share-level permissions are rarely modified. NTFS permissions are more configurable, so that is where the bulk of your time configuring permissions will go.

34. Answer: D

Explanation: Always explain specifically and exactly what you must do and what the ramifications are. Verify that the customer agrees to the proposed work (in writing).

Incorrect answers: Try to avoid being vague ("I need to rebuild the computer"), and conversely, avoid technical acronyms or jargon. Always make sure the customer is fully aware of the situation.

35. Answer: B

Explanation: The type of authentication method being used here is single-factor. The only factor of authentication is something the users know—usernames and passwords.

Incorrect answers: MFA stands for multifactor authentication, which is when two or more types of authentication methods are combined—for example, a password and a fingerprint. RADIUS and TACACS+ are authentication protocols, not authentication methods, and are often involved with single sign-on (SSO), federated identity management (FIM), and MFA authentication schemes. Regardless, the scenario said that the users were logging in to a payroll system, which is a separate entity from any authentication servers.

36. Answer: B

Explanation: `Copy` is used to make a duplicate of the file in another location.

Incorrect answers: `Move` enables you to take a file and shift it to another location. `Dir` gives you the contents of a specific folder. `Copy`, `move`, and `dir` are Windows commands. `Ls` lists the directory contents on a Linux-based system (as does `dir` in many Linux distros).

37. Answer: C

Explanation: The Task Manager enables a user to see the amount of memory and the percentage of processing power a particular process uses in real time. This can be done on the Processes tab.

Incorrect answers: System Information gives you information about the hardware and software of the computer, but it is static (text only) and doesn't change in real time. The Registry stores all of the settings of Windows and is modified with the Registry

Editor. Performance Monitor can graph the performance of the different components in the computer and, if configured properly, can do the same thing as the Task Manager in this scenario, but not as easily.

38. **Answer: A**

    Explanation: By moving the paging file (or swap file, aka virtual memory) to the D: drive, you are freeing up C: to deal with those drive-intensive programs.

    Incorrect answers: Reinstalling Windows is a huge process that you should avoid at all costs, especially when unnecessary, such as in this example. Defragging the C: drive would help if that is where the OS and applications are, but defragging the D: drive will not speed up the applications. Decreasing the page file size never helps. However, increasing the size, moving it, and adding RAM are all ways to make applications run faster.

39. **Answer: C**

    Explanation: Use an antistatic wrist strap when working inside a computer to protect against electrostatic discharge (ESD). Other ways to prevent ESD include using an anti-static mat, touching the chassis of the case (self-grounding), and using antistatic bags.

    Incorrect answers: A multimeter is used to run various electrical tests. A crimper is used to connect plugs and other connectors to the ends of a cable—for example, crimping RJ45 plugs on to the ends of a twisted-pair cable. A PSU tester is used to test the voltage of a power supply unit and other electrical connections inside the computer.

40. **Answer: C**

    Explanation: If something is immediately hazardous to you, you must leave the area right away.

    Incorrect answers: Afterward, you can call 911, the building supervisor, or your man-ager, depending on the severity of the situation. Computers and all other technology come second after human life. Remember that. Plus, if backup systems have been implemented properly, you have nothing to lose if a computer is damaged. If the situ-ation is not an emergency, be sure to reference the material safety data sheet (MSDS) for the substance you encounter.

41. **Answer: B**

    Explanation: You need to explain to the customer that there is a safer way. Cable man-agement is very important when it comes to the safety of employees. Trip hazards such as incorrectly routed network cables can have devastating effects on a person.

    Incorrect answers: Never ignore the problem. It is not your place to notify the building supervisor or administrator because this is not your company. However, you might opt to tell your manager about the event. A wise consulting company wants to protect its employees and should want to know of potential hazards at customer locations.

42. **Answer: C**

    Explanation: Every municipality has its own way of recycling batteries. They might be collected by the town or county yearly, or perhaps there are other recycling programs that are sponsored by recycling companies. Always call the municipality to find out exactly what to do.

    Incorrect answers: You should definitely recycle batteries and not throw them in the trash. Manufacturers probably won't be interested in batteries that don't charge any longer. It is more likely that you will recycle them. Be safe—never open a battery!

43. **Answer: C**

    Explanation: Asking a customer if employees always cause issues is just plain rude; this type of communication should be avoided.

    Incorrect answers: The other three statements are positive and helpful, or at least consoling. Stay away from being judgmental of the customer.

44. **Answer: C**

    Explanation: Ask if the server problem is related to the PC problem. Try to understand the customer before making any judgments about the problems. Make sure it isn't a bigger problem than you realize before making repairs that could be futile. If you find out that it is a separate problem, ask the customer which issue should be resolved first.

    Incorrect answers: You never know if problems are interrelated, so always listen to the customer and be patient before starting any work. If necessary—and if it is a separate problem—you can escalate the server issue to another technician, but state that you will do that. Statements about what you know and don't know are rarely necessary. You might have to ultimately call your supervisor about the server issue. But as an A+ technician you might have the server knowledge required. It depends on the problem. Find out the entire scope of the issues at hand and whether or not they are related before beginning any work.

45. **Answer: B**

    Explanation: Chain of custody is the chronological paper trail of evidence that may or may not be used in court.

    Incorrect answers: First response describes the steps a person takes when first responding to a computer with prohibited content or illegal activity: it includes identifying what exactly is happening, reporting through proper channels, and preserving data and devices. Setting and meeting expectations deal with customer service; this is something you should do before you start a job for a customer. Data (and device) preservation is a part of first response; a person who first arrives at the scene of a computer incident will be in charge of preserving data and devices in their current state.

46. **Answer: B**

    Explanation: Don't attempt to move heavy objects by yourself. Ask someone to help you.

    Incorrect answers: Removing jewelry, disconnecting power, and bending at the knees and lifting with the legs are all good safety measures.

47. Answer: C

Explanation: One example of active communication is clarifying a customer's statements. For instance, if you are unsure exactly what the customer wants, always clarify the information or repeat it back to the customer so that everyone is on the same page.

Incorrect answers: Never declare that the customer doesn't know what he is doing. This is a surefire way to lose the customer and possibly your job. It should go without saying: mouthing off could be the worst thing you could do. Save that for the drive home on the freeway—I'm just kidding! Be professional at all times when working with customers and perhaps while driving as well.

48. Answer: C

Explanation: The next attempt you should make (from the listed answers) is a soft reset of the device. Resetting often requires pressing a special combination of buttons. That keypress (hopefully) restarts the device with the RAM cleared. Then you can troubleshoot the problem application further if necessary.

Incorrect answers: A hard reset is not recommended (yet) because that will wipe the data, and a soft reset hasn't been attempted yet in the scenario. Force-quitting the app is the same as ending the task for the application. Always try to fix the problem yourself, and always attempt a soft reset, before bringing the device to an authorized service center.

49. Answer: A

Explanation: The first step in the malware removal best practices procedure is to identify malware symptoms.

Incorrect answers: The other steps are (2) quarantine infected systems; (3) disable System Restore; (4) remediate infected systems; (5) schedule scans and run updates; (6) enable System Restore; and (7) educate the end user.

50. Answers: B and D

Explanation: The best listed answers are dism and chkdsk. For a computer that is running slow, try using the chkdsk (check disk) and SFC (system file checker) commands. Then, if those run into problems, try using the dism (Deployment Image Servicing and Management) command. Chkdsk and SFC can repair problems with the drive and with system files. Dism can repair problems with the system image (where SFC will draw information from).

Incorrect answers: Format is used to ready a partition for files. Ipconfig is used to view network IP configuration data on a Windows system. Dir lists the files and folders within a current folder (directory). Diskpart is used to make modifications to the partitions on a hard drive; it is the command-line equivalent of Disk Management. Know your command line!

51. Answer: A

Explanation: You should first ask if anything has changed since the optical drive worked properly.

Incorrect answers: Don't blame the user by asking what "you" modified; it implies that you think the user caused the issue. Always ask if anything has changed before any other questions. Try not to accuse a user of accessing inappropriate websites because this could be considered inflammatory and harassment. Think like a robot with the single purpose of fixing the problem, but act like a professional and courteous human being.

52. Answer: B and D

Explanation: Your coworker might need an adapter; otherwise, the plug may not fit in some countries' outlets. Some power supplies have selectors for the United States and Europe (115 and 230 volts). If the wrong voltage is selected, the power supply will not work and the computer will not boot; it can also be a safety concern if the voltage is set incorrectly. Newer power supplies might auto-sense the voltage. If the power supply doesn't have one of those red switches, check the documentation to see if it can switch the voltage automatically.

Incorrect answers: A computer most certainly can be used in other countries, as long as it is configured properly and you have the right adapter. Line conditioners simply clean the power for a specific voltage. If your circuit has dirty power (for example, it is fluctuating between 113 and 130 volts), a line conditioner will keep it steady at 120 volts.

53. Answer: C

Explanation: Teach the user how to avoid this problem by recommending safe computing practices. The customer will then be more likely to come back to you with other computer problems. 'Nuff said.

Incorrect answers: Avoid saying "can't"; it's a negative expression that belittles your own ability, which is most likely greater than that. Embrace the teaching method. Over time, it means that you will encounter the same problem less often, and the customer will ultimately thank you for your input. Changing user permissions might help if the person was an administrator. Better yet, you could urge the customer to use a standard user account by default.

54. Answer: D

Explanation: Make sure that the customer has a path toward a solution before dismissing the issue.

Incorrect answers: Do *not* try to fix the problem if the scope of work is outside your knowledge. Some PC technicians might not work on domain controllers because they are advanced Microsoft servers that are used in client/server networks.

55. Answers: C and D

Explanation: The power cord carries 120 volts at 15 amps or 20 amps, with all of the obvious danger that such voltage and amperage entails. While normally low voltage, a landline telephone cord carries 80 volts when the phone rings. That and network cables can also be the victims of power surges from central office or networking equipment. It is important to disconnect these before servicing a computer.

Incorrect answers: Now, if you were opening the computer, you would disconnect everything. However, you might be fixing something that doesn't require you to open the computer—for example, connecting a network cable. Remember to always disconnect any power, data, or telecommunications cables before working on the system.

56. **Answers: A and D**

Explanation: You should attempt to identify the problem and call Microsoft tech support (or contact them in another manner). The message tells you that the DHCP partner is down. This means that there are two DHCP servers, one acting as a failover. As part of your identification of the problem, you should access the TechNet, for example:

https://docs.microsoft.com/en-us/previous-versions/windows/it-pro/windows-server-2012-R2-and-2012/dn338985(v=ws.11).

You will find out more about the problem and possibly learn that it isn't as bad as it might seem, and your manager might be overreacting slightly. (These things happen.) In reality, this message means that the partner DHCP server is down, but the one you are working at locally is still functional and is responding to all DHCP requests. You should indeed fix the problem, of course, but now you can call Microsoft tech support in a methodical and calm way, armed with information about what you think the problem is. When a company purchases a Windows Server operating system, it comes with tech support, either from Microsoft or from the company that built the server. Because your knowledge of Windows Server is limited, tech support is a great way to not only fix the problem but also learn a thing or two from the people who work with the system all the time.

Incorrect answers: Escalating the problem is impossible because no other technicians are available to help you. The other answers refer to the CompTIA troubleshooting process, none of which you should attempt until you have called tech support. Now, if your knowledge of Windows Server is sufficient, you could attempt to solve the problem yourself. Though this might have seemed like a more complex question, it really isn't. Trust in your fundamentals!

57. **Answer: A**

Explanation: The classification of data helps prevent confidential information from being publicly disclosed. Some organizations have a classification scheme for their data, such as normal, secret, and top secret. Policies are implemented to make top secret data the most secure on the network. By classifying data, you are determining who has access to it. This is generally done on a need-to-know basis.

Incorrect answers: Social engineering is the art of manipulating people into giving classified information. A remote access server (RAS) allows users to connect remotely to the network. To protect a web-based connection (and data that passes through it), an organization would use HTTPS (and an encrypted certificate), not HTTP. Wiping a hard drive is a vague response. How is it being wiped? If it is being formatted, that is not enough to protect confidential information. You need to perform bit-level erasure with third-party software, degauss the drive, or destroy it to make sure that no one can access the data. The thing is that data is always stored somewhere on a server or NAS device, so properly disposing of a single hard drive doesn't protect any and all confidential information from being publicly disclosed.

58. Answer: C

Explanation: HKEY_LOCAL_MACHINE is the Registry hive that stores information about the programs Windows runs when it starts. The actual hives are stored in \%windir%\System32\Config, but it's okay to call HKEY_LOCAL_MACHINE and the other HKEYs *hives*. Most technicians do it, and you might see them referred to that way on the exam as well. The HKEY_LOCAL_MACHINE hive is the one you will access the most often. You can configure advanced settings for TCP/IP, the GUI of the OS, and lots more from here.

Incorrect answers: HKEY_CURRENT_CONFIG contains data that generated when the system boots; nothing is permanently stored. HKEY_USERS stores the information for each user profile. HKEY_CLASSES_ROOT contains information about registered applications and file associations.

59. Answer: A

Explanation: A web browser such as Edge, Internet Explorer, Firefox, or Chrome (or any other web browser) is normally used to configure a router. You can type the IP address of the router into the Windows Explorer/File Explorer address bar, but that will simply open an IE (or other browser) tab.

Incorrect answers: In the Device Manager you enable and disable devices and install, update, and roll back drivers for devices. Msconfig is used to modify how the computer boots and to enable/disable programs and services.

60. Answer: D

Explanation: The first thing you need to supply is the driver for any special drives, such as new SCSI drives, SAS drives, or RAID controllers. That, of course, is optional. If you have a typical SATA drive, Windows should recognize it automatically.

Incorrect answers: Once Windows knows which hard drive to install to, partitioning, then formatting, and then configuration of settings can commence, in that order.

61. Answer: A

Explanation: Although Windows has the Reconnect at Sign In check box selected by default, it could have been disabled.

Incorrect answers: You don't need to select the drive letter each time a connection is made; once you set up the mapped network drive, it uses that drive letter each time automatically. You should check the connection to the folder when mapping the drive, but based on the scenario, this worked fine when the drive was mapped; it was the reboot that caused the issue. If you do choose to use the net use command, be sure to make persistent connections. This is done by adding /persistent:yes to the command syntax.

62. Answer: C

Explanation: MAC filtering is used to restrict computers from connecting to a network; it is based on the physical Media Access Control (MAC) address of the computer's network adapter. It works with wired or wireless connections.

Incorrect answers: WPA is used to encrypt the wireless session between a computer and the wireless access point (WAP); its key code is required to gain access to the network. DHCP settings simply allow a specific range of IP addresses and other IP data, such as gateway address and DNS server address, to be handed out to clients. The SSID broadcast is the name of the wireless network as broadcast out over radio waves by the WAP.

63. **Answer: B**

Explanation: The Print Spooler needs to be restarted on the computer that started the print job or the computer that controls the printer. This can be done in the Services console window or in the Command Prompt with the `net stop spooler` and `net start spooler` commands, or anywhere else that services can be started and stopped, such as the Task Manager.

Incorrect answers: Print drivers are not services; they are not started, stopped, or restarted. Instead, they are either installed, uninstalled, updated, or rolled back. The network adapter and the printer are devices, not services. Okay, that was an easy one, but the real exam will have a couple easy ones thrown in as well. Don't think too hard when you actually do receive an easier question.

64. **Answer: C**

Explanation: Adding the port number and name of service to the Windows Defender Firewall Exceptions list is the correct answer. But I'm going to pontificate more, as I usually do.

Incorrect answers: Uninstalling and reinstalling the service pack or security update do not help this particular situation. Remember that Windows 7 has a service pack, but Windows 8 and newer do not use service packs and simply use "updates." By default, any of today's Windows OS versions enable the Windows Defender Firewall automatically and don't allow inbound connections from the server to the network application. Therefore, you need to make an "exception." In Windows, use the Windows Defender Firewall with Advanced Security, either from Administrative Tools or by typing `wf.msc` at the Run prompt. If you decide to add a port, you need to know the port number of the application. For example, VNC applications might use port 5900 or port 5901 for incoming connections.

65. **Answer: B**

Explanation: The PC air intakes are probably clogged with cement dust. This stops fresh, cool air from entering the PC and causes the CPU to overheat. That's why the system doesn't reboot immediately; the CPU needs some time to cool down. You should install a filter in front of the PC air intake and instruct the customer to clean the filter often. While you are working on the computer, you should clean out the inside of the system and vacuum out the exhaust of the power supply (without opening the power supply, of course).

Incorrect answers: If the PC had a virus, that might cause it to lock up or shut down, but you would be able to reboot the computer right away. Plus, there would probably be other indicators of a virus. The CPU heat sink could be an issue and could cause the same results, but this scenario is less likely. Companies often buy computers from popular manufacturers such as Dell and HP; these computer manufacturers spend a lot of time designing their heat sink/fan combinations to work with the CPU. If the power supply were underrated, it would cause intermittent shutdowns but not lockups. Nothing in the scenario would lead you to believe that the computer uses so many powerful components as to make the power supply underrated.

66. Answer: C

Explanation: The Guest account is the most likely answer here. This account has the fewest privileges of all Windows accounts. It cannot install printers or printer drivers. By the way, Standard users can also have issues with printers depending on the version of Windows and the policies involved. But the Guest has absolutely no administrative powers whatsoever.

Incorrect answers: Power Users don't really have power anymore. They are included for backward compatibility with older versions of applications and how they interact with Windows. The administrator account is the most powerful account on a local Windows system and has complete control over everything, unless there is a domain involved. Then you would want a Domain Administrator account.

67. Answers: B and D

Explanation: The share-level permissions must first be set to enable access to the user. Then the NTFS file-level "user" permissions must also be set; the most restrictive of the two will take precedence (usually this is configured as NTFS being more restrictive).

Incorrect answers: Certificates are normally used in Internet or VPN sessions. Local user access is somewhat vague but doesn't apply here; the reason is that when a user connects to a shared resource, that person does so over the network to a remote computer.

68. Answers: C and D

Explanation: Pictures and email are possibly valuable, and definitely irreplaceable, if there is no backup.

Incorrect answers: The rest of the answers mention things that can be restored or reinstalled from the operating system disc or image.

69. Answer: B

Explanation: Of all the answers, the only one that deals with the local level is Local Security Policy.

Incorrect answers: Organizational Unit (OU) Group Policy, Active Directory Policy, and Site Policy all require at least one domain controller on the network. You should know some domain-based policy terminology to compare them to security options on the local computer. You can access the Local Security Policy from Administrative Tools or by typing `secpol.msc` at the Run prompt.

70. Answer: B

Explanation: In many cases, passwords cannot be reset by the user or by the systems admin. If that is the case, you need to verify the identity of the person first. You might need to do so just as a matter of organizational policy.

Incorrect answers: Telling the person not to do that or to simply remember the password is just rude. If the password could be reset and you are allowed to do so, you should reset it immediately.

71. **Answer: C**

   Explanation: GPS can help to locate a stolen or lost mobile device. Plenty of third-party programs allow the user to track the device, as long as it is on and has GPS installed and functioning. If the device is off, the program will display the last known good location.

   Incorrect answers: Passcodes are used to secure the device in the event that it is stolen or lost. Auto-erase is used to wipe the contents of the device if lost or stolen. Encryption protects the data in the case that the user no longer has possession of it.

72. **Answer: B**

   Explanation: To aid in preventing access to a wireless network, disable the SSID. But only do this when all computers have been connected. If more computers need to be connected later, they will have to connect manually, or the SSID will have to be reenabled.

   Incorrect answers: Although this is an okay security method, it won't keep smart attackers out of your network. MAC filtering and WPA2 encryption do a much better job at that than disabling the SSID.

73. **Answer: A**

   Explanation: If you are just setting the time on the computer, use the time command. Time can also be set in Windows within the Notification Area. This is a bit of a trick question because you are dealing only with local time, not anything network-related. So the rest of the answers are incorrect.

   Incorrect answers: The `net time` command is needed if you want to synchronize the local computer's time to another system or just find out the time on a remote system. `net timer` is not a valid command. The `net time` command uses the `/set` option if you wish to synchronize time to another computer.

74. **Answer: D**

   Explanation: The Character Map enables you to copy characters from any font type. To open it, go to Run and type `charmap`. In Windows 10, go to Start > Windows Accessories > Character Map. In Windows 7, go to Start > All Programs > Accessories > System Tools > Character Map. Otherwise, in any version of Windows, you can locate it simply by searching for it by name.

   Incorrect answers: The Language Bar automatically appears when you use handwriting recognition or speech recognition. It can be configured within Region and Languages. Sticky keys is a feature that helps users with physical disabilities; it can be turned on by rapidly pressing the Shift key five times and agreeing Yes. Control Panel > Fonts opens the Fonts folder, where you can add or remove text fonts.

75. Answer: B

Explanation: Jailbreaking is the process of removing the limitations of an Apple device's iOS. It enables a user to gain root access to the system and download previously unavailable applications, most likely unauthorized by Apple.

Incorrect answers: Rooting is similar, but it is a term typically used with Android-based devices. It gives administrative capabilities to users of Android-based devices. Both jailbreaking and rooting are not recommended and may void device warranties. VirusBarrier was the first AV software designed for iOS; it was developed in response to a particularly nasty jailbreak. Super-admin powers is just a colorful term for what you get when you root or jailbreak a mobile device.

76. Answer: D

Explanation: The Sync Center is located within the Control Panel or can be found using the search tool. It allows you to set up synchronization partnerships with external devices and enables you to manage offline files. Sometimes, the individual icons within the Control Panel are referred to as applets.

Incorrect answers: File History is the name of the backup program in Windows 8/8.1 and Windows 10. The command-line–based User State Migration Tool (USMT) is used to move files and user settings from multiple computers at once. Robust file copy is a Command Prompt tool (Robocopy) that is used to move large amounts of data; it is the successor to xcopy, though xcopy is still available in Windows.

77. Answer: A

Explanation: Unicode is the code used to represent characters among multiple computers' language platforms. It is commonly used in Microsoft Word and other Office programs. For example, to show the logical equivalence symbol ($\equiv$), you would type U+2261, then highlight that text, and then press the Alt+X shortcut on the keyboard, which changes the text into the symbol ($\equiv$).Unicode works regardless of the language a person is working in.

Incorrect answers: ASCII and EBCDIC are different types of character encoding sets in the English language only. ITU-T deals with standards for telecommunications. .ps1 is the main file extension used for PowerShell scripts.

78. Answer: B

Explanation: New malicious software (malware) is always being created. Because of this, the best place to find information about spyware, a virus, rootkit, ransomware, or other malware is at a place that can be updated often and easily: the anti-malware company's website.

Incorrect answers: Operating system documentation usually does not have this kind of information. In addition, the OS documents and the anti-spyware readme.txt file will be outdated soon after they are written. Never trust in what a user has to say about malware. The user is not the person who would remove it—a technician would.

79. **Answers: A and D**

    Explanation: The Windows PCs have probably been infected by a worm and have been compromised and turned into zombies (bots). Trojans could also be involved in this scenario. The Windows PCs are probably part of a botnet that includes other computers as well. The botnet is orchestrated by a master computer that initiates the DDoS (distributed denial-of-service) attack. The infections that you as the technician will have to remove include the worm and the zombie program (or script).You might also be informed that the systems need to be isolated, wiped, and re-imaged before they can be used again.

    Incorrect answers: Spyware is software installed on a computer to track the user/computer. Ransomware is malware that is used to encrypt the files on a user's computer. A virus is similar to a worm, but it does not self-replicate to other systems; also, the worm (or Trojan) is more commonly used as a mechanism to deliver a zombie script or other payload. You as a PC technician won't be able to do much about the entire botnet.

80. **Answer: D**

    Explanation: Use the Registry Editor (regedit.exe) to try troubleshooting the problem if typical GUI-based and Command Prompt methods have provided no resolution. The Registry Editor allows you to do any configuration necessary in Windows, and using it may be necessary for more complex troubleshooting problems. At this point you are testing the theory to determine cause because you have already identified the problem and established a theory of probable cause. Remember your CompTIA A+ troubleshooting theory from the 220-1001 objectives. I've listed them below.

    1. Identify the problem.

       Question the user and identify user changes to computer and perform backups before making changes.

       Inquire regarding environmental or infrastructure changes.

       Review system and application logs.

    2. Establish a theory of probable cause (question the obvious).

       If necessary, conduct external or internal research based on symptoms.

    3. Test the theory to determine cause.

       Once theory is confirmed, determine next steps to resolve problem.

       If theory is not confirmed, reestablish new theory or escalate.

    4. Establish a plan of action to resolve the problem and implement the solution.

    5. Verify full system functionality and, if applicable, implement preventive measures.

    6. Document findings, actions, and outcomes.

    Incorrect answers: Regsvr32 is used to register/unregister ActiveX controls and DLLs in the Registry. GPUpdate enables policy changes to take effect without the need for a logoff or restart. USMT is used to migrate user accounts. Boot Camp is a tool used in macOS to dual-boot Mac computers to Windows. It is the only answer listed that is not a Windows-based command.

YOU ARE ON YOUR WAY!

That wraps up Exam B. Take a nice long break before moving on to the last 220-1002 exam in this book.

If you scored 90 percent or higher on this 220-1002 practice exam, move on to the next one! If you did not, I strongly encourage you to study the material again and retake the first couple practice exams until you get 90 percent or higher on each. Keep going; you are doing awesome!

CHAPTER NINE

220-1002 Practice Exam C

Let's turn up the heat a bit more. The previous 220-1002 exam was the intermediate test. This third and final test could be considered an advanced practice test. A large percentage of the questions have a higher difficulty rating. Be ready for questions with longer, more in-depth scenarios and more complex answers.

If you haven't taken a break already, I suggest taking one between exams. If you just completed the second exam, give yourself a half hour or so before you begin this one. If you didn't score 90 percent or higher on exam B, go back and study; then retake exam B until you pass with 90 percent or higher.

Write down your answers and check them against the Quick-Check Answer Key, which immediately follows the exam. After the answer key, you will find the explanations for all of the answers. Good luck!

Practice Questions

1. You work as a technician for an organization that has a custom web-based application that is used for the monitoring of networking devices. While using a web browser to access the application, you press F12, and within the js folder, you see the following code:

```
$(function() {
// Attach collapsible behavior to select options
(function()
{
    var selects = $('select[data-toggle="collapse"]');
```

Which of the following script types is being used?

○ **A.** Python

○ **B.** PowerShell

○ **C.** Bash

○ **D.** JavaScript

○ **E.** Visual Basic Script

2. Viruses have been detected and removed on a customer's computer several times during the course of several weeks. Which of the following methods will best help prevent future occurrences?

○ **A.** Delete temporary files, cookies, and browser history.

○ **B.** Defragment the hard drive.

○ **C.** Install antivirus software that uses manual updates.

○ **D.** Discuss safer web browsing habits with the customer.

Quick Answer: **233**
Detailed Answer: **234**

3. Which of the following sends an invitation by email asking for help?

○ **A.** Remote Desktop Connection

○ **B.** Service call

○ **C.** VNC

○ **D.** Remote Assistance

Quick Answer: **233**
Detailed Answer: **234**

4. When you are performing a clean installation, which of the following is the default location for the system files of Windows?

○ **A.** C:\Windows

○ **B.** C:\Windows\System32\Config

○ **C.** C:\Windows\System32

○ **D.** C:\System Files

Quick Answer: **233**
Detailed Answer: **235**

5. You are required to set up a remote backup solution for music and photos stored on an Android tablet. The files cannot be stored at any company location. Which technology should be used?

○ **A.** iCloud

○ **B.** Google Cloud

○ **C.** Microsoft OneDrive

○ **D.** Local NAS device

Quick Answer: **233**
Detailed Answer: **235**

6. You have been contracted to repair a computer at an organization that has strict rules about information leaving the premises. While troubleshooting the computer, you determine that the computer should be taken offsite to complete the repair. Which of the following should you do next?

   ○ **A.** Get authorization from your manager.

   ○ **B.** Delete proprietary information before leaving the building.

   ○ **C.** Check corporate policies for guidance.

   ○ **D.** Remove the HDD and send the computer for repair.

Quick Answer: **233**
Detailed Answer: **235**

7. You need to copy and paste information from a web page, but you want to remove all formatting so that it can be pasted cleanly into Word. Which program should be used as an intermediary?

   ○ **A.** CMD

   ○ **B.** Excel

   ○ **C.** Notepad

   ○ **D.** MMC

Quick Answer: **233**
Detailed Answer: **235**

8. A computer is responding slowly, and the Windows Task Manager shows that spoolsv.exe is using 95 percent of system resources. Which of the following is most likely the cause of this problem?

   ○ **A.** Windows Update is running.

   ○ **B.** A virus infection has occurred.

   ○ **C.** Hyper-Threading has been disabled.

   ○ **D.** The printing subsystem.

Quick Answer: **233**
Detailed Answer: **236**

9. Which of the following descriptions classifies the protocol IMAP?

   ○ **A.** A protocol that allows real-time messaging

   ○ **B.** An email protocol that allows users to selectively download messages

   ○ **C.** An email protocol that allows users to send but not to receive messages

   ○ **D.** A protocol that authenticates users who are sending email

Quick Answer: **233**
Detailed Answer: **236**

10. From which of the following locations could you disable a hardware component on a laptop in Windows?

    ○ **A.** Device Manager

    ○ **B.** Task Manager

    ○ **C.** File Explorer

    ○ **D.** Services console

Quick Answer: **233**
Detailed Answer: **236**

11. Which command-line tool in Windows finds all of the unsigned drivers in the computer?

Quick Answer: **233**
Detailed Answer: **236**

   - ○ **A.** Sigverif
   - ○ **B.** Dxdiag
   - ○ **C.** Ping
   - ○ **D.** Msconfig

12. Users are reporting to you that a Windows feature asks them for confirmation before running certain applications or when making system changes. What is the name of this Windows feature, and where should you direct users to turn the functionality off?

Quick Answer: **233**
Detailed Answer: **237**

   - ○ **A.** Security Center; it can be turned off in the Services console window.
   - ○ **B.** User Account Control; it can be turned off under Security in the Control Panel.
   - ○ **C.** Windows Defender Firewall; it can be turned off under System Properties.
   - ○ **D.** User Account Control; it can be turned off under User Accounts in the Control Panel.

13. James is a LAN administrator in charge of printers. Which of the following should he check first when a Windows user is trying to print a document and gets the error message "Print sub-system not available"?

Quick Answer: **233**
Detailed Answer: **237**

   - ○ **A.** Correct printer driver is installed.
   - ○ **B.** Printer has been added.
   - ○ **C.** Spooler service is running.
   - ○ **D.** Printer has power from the jack.

14. Your manager's Windows computer locks up after the graphical user interface starts to load. However, the computer will boot in Safe Mode. When you access the Event Viewer, you see an entry stating that a driver failed. Which of the following steps will help you further diagnose the problem?

Quick Answer: **233**
Detailed Answer: **237**

   - ○ **A.** Running sigverif
   - ○ **B.** Enabling Boot Logging and then in Safe Mode analyzing the ntbtlog.txt file
   - ○ **C.** Disabling Driver Signature Enforcement
   - ○ **D.** Accessing Debugging Mode

15. Which of the following commands is used to fix errors on the system disk?

Quick Answer: **233**
Detailed Answer: **238**

- ○ **A.** robocopy
- ○ **B.** tracert /w
- ○ **C.** diskpart
- ○ **D.** chkdsk /F

16. You are troubleshooting a computer that has a web browser issue. The end user says that multiple browser pages open by themselves when surfing the Internet. Also, you observe that the computer is running slowly. Which of the following actions should you perform first?

Quick Answer: **233**
Detailed Answer: **238**

- ○ **A.** Install anti-malware software.
- ○ **B.** Update antivirus definitions.
- ○ **C.** Reboot the computer.
- ○ **D.** Enable a pop-up blocker.

17. A new program is crashing and causing the computer to lock up. What is the best location to check for further information about the cause of the crash?

Quick Answer: **233**
Detailed Answer: **238**

- ○ **A.** System log
- ○ **B.** Security log
- ○ **C.** Application log
- ○ **D.** Setup log

18. You are tasked with disabling services from starting on a Windows PC. Which command should be run to bring up a window to make these changes?

Quick Answer: **233**
Detailed Answer: **238**

- ○ **A.** SFC
- ○ **B.** Chkdsk
- ○ **C.** Msconfig
- ○ **D.** Gpupdate

19. In Windows, which of the following folders might be stored in a hidden partition by default?

Quick Answer: **233**
Detailed Answer: **238**

- ○ **A.** \Boot
- ○ **B.** \Windows
- ○ **C.** \Documents and Settings
- ○ **D.** \Bootmgr

20. One of your customers has a wireless network that is secured with WEP. The customer wants to improve data encryption so that the transmission of data has less of a chance of being compromised. Which of the following statements best describes the recommended course of action?

Quick Answer: **233**
Detailed Answer: **239**

- ○ **A.** Reconfigure the network to use WPA2.
- ○ **B.** Use MAC address filtering.
- ○ **C.** Modify the WEP key every week.
- ○ **D.** Disable the SSID broadcast.

21. Which of the following commands is used to display hidden files?

Quick Answer: **233**
Detailed Answer: **239**

- ○ **A.** `dir /o`
- ○ **B.** `dir /a`
- ○ **C.** `dir /d`
- ○ **D.** `dir /?`

22. After you install a new video card, the PC loads Windows and continuously reboots. Which of the following statements best describes the first course of action?

Quick Answer: **233**
Detailed Answer: **239**

- ○ **A.** Go into Safe Mode.
- ○ **B.** Run `Chkdsk`.
- ○ **C.** Run `Msconfig`.
- ○ **D.** Check the System log.

23. Which of the following statements best describes how to prepare a mobile device in case it is stolen or lost? (Select the three best answers.)

Quick Answer: **233**
Detailed Answer: **239**

- ❏ **A.** Disable Bluetooth.
- ❏ **B.** Configure remote backup.
- ❏ **C.** Enable Wi-Fi encryption.
- ❏ **D.** Enable GPS.
- ❏ **E.** Enable Wi-Fi tethering.
- ❏ **F.** Configure a pattern screenlock.

24. Two coworkers share the same file inside a folder. User A works on the file, makes changes, and saves the file. User B then works on the file, makes changes, and saves the file as well. The next time User A attempts to open the file, she receives an access denied error. Which of the following statements best describes the most likely cause of this error message?

    ○ **A.** The NTFS permissions were changed on the file to allow only execute.

    ○ **B.** The file was set with the system and hidden attributes.

    ○ **C.** The file was set to read only by the Accounts Receivable administrator.

    ○ **D.** The file was moved before being modified and then moved back to the share.

25. In Windows, which of the following commands should be used to verify that a previous system shutdown was completed successfully?

    ○ **A.** `Ipconfig`

    ○ **B.** `Chkntfs`

    ○ **C.** `Chkdsk`

    ○ **D.** `SFC`

26. Which of the following are the best answers for securing a data center? (Select the two best answers.)

    ❑ **A.** Bollard

    ❑ **B.** Badge reader

    ❑ **C.** Cable lock

    ❑ **D.** USB-based hardware token

    ❑ **E.** Biometric lock

    ❑ **F.** Privacy shades

27. Which of the following is the best Windows utility to use if an administrator wants to perform administrative tasks that integrate scripts over a network?

    ○ **A.** PowerShell

    ○ **B.** Command Prompt

    ○ **C.** Command-line

    ○ **D.** Bash

28. Which of the following can be used to kill a running process?

    ○ **A.** Task Manager

    ○ **B.** Computer Management

    ○ **C.** Control Panel

    ○ **D.** Tasklist

29. Which of the following file systems is suited specifically for USB flash drives?

    ○ **A.** FAT32

    ○ **B.** exFAT

    ○ **C.** NTFS

    ○ **D.** ext4

30. A program has been detected collecting information such as the computer name and IP address and sending that information to a specific IP address on the Internet. Which kind of threat is this an example of?

    ○ **A.** Spyware

    ○ **B.** Virus

    ○ **C.** Rootkit

    ○ **D.** Spam

31. You are required to stop the Windows Defender Firewall service. Which of the following best describes how to accomplish this? (Select the three best answers.)

    ❏ **A.** In Performance Monitor

    ❏ **B.** With the `net stop mpssvc` command

    ❏ **C.** Within `Msconfig`

    ❏ **D.** Within the Task Manager

    ❏ **E.** In System Information

    ❏ **F.** With Gpedit.exe

    ❏ **G.** In Services.msc

32. You spill a chemical on your hands. It does not appear to be life threatening. Which of the following statements best describes the recommended course of action?

    ○ **A.** Call 911.

    ○ **B.** Call the building supervisor.

    ○ **C.** Consult the MSDS for the chemical.

    ○ **D.** Ignore it.

33. Which command allows a user to change a file's permissions in Linux?

Quick Answer: **233**
Detailed Answer: **242**

- ○ **A.** Chown
- ○ **B.** Passwd
- ○ **C.** Ls
- ○ **D.** Chmod

34. While you are working on a computer at a customer's home, the customer informs you that he needs to leave for about 10 minutes and that his eight-year-old son can help you with anything if you need it. Which of the following statements best describes the recommended course of action??

Quick Answer: **233**
Detailed Answer: **242**

- ○ **A.** Tell the customer to get back home as soon as possible.
- ○ **B.** Tell the customer that you are not responsible for the child.
- ○ **C.** Tell the customer that an adult must be home while you work.
- ○ **D.** Tell the customer that the child must be removed.

35. You want a cloud provider that will offer you service which is quickly scalable. Which of the following should be requested when you contact potential cloud providers?

Quick Answer: **233**
Detailed Answer: **242**

- ○ **A.** Measured services
- ○ **B.** Rapid elasticity
- ○ **C.** On-demand service
- ○ **D.** Resource pooling

36. You have been asked to recommend an anti-malware program for a home user. However, the user does not want to pay for a license. Which of the following should you suggest?

Quick Answer: **233**
Detailed Answer: **242**

- ○ **A.** Personal license
- ○ **B.** Corporate license
- ○ **C.** Open license
- ○ **D.** Enterprise license

37. A customer experiences a server crash. When you arrive, the manager is upset about this problem. Which of the following statements best describes the recommended course of action?

Quick Answer: **233**
Detailed Answer: **243**

- ○ **A.** Stay calm and do the job as efficiently as possible.
- ○ **B.** Take the customer out for a cup of coffee.
- ○ **C.** Avoid the customer and get the job done quickly.
- ○ **D.** Refer the customer to your supervisor.

38. Which type of web server is designed to resolve hostnames to IP addresses?

Quick Answer: **233**
Detailed Answer: **243**

- ○ **A.** DHCP server
- ○ **B.** Web server
- ○ **C.** Proxy server
- ○ **D.** DNS server

39. As you are servicing a manager's PC at your company, you run across a list of names of employees who are supposedly about to be let go from the company. Some of these people are coworkers. Which of the following statements best describes the recommended course of action?

Quick Answer: **233**
Detailed Answer: **243**

- ○ **A.** Shred the list.
- ○ **B.** Act as if you never saw the list.
- ○ **C.** In secret, tell everyone who was on the list.
- ○ **D.** Yell at the manager for having that list out.

40. Which macOS utility is most like Windows' "end task" feature?

Quick Answer: **233**
Detailed Answer: **243**

- ○ **A.** Time Machine
- ○ **B.** Finder
- ○ **C.** Taskkill
- ○ **D.** Force quit

41. Which of the following statements best describes how to reduce the chance of ESD? (Select the three best answers.)

Quick Answer: **233**
Detailed Answer: **244**

- ❏ **A.** Use an antistatic strap.
- ❏ **B.** Use an antistatic mat.
- ❏ **C.** Raise the temperature.
- ❏ **D.** Raise the humidity.
- ❏ **E.** Lower the humidity.
- ❏ **F.** Work in a carpeted area.

42. While you explain a technical concept to a customer, which of the following statements best describes the recommended course of action?

Quick Answer: **233**
Detailed Answer: **244**

- ○ **A.** Recommend a training class.
- ○ **B.** Sit next to the customer.
- ○ **C.** Use acronyms so that the customer feels comfortable about your knowledge.
- ○ **D.** Tell the customer to read the manual.

43. You are viewing the contents of an `ipconfig /all` on a Windows computer. You see the name *dpro42.com* toward the beginning of the results. Which type of network is this Windows computer most likely a part of?

- ○ **A.** Workgroup
- ○ **B.** Homegroup
- ○ **C.** Domain
- ○ **D.** VPN

Quick Answer: **233**
Detailed Answer: **244**

44. Which of the following should be used to clean a monitor's screen when you are not sure how to do so?

- ○ **A.** Isopropyl alcohol
- ○ **B.** Mild detergent
- ○ **C.** Water
- ○ **D.** Boric acid

Quick Answer: **233**
Detailed Answer: **244**

45. You are required to register an ActiveX control in the Command Prompt. Which utility should be used?

- ○ **A.** Regsvr32
- ○ **B.** Regedit.exe
- ○ **C.** MMC
- ○ **D.** MSTSC

Quick Answer: **233**
Detailed Answer: **244**

46. As part of the risk management of your company, you have been tasked with backing up three physical servers on a daily basis. These backups will be stored to a NAS device on the LAN. Which of the following can you do to make sure the backup will work if needed?

- ○ **A.** Create alerts to let the administrators know when backups fail.
- ○ **B.** Set up scripts that will automatically rerun failed backup jobs.
- ○ **C.** Store copies of the backups offsite at a data center.
- ○ **D.** Frequently restore the servers from the backup files and test them.
- ○ **E.** Configure the backups to restore to VMs for rapid recovery.

Quick Answer: **233**
Detailed Answer: **245**

47. You have an Intel Core i7 system with a UEFI-enabled mother-board. Which of the following types of hard drive partitioning schemes should be selected when installing Windows?

Quick Answer: **233**
Detailed Answer: **245**

   ○ **A.** MBR

   ○ **B.** FAT32

   ○ **C.** Dynamic drive

   ○ **D.** GPT

48. Which of the following statements best describes the recom-mended course of action to take prior to attempting to remediate infected Windows systems of malware?

Quick Answer: **233**
Detailed Answer: **245**

   ○ **A.** Educate the end user.

   ○ **B.** Disable System Restore.

   ○ **C.** Schedule scans.

   ○ **D.** Update the anti-malware program.

49. A customer's mobile device cannot connect to Wi-Fi. According to the customer, it was working fine yesterday. Troubleshoot! Which of the following statements best describes the recommended course of action? (Select the three best answers.)

Quick Answer: **233**
Detailed Answer: **246**

   ❏ **A.** Power cycle the device.

   ❏ **B.** Re-pair the device.

   ❏ **C.** Perform a hard reset.

   ❏ **D.** Forget the Wi-Fi network.

   ❏ **E.** Check if the correct SSID was entered.

   ❏ **F.** Change the IP address.

50. Which of the following utilities enables a Windows user to edit a file offline and then automatically update the changes when the user returns to the office?

Quick Answer: **233**
Detailed Answer: **246**

   ○ **A.** Sync Center

   ○ **B.** Windows Aero

   ○ **C.** Windows Defender

   ○ **D.** HomeGroup

51. A help desk phone support technician is finding it difficult to understand the customer due to a heavy accent. Which of the following statements best describes the first course of action the technician should take to help the customer resolve the problem?

    ○ **A.** Repeat the problem back to the customer.

    ○ **B.** Have the customer call back at a later time.

    ○ **C.** Ask the customer to not speak with an accent.

    ○ **D.** Tell the customer that her accent is preventing the problem from being solved.

Quick Answer: **233**
Detailed Answer: **246**

52. Which of the following relies on PPTP to create a secure tunnel?

    ○ **A.** WWAN

    ○ **B.** 4G LTE

    ○ **C.** VPN

    ○ **D.** WLAN

Quick Answer: **233**
Detailed Answer: **247**

53. Which of the following will occur if %temp% is executed from Run?

    ○ **A.** Applications located in the %temp% folder will be executed.

    ○ **B.** The operating system's temporary folder will be opened.

    ○ **C.** The current user's temporary folder will be opened.

    ○ **D.** Applications will be deleted in the %temp% folder.

Quick Answer: **233**
Detailed Answer: **247**

54. Which group is best to assign to a home user to prevent software installation?

    ○ **A.** Administrators

    ○ **B.** Power users

    ○ **C.** Remote Desktop users

    ○ **D.** Users

Quick Answer: **233**
Detailed Answer: **247**

55. A Windows PC is not booting correctly. You need to locate bad sectors and recover information. Which command is best?

    ○ **A.** `chkdsk C: /R`

    ○ **B.** `chkdsk C: /F`

    ○ **C.** `chkdsk C: /C`

    ○ **D.** `chkdsk C: /I`

Quick Answer: **233**
Detailed Answer: **247**

56. One of your coworkers has a smartphone that contains PII. Because the data is required for use and is valuable, the coworker cannot have the phone automatically wiped if it is lost or stolen. Which of the following is the best way to secure the device?

Quick Answer: **233**
Detailed Answer: **247**

- ○ **A.** Passcode
- ○ **B.** Swipe
- ○ **C.** PIN
- ○ **D.** Fingerprint

57. Where can a user's Desktop folder be found in Windows by default?

Quick Answer: **233**
Detailed Answer: **248**

- ○ **A.** C:\Users\%username%\desktop
- ○ **B.** C:\Documents and Settings\%username%\desktop
- ○ **C.** C:\System Volume Information\%username%\desktop
- ○ **D.** C:\Users\System32\%username%\desktop

58. A user who is part of a workgroup reports that she cannot print to a new printer. Everyone else in the workgroup can print to the new printer, and the user can still automatically send print jobs to the old printer. Which of the following statements describes how to remedy the problem? (Select the two best answers.)

Quick Answer: **233**
Detailed Answer: **248**

- ❏ **A.** Add the new printer to the user's computer.
- ❏ **B.** Clear the print queue on the new printer.
- ❏ **C.** Change the user's password and permissions.
- ❏ **D.** Set the new printer as the default printer.

59. Your organization has an Active Directory domain. One of the users, Bill, should not have read access to a folder named Accounting. The Accounting folder is shared on a network server, on a partition formatted as NTFS. Which of the following statements best describes how to stop Bill from having read access to the folder without impacting any other users on the network?

Quick Answer: **233**
Detailed Answer: **248**

- ○ **A.** Remove Bill from all domain groups that have access to the Accounting folder.
- ○ **B.** Deny read access to the Accounting folder for Bill through local access security.
- ○ **C.** Deny read access to the Accounting folder for any group that Bill is a member of.
- ○ **D.** Deny read access to the Accounting folder for Bill through shared access security.

60. Examine the following figure. Then answer the question that follows.

Quick Answer: **233**
Detailed Answer: **248**

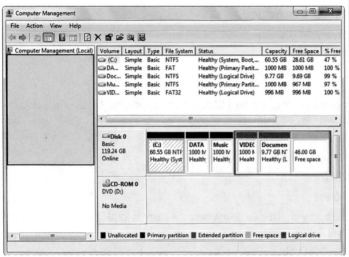

Which portion of Computer Management is displayed in the figure?

○ **A.** Event Viewer

○ **B.** Disk Management

○ **C.** Gparted

○ **D.** DiskPart

61. Which of the following is the best Windows utility to back up important system settings without requiring external storage?

Quick Answer: **233**
Detailed Answer: **248**

○ **A.** Msconfig

○ **B.** Task Manager

○ **C.** System Protection

○ **D.** Robocopy

62. Your boss wants to encrypt a hard drive that will store critical data. Your boss needs to be able to drag and drop folders onto the volume and have them encrypted in real time. Which encryption technique should you suggest?

Quick Answer: **233**
Detailed Answer: **249**

○ **A.** BitLocker

○ **B.** PKI

○ **C.** TPM

○ **D.** Kerberos

Quick Check

63. Your boss asks you to troubleshoot a computer with a virus. Which of the following statements best describes the first step you should take to remedy the problem?

Quick Answer: **233**
Detailed Answer: **249**

  ○ **A.** Run a System Restore.

  ○ **B.** Identify the malware.

  ○ **C.** Roll back drivers.

  ○ **D.** Research malware types.

64. User A is part of the Users Group on a Windows computer. User A attempts to access files on a UNC path: \\server\fileshare. Fileshare has the following share permissions:

Quick Answer: **233**
Detailed Answer: **249**

Administrators—Full Control

Users—Read Only

Guests—No Access

However, the directory on the hard drive where the share is located has the following permissions:

Administrators—Full Control

Users—Change

Guests—No Access

Which level of access will the account User A have?

  ○ **A.** Read Only

  ○ **B.** Change

  ○ **C.** Full Control

  ○ **D.** No Access

65. Your boss wants to implement BitLocker on yet a second laptop for traveling purposes. Which of the following should be performed before implementing BitLocker?

Quick Answer: **233**
Detailed Answer: **249**

  ○ **A.** Enable TPM in the BIOS/UEFI.

  ○ **B.** Disable UAC.

  ○ **C.** Defrag the hard drive.

  ○ **D.** Convert the file system to NTFS.

66. You need to edit a protected .dll file on a Windows 8.1 Pro PC, but you cannot find the file you are looking for in the System32 folder. Which of the following Control Panel utilities should you configure?

Quick Answer: **233**
Detailed Answer: **250**

  ○ **A.** Display

  ○ **B.** System

  ○ **C.** Indexing Options

  ○ **D.** Folder Options

67. One of your customers has a defective disk. Which command can be used to extract readable information?

   ○ **A.** Recover

   ○ **B.** Replace

   ○ **C.** Convert

   ○ **D.** REM

68. You have been asked to load a copy of the company's purchased software on a personal computer. Which of the following statements best describes the first step you should take to remedy the problem?

   ○ **A.** Verify that the install is allowed under the company's licensing agreements.

   ○ **B.** Notify the company's owner of the breach.

   ○ **C.** Advise the individual that downloading unlicensed software is illegal.

   ○ **D.** Leave the premises and call local law enforcement.

69. Your friend is playing the latest first-person game on a PC, but the screen is pausing during game play. Your friend has a high-end graphics card and the maximum memory for the motherboard. Which of the following statements best describes how to remedy the problem?

   ○ **A.** Upgrade the drivers.

   ○ **B.** Reinstall the OS.

   ○ **C.** Replace the hard drive.

   ○ **D.** Reinstall the game.

70. You have been asked to move data from one user's laptop to another user's laptop, each of which has EFS functioning. Which of the following statements best describes the first step you should take to remedy the problem?

   ○ **A.** Give the user of the second laptop administrator privileges.

   ○ **B.** Export the user's certificate.

   ○ **C.** Disable networking.

   ○ **D.** Convert the partition to FAT32.

71. Which of the following statements is true?

Quick Answer: **233**
Detailed Answer: **251**

- ○ **A.** Authentication can be something a user knows, such as a smart card.
- ○ **B.** Authentication can be something a user is, such as a fingerprint.
- ○ **C.** Authentication can be something a user does, such as a PIN or password.
- ○ **D.** Authentication can be something a user has, such as signature.

72. You are required to implement an organizational policy that states user passwords can't be used twice in a row. Which of the following policies should be configured?

Quick Answer: **233**
Detailed Answer: **251**

- ○ **A.** Minimum password length
- ○ **B.** Enforce password history
- ○ **C.** Minimum password age
- ○ **D.** Complexity requirements

73. You are working on a computer in which you just installed a new hard drive. The system already runs Windows. The new hard drive does not appear in Explorer. Which of the following statements best describes the next step you should take to ensure the drive will be recognized by the operating system?

Quick Answer: **233**
Detailed Answer: **251**

- ○ **A.** Reboot the computer.
- ○ **B.** Initialize and format the hard drive in Disk Management.
- ○ **C.** Configure the drive in the BIOS/UEFI.
- ○ **D.** Assign a drive letter to the hard drive in Disk Management.
- ○ **E.** Set the drive to active.

74. An attacker is constantly trying to hack into one of your customer's SOHO networks. Which of the following statements best describes the easiest, most practical way to protect the network from intrusion?

Quick Answer: **233**
Detailed Answer: **252**

- ○ **A.** Disable the SSID broadcast.
- ○ **B.** Install an antivirus server application.
- ○ **C.** Disconnect the Internet connection.
- ○ **D.** Install a firewall.
- ○ **E.** Install an IDS.

75. One of the administrators recently moved a large chunk of data from one server to another. Now, several users are reporting they cannot access certain data shares and get the following error: Access Denied. The admin confirms that the users are in the proper security groups, but the users are still unable to access the shares. Which of the following are the most likely causes of the problem? (Select the two best answers.)

   ❏ **A.** Denied permissions
   ❏ **B.** User account time of day restriction
   ❏ **C.** Mapped drives
   ❏ **D.** Administrative share permissions
   ❏ **E.** Disabled proxy settings

76. Which command in the Linux terminal enables you to find out information about a wireless network adapter?

   ○ **A.** Ipconfig
   ○ **B.** Regedit
   ○ **C.** Apt-get
   ○ **D.** Iwconfig

77. You have a Windows computer for which you wish to write a batch file. You want the batch file to turn off the computer after a certain amount of time. Which main command should be run in the batch file?

   ○ **A.** Taskkill
   ○ **B.** Down
   ○ **C.** Kill
   ○ **D.** Shutdown

78. Which switch of the Robocopy command copies subdirectories but skips empty ones?

   ○ **A.** /E
   ○ **B.** /B
   ○ **C.** /S
   ○ **D.** /DCOPY:T

79. Which of the following are components of dealing with prohibited content? (Select the three best answers.)

Quick Answer: **233**
Detailed Answer: **253**

- ❏ **A.** First response
- ❏ **B.** Maintaining a positive attitude
- ❏ **C.** Preserving data
- ❏ **D.** Creating a chain of custody
- ❏ **E.** Avoiding distraction

80. You are designing the environmental controls for a server room that contains several servers and other network devices. Which of the following statements best describes the role of an HVAC system in this environment? (Select the two best answers.)

Quick Answer: **233**
Detailed Answer: **253**

- ❏ **A.** It shields equipment from EMI.
- ❏ **B.** It provides isolation in case of a fire.
- ❏ **C.** It provides an appropriate ambient temperature.
- ❏ **D.** It maintains appropriate humidity levels.
- ❏ **E.** It vents fumes from the server room.

Quick-Check Answer Key

1. D	28. A	55. A
2. D	29. B	56. D
3. D	30. A	57. A
4. C	31. B, D, G	58. A, D
5. B	32. C	59. D
6. C	33. D	60. B
7. C	34. C	61. C
8. D	35. B	62. A
9. B	36. C	63. B
10. A	37. A	64. A
11. A	38. D	65. A
12. D	39. B	66. D
13. C	40. D	67. A
14. B	41. A, B, D	68. A
15. D	42. B	69. A
16. A	43. C	70. B
17. C	44. C	71. B
18. C	45. A	72. B
19. A	46. A	73. B
20. A	47. D	74. D
21. B	48. B	75. A, C
22. A	49. A, D, E	76. D
23. B, D, F	50. A	77. D
24. D	51. A	78. C
25. B	52. C	79. A, C, D
26. B, E	53. C	80. C, D
27. A	54. D	

Answers and Explanations

1. Answer: D

Explanation: The snippet of code shown is an example of JavaScript. When you press F12 in a web browser, it displays the code used by the web page. This often includes HTML, CSS, and JavaScript. For this question, you don't even need to look at the code because the question states that you are looking in the js folder, which is short for JavaScript. However, you could also tell by the code. For example, `$(function()` is a jQuery, an easier way of using JavaScript. Also, `var` is commonly used in JavaScript; it is a statement that declares a variable. In this example, a table or other data structure is "collapsible," which means it can be shrunk into a smaller space. So this question might seem complex, but it really isn't. Remember, .js is normally associated with JavaScript.

Incorrect answers: As for the others, .py is associated with Python; .ps1 is associated with PowerShell; .sh is associated with Bash and the Terminal (Linux/Unix); and .vbs is associated with Visual Basic Script (or VBscript).

2. Answer: D

Explanation: Because this situation happens often, you should school the user on safer web browsing habits such as being very careful when clicking on links brought up by search engines, not clicking on pop-up windows, and being conservative about the websites that are accessed. Also, the browser can be updated, add-ons can be installed to the web browser for increased protection, phishing filters can be enabled, and so on.

Incorrect answers: Deleting temporary files won't stop the user from visiting the same websites that probably caused the problem in the first place. Defragmenting the hard drive will help the drive and the OS perform better but won't help in the malware department. The computer should have an antivirus solution or, better yet, an anti-malware solution, but it should be set to update automatically every day.

3. Answer: D

Explanation: Connections can be made by sending Remote Assistance invitations by email (Outlook or other email client) or Easy Connect. These invitations could be to ask for help or to offer help. This approach is often implemented in help desk scenarios in which a user invites a technician to take control of his computer so that it can be repaired. It's effectively a virtual service call. The technician doesn't need to come physically to the user's desk but instead connects remotely.

Incorrect answers: You can also take control of a computer without an invitation (and if you are an administrator or a user with permissions); this can be done only if the computer to be controlled has the Remote Desktop feature turned on. Virtual network computing (VNC) is similar to Remote Desktop; it enables control of a computer remotely. Several third-party VNC companies offer free software. Microsoft doesn't refer to its software as VNC though. Collectively, the client software is also referred to as either Remote Desktop or Microsoft Terminal Services Client (MSTSC). Mstsc.exe is the executable that can also be used in the Command Prompt.

4. **Answer: C**

   Explanation: The default folder location for Windows system files is C:\Windows\System32—that is, if C: is the drive being installed to (which is the default). You might also see this referred to as X:\%windir%\System32 or simply \%windir%\System32. The X: is a variable meaning whichever volume is installed to. %windir% is a variable referring to the name of the main installation folder (usually Windows). %windir% is also expressed sometimes as %systemroot%.

   Incorrect answers: C:\Windows is the systemroot, where the OS is installed (though it also inhabits subfolders). C:\Windows\System32\Config is the folder where the Registry hives are stored. There is no C:\System Files folder, unless you were to create it yourself.

5. **Answer: B**

   Explanation: You would use the Google Cloud solution so that files can be backed up to a location outside the company. This backup—or full synchronization method—is great for Android-based smartphones or tablets as well as Google Chromebooks. Several other third-party solutions are available as well.

   Incorrect answers: iCloud is the Apple solution for file backup, apps, and so on. Microsoft OneDrive has the same types of features in a variety of solutions. Though there is some crossover between cloud platforms, generally Android users would back up to the Google Cloud. A company-based local network-attached storage (NAS) device would go against what you have been asked to do in the scenario. If the NAS were on the Internet or part of a cloud, that would be a different story.

6. **Answer: C**

   Explanation: You should check the company's policies and procedures first (or inquire with a compliance officer). If there is confidential or proprietary information that should not leave the premises (under normal circumstances), the company guidelines should define what to do in a repair situation.

   Incorrect answers: If the computer ultimately does have to leave the premises, you will probably have to obtain authorization and signatures from one or more people who work at the company; this goes beyond *your* manager, who works at your company, not the company you have been contracted to help. You should never delete any information from computers that you work on unless, of course, doing so is required as part of a hard drive scrub or hard drive replacement, and the data has been backed up. Removing the hard drive is not enough; there could be data elsewhere in the computer. Also, repairing a system without a hard drive can, in many cases, prove to be difficult.

7. **Answer: C**

   Explanation: Use Notepad. This text-based editor applies virtually no formatting. Text and other information can be copied from a web page, pasted to a Notepad document, and then copied again and pasted into Word; all formatting is removed. Notepad (and third-party tools such as Notepad++) can also be used for scripting and web page development.

Incorrect answers: CMD, or more specifically cmd.exe, is the executable that opens the Microsoft Command Prompt. Excel is a program by Microsoft that enables you to create and modify spreadsheets. The MMC is the Microsoft Management Console. It is a utility in Windows that enables you to work with several console windows within the same program; it saves the last place you were working.

8. **Answer: D**

   Explanation: The printing subsystem is most likely failing for one of a variety of reasons. The first solution is to terminate spoolsv.exe (which is the Print Spooler service) in the Task Manager or in the Command Prompt with the `taskkill` command. Then restart the computer. If that approach doesn't work, the system may have to be repaired, restored, or modified in the Registry (which could be an in-depth process). It is also possible that a virus has compromised the system. There are viruses that are also called spoolsv.exe; a quick sweep of the system folders with AV software should uncover this…hopefully.

   Incorrect answers: If Windows Update was running, it should not take up that many resources—not nearly so. FYI, the executable for that is wuauclt.exe. Hyper-Threading can be disabled in the BIOS/UEFI on some systems. This should have no effect on the system's ability to multitask, though, and multiple processes should be able to run simultaneously without a problem.

9. **Answer: B**

   Explanation: IMAP is the Internet Message Access Protocol, which allows an email client to access email on a remote mail server. Generally, the email client software leaves the messages on the server until the user specifically deletes them. So, the user can selectively download messages. This allows multiple users to manage the same mailbox.

   Incorrect answers: Real-time messaging can be accomplished by using instant messaging and chat programs. IMAP, like POP3, allows users to download or receive messages, but it does not send messages; a protocol such as SMTP would be used to send mail. IMAP, like POP3, authenticates the user, but again not for sending email—just when receiving email.

10. **Answer: A**

    Explanation: Use the Device Manager to disable a component in Windows, regardless of whether it is a laptop or a PC. When you disable a device, a down arrow appears over the icon of the device, next to the name.

    Incorrect answers: Use the Task Manager to analyze basic system performance and stop processes. Use File Explorer to view folders, files, and other computers. Use the Services console (services.msc) to stop and start and modify the startup type of services.

11. **Answer: A**

    Explanation: The sigverif.exe tool can be used to check for unsigned drivers within your Windows operating system. Unsigned drivers are those that have not been verified by Microsoft. If you receive error messages and are troubleshooting, run this command from the Run prompt. When the check is finished, unsigned drivers are displayed. This list is also stored in a file called sigverif.txt within the %windir% (%systemroot%).

Incorrect answers: The `dxdiag` command is the executable for the DirectX Diagnostic Tool. It is used to test the functionality of audio and video devices. `Ping` is used to test whether or not another host is on the network. `Msconfig` (the Microsoft System Configuration Utility) is a tool used to troubleshoot the startup process of Windows.

12. **Answer: D**

    Explanation: User Account Control (UAC) is the portion of Windows that asks for confirmation of administrative rights before allowing a user to make system changes or run certain applications. It can be disabled within the User Accounts applet within the Control Panel by clicking the Change User Account Control Settings link. But beware; only users who have administrative rights should even be permitted to turn off this setting. UAC can be further configured in the Group Policy Editor and in the Registry Editor. For more information about how UAC works, see the following link:

    https://docs.microsoft.com/en-us/windows/security/identity-protection/user-account-control/how-user-account-control-works

    Incorrect answers: UAC is not turned off in the Security Center or with the Windows Defender Firewall. It has separate functionality that is built into Control Panel > User Accounts. It cannot be turned off as a service in the Services console window (services.msc), though there is a related service called the Application Information service (using the service name *appinfo*), which deals with the usage of additional administrative privileges.

13. **Answer: C**

    Explanation: If a "print sub-system not available" message or similar message appears, it most likely means the spooler has stalled. You can turn it back on within the Services section of Computer Management or by issuing the command `net start spooler` at the Command Prompt.

    Incorrect answers: If the wrong printer driver was installed, either the user would get a message stating that the printer is not available, or the document would print but the information would be garbled. If the printer was not added, the user would not be able to print any documents to any printers and therefore should not get an error message. If the printer was not getting power, the user would most likely get a message stating that the printer is not available.

14. **Answer: B**

    Explanation: Boot Logging can be enabled from the Windows Recovery Environment (WinRE) in Startup Settings or in the Windows Advanced Boot Options menu. After this option is enabled, the system automatically creates a file called ntbtlog.txt. Afterward, you can access the system by booting into Safe Mode, once again from the recovery environment.

    Incorrect answers: Sigverif is a program that can be run in Windows that verifies whether drivers have been signed by Microsoft. Disabling Driver Signature Enforcement is another Startup Settings (WinRE) option; you might use this to help fix the issue but not to diagnose the problem. Debugging Mode is another option. In this scenario you don't necessarily need to debug the system, but rather you should repair the individual driver that failed to load.

15. **Answer: D**

    Explanation: `Chkdsk /F` allows you to fix errors on a disk. It does not fix all errors, but it checks for disk integrity, bad sectors, and similar issues.

    Incorrect answers: `Robocopy` copies files and directory trees. `Tracert /w` analyzes the path to another computer with a specific timeout per reply. `Diskpart` is the command-line tool that enables you to make changes to the operating system's partition table.

16. **Answer: A**

    Explanation: The first thing you should do is install anti-malware software. It would be surprising if the computer doesn't have any, but it happens.

    Incorrect answers: This could be a virus issue or other malware issue; you wouldn't know until you investigate further. So, anti-malware is a better solution than just *anti-virus*. After installing the software, you should scan the system for malware, update that software, and then reboot the computer. Use the CompTIA A+ malware removal process to aid in this process. A pop-up blocker is good for ads, but not necessarily for full pages that open by themselves. Plus, because the system is running slowly, the problem appears to be more than just pop-ups and is probably malware related.

17. **Answer: C**

    Explanation: The Application log is the location for all events concerning Windows applications and third-party programs.

    Incorrect answers: The System log contains information about drivers, system files, and stop errors, but not application crashes. The Security log contains information regarding auditing events. The Setup log stores information of events that occurred during the installation of Windows.

18. **Answer: C**

    Explanation: `Msconfig` is the only option listed where you can disable services. The key in the question is the phrase "bring up a window." `Msconfig` runs in a window, whereas the rest of the answers run as text on the command line. `Msconfig` can also be used to modify how the system boots. (The Services console window can also be used to disable services, as well as start and stop them.)

    Incorrect answers: `SFC` is the System File Checker; it scans the integrity of protected system files and repairs problems if necessary and if possible. Contrast this with `chkdsk`, which can locate and repair errors on the disk, but not within system files. `GPUpdate` can update user and computer policy settings on the local computer or on remote computers.

19. **Answer: A**

    Explanation: The \Boot folder can be located in a hidden partition (100 MB in size), by default, which is separate from the C: drive.

    Incorrect answers: The \Windows folder is the place where the operating system is installed; it is also known by the variable %systemroot% or %WINDIR% and is located in the C: drive by default. \Documents and Settings is also located in C: by default. Bootmgr is the Windows Boot Manager, which is the Windows loader program; it is a file, not a folder.

20. **Answer: A**

Explanation: The best solution is to upgrade the wireless network from WEP to at least WPA2. WEP is a deprecated wireless encryption protocol and should be updated to a newer and more powerful protocol if at all possible. If this is not possible, it would be wise to use a strong WEP key and modify it often.

Incorrect answers: MAC address filtering does not increase the level of data encryption, but it does filter out unwanted computers when they attempt to connect to the wireless access point. Disabling the SSID broadcast deters new computers from making initial connections to the wireless access point.

21. **Answer: B**

Explanation: Dir /a can be used to display hidden files. Specifically, dir /ah can be used to show hidden files only.

Incorrect answers: Dir /o deals with various sort orders of files—for example, alphabetical. Dir /d sorts files by column in wide format, and dir /? displays the help file for the dir command.

22. **Answer: A**

Explanation: Try accessing Safe Mode first and see if the problem continues. It probably won't, and you will need to roll back the driver and locate, download, and install the correct one. Remember to get your drivers from the manufacturer's website, and don't forget to download the correct driver for your particular operating system.

Incorrect answers: Chkdsk checks the integrity of files and fixes them if necessary. Msconfig is used to boot the computer in different ways. Although you normally could select Safe Boot in msconfig, it is not possible in this scenario because the system won't boot into Windows properly. You could check the System log while in Safe Mode, but it won't explain much except that the system shut down improperly and rebooted continuously.

23. **Answers: B, D, and F**

Explanation: First, you should configure some kind of remote backup. This way, if the device is compromised, you have the confidential data backed up outside of the device at another location. The other half of this solution (not mentioned in the answers) is remote wipe. When you are positive that the device is stolen or lost, and you know the data was backed up at some point, trigger a remote wipe to remove all data from the device. Second, enable GPS on the device so that it can be tracked if it is lost or stolen. Third, configure a screenlock of some sort, be it a pattern that is drawn on the display, a PIN, or a password. A strong password is usually the best form of screenlock and the hardest to crack.

Incorrect answers: It doesn't make a difference how Bluetooth and Wi-Fi are configured. They won't help protect confidential data in the case of theft. Instead of Wi-Fi encryption, a mobile device should be prepared with a file encryption or full drive encryption tool.

24. Answer: D

Explanation: Most likely User B moved the file to another location outside of the current partition, made the changes (which is possible since User B is the one who moved it), and then moved it back to the original location. Whenever a file is moved to another partition or volume, the file takes on the permissions of the parent folder. However, if the file had been moved *within* the volume, the permissions would have been retained. Tricky. Remember this: If the file is moved within the same volume, it retains permissions, so the permissions don't change. But if a file is moved to another volume, it takes on the permissions of the folder it is moved into. As for copying, the file's copy always takes on the permissions of the parent regardless of where that copy is placed.

Incorrect answers: If NTFS permissions were changed to allow execute, User A should have been able to open the file. If the file was set with the hidden attribute, User A should not have been able to see the file. Accounts Receivable might or might not set a file to read-only. However, User A should still be able to open the file, but in read-only mode.

25. Answer: B

Explanation: Chkntfs can check to see whether a previous system shutdown completed successfully. This command must be run in elevated mode to function properly. Generally, you would check this on the system drive (for example, C:). If the drive is okay and the system did complete the shutdown successfully, you'll get a message such as "C: is not dirty." Otherwise, you'll get a message telling of the error.

Incorrect answers: Chkdsk checks the integrity of the disk. Ipconfig displays the configuration of your network adapters. SFC scans the integrity of all protected system files and can replace them with the correct versions if necessary.

26. Answers: B and E

Explanation: The badge reader and biometric lock are the best of the listed answers (although all kinds of other security methods are possible). This scenario is an example of multifactor authentication (MFA). An RFID-based badge reader relies on something a person *has*, and the biometric lock system relies on something the user *is*. MFA systems are more secure because they *layer* the security.

Incorrect answers: A bollard is a physical obstacle, often seen in parking lots; it is used to block cars from driving onto a sidewalk or into a building. Cable locks are a good idea for servers and other equipment in a server room or data center, but they don't secure the data center itself. A USB token is used for authentication to a computer, but not to the data center. Privacy (window) shades work well for blocking people from seeing what is inside a room, but don't do much to actually secure the room. Plus, I haven't seen too many windows in the data centers and server rooms I have worked in!

27. Answer: A

Explanation: The Windows PowerShell is the best of the listed Windows utilities that enables administrators to perform administrative tasks that integrate scripts and executables and can be run over a network. For even more power and flexibility, use the PowerShell Integrated Scripting Environment (PowerShell ISE).

Incorrect answers: The Command Prompt is the basic version of a command line in Windows. It is not as functional as the PowerShell. *Command line* is a generic term that refers to any command-line interpreting program regardless of the OS used. Bash is the shell used by Linux/Unix; for example, in Ubuntu Linux, you would access it from the Terminal.

28. Answer: A

Explanation: The Task Manager can end (or "kill") a running process. It is also used to end applications that lock up, and it analyzes the performance of the system.

Incorrect answers: Computer Management is the main configuration console window; it contains the Device Manager, Event Viewer, and Services, among other things. The Control Panel lists all of the configuration applets available in Windows, such as Power Options, User Accounts, and Windows Defender Firewall. `Tasklist` is a command in Windows that displays a list of the running processes. To kill a process in the Command Prompt, first find out the name of the process and/or process ID (PID) with `tasklist` and then use the `taskkill` command to end the process.

29. Answer: B

Explanation: exFAT (also known as FAT64) is suited specifically for USB flash drives and many other mobile storage solutions. It is the successor to FAT32 and can format media that is larger than 32 GB with a single partition.

Incorrect answers: Older file systems such as FAT32 are very limited as to the partition size. NTFS can be a good solution for USB flash drives, but exFAT was developed specifically for USB flash drives and is the better solution if you have an operating system that supports it. Ext4 is a commonly used file system in Linux-based systems.

30. Answer: A

Explanation: Spyware is a type of malicious software that is usually downloaded unwittingly by a user or is installed by third-party software. It collects information about the user and the user's computer without the user's consent.

Incorrect answers: A virus is code that runs on the computer without the user's knowledge; it infects a computer when the code is accessed and executed. A rootkit is software designed to gain administrator-level control over a computer system without being detected. Spam is the abuse of electronic messaging systems such as email.

31. Answers: B, D, and G

Explanation: You can stop a service in a variety of ways. The easiest and most common is to go to the Services console window. You can do this by typing `services.msc` at the Run prompt. You can also stop services in the Task Manager by accessing the Services tab and right-clicking the service in question. But in the Task Manager you have to know the executable name of the service. The name of the Windows Firewall service is mpssvc. So, the third way (of the listed answers) is to use the `net stop mpssvc` command in the Command Prompt.

Incorrect answers: Performance Monitor, System Information, and Gpedit do not allow you to stop services.

32. Answer: C

Explanation: If the chemical spill is not life threatening, consult the material safety data sheet (MSDS) to determine the proper first aid (if any).

Incorrect answers: If it is an emergency, call 911. If you cannot get access to the MSDS, contact the facilities department of your organization or try your building supervisor. Never ignore a chemical spill. Take action before it becomes a problem.

33. Answer: D

Explanation: The chmod command allows a user to modify file and folder permissions at the Linux command line.

Incorrect answers: The chown command allows a user to change the ownership settings of a file. Passwd enables a user to change the password in the command line. Ls displays the contents of a directory in Linux. These commands can also be used in macOS.

34. Answer: C

Explanation: Whenever you're working in someone's home, make sure that an adult is available.

Incorrect answers: You cannot take on the type of responsibility for watching a child; there could be legal consequences. Plus, there is no point in discussing the matter. Most companies have policies that simply state the terms of your visit to a customer. It is not your responsibility to watch over children, nor should any company agree to have its consultants do this. If the person insists on leaving, and you can pack up your things before that happens, do so, and then call your supervisor to inform him or her of the event.

35. Answer: B

Explanation: Rapid elasticity means that the service can be scalable at need and can grow in real time with your company's growth.

Incorrect answers: In measured services, the provider monitors the services rendered so that the provider can properly bill the customer. On-demand service simply means that users can get cloud connectivity at any time, 24/7. Resource pooling is the grouping of servers and infrastructure for use by multiple customers but in a way that is on demand and scalable. All of these terms are interconnected, and a customer should be concerned with all of them.

36. Answer: C

Explanation: An open license means that the software can be downloaded and used for free.

Incorrect answers: Often, anti-malware suites offer advanced versions of the software for a fee. At that point, it would become a personal license. Corporate and Enterprise licenses are not for home users; they are often bulk discount licensing for multiple seats.

37. Answer: A

Explanation: Stay calm and do the job as efficiently as possible. There isn't much you can do when a customer is upset except fix the problem.

Incorrect answers: I'd be interested to see what would happen if a person asked the owner of the server out for a cup of coffee, but I'm pretty sure the reaction would be negative. You don't want to avoid the customer, but you don't have to engage in anything except fixing the problem. You should refer the customer to your supervisor only if the person gets in the way of you doing your work.

38. Answer: D

Explanation: A Domain Name System (DNS) server is designed to translate hostnames (such as *dprocomputer.com*) to their corresponding IP addresses (for example, 65.18.242.1).

Incorrect answers: A DHCP server is used to automatically assign IP addresses and client-side DNS settings to client computers. A web server houses websites for people to access on the Internet (or intranet or extranet). A proxy server is a go-between server that has several functions, the primary of which is to cache HTTP or FTP information for clients on the network (as well as secure derivatives of those: HTTPS, SFTP, and so on).

39. Answer: B

Explanation: There isn't much you can do in a situation like this, especially if you already saw what was printed on the document. The best thing is to ignore it and act as if it never happened. It's not your place to take action based on a document that is lying around. Without intense scrutiny, it is hard to know exactly what a document is. The purported list might be real, but it might not be. It isn't your call to make. However, before working at a *customer* site, you should ask that all confidential materials be removed before you begin work. If something is left out in plain sight, you could let a manager know that there could be confidential data lying around.

Incorrect answers: Technicians must be security-minded. Any documents owned by the company and printed by another user are not your property or your concern; they should not be handled or shredded. It could be a bad situation, but the right course of action is to not discuss it. As mentioned, the list could be real, or it could be a draft or a prank; either way, telling everyone about it could cost you your job. It is, however, something that you could bring up to a member of Human Resources, if necessary. Yelling is never a recommended course of action at the office. Save that for construction zones, demolition derbies, and heavy metal bands; or just avoid it altogether.

40. Answer: D

Explanation: The force quit option in Apple's macOS is most like the "end task" feature in the Windows Task Manager. It helps when an application is not functioning as intended and is either frozen or intermittently slows down the system.

Incorrect answers: Time Machine is the macOS backup utility, similar to Windows File History and Windows System Restore. Finder is the macOS file and application exploration tool, similar to the Windows File Explorer. `Taskkill` is actually a Windows command, but it does the same thing as the end task feature in the Task Manager—only it does it in the Command Prompt.

41. Answers: A, B, and D

Explanation: To reduce the chance of electrostatic discharge (ESD), use an antistatic wrist strap and mat. If connected properly, they become suitable methods of self-grounding. Also, consider raising the humidity. The more humidity there is, the less friction, and ultimately, less ESD.

Incorrect answers: Raising the temperature has no effect. Lowering the humidity increases the chances of ESD. Working in a carpeted area also increases the chance of ESD; try to work in a noncarpeted area. You should also touch the chassis of the computer before handling any components (a basic example of self-grounding). In addition, place components in antistatic bags when they are not in use.

42. Answer: B

Explanation: Make the customer truly feel comfortable by sitting down next to her and taking the time to explain the technical concept from a simple and concise point of view. The less jargon, the better.

Incorrect answers: Recommending a training class is tantamount to dismissing the customer off-hand. Telling the customer to read the manual is just downright rude. I know, I say this often to you; however, you are a tech, so reading the manual is what you do. The customer is not supposed to be super-technically oriented. The acronym RTM should be kept within technical circles!

43. Answer: C

Explanation: If you see the name *dpro42.com* toward the beginning of the results of an `ipconfig /all` command, the computer is most likely a part of the dpro42.com domain. This would be listed in the Primary DNS Suffix entry, which is usually directly after the Host Name entry. The .com is the giveaway. Some kind of DNS extension (such as .com or .net) is necessary when you have a domain.

Incorrect answers: If the computer were simply part of a workgroup or homegroup, the Primary DNS Suffix entry would be left blank (by default). If the computer was connected to a VPN, you would see IP configuration details for a "Tunnel adapter" connection farther down the list of results of the `ipconfig /all`.

44. Answer: C

Explanation: If you are not sure about what to clean a screen with, use water. Water will most likely not damage the screen.

Incorrect answers: However, if the user manual for the monitor calls for it, you might see that you can use a half-and-half mixture of water and isopropyl alcohol. Do not use detergents on a screen; they are okay for the outside of a computer case but not the display. And boric acid could be quite dangerous.

45. Answer: A

Explanation: The `regsvr32` command is used to register and unregister ActiveX controls and Dynamic-Link Libraries (DLLs). For example, to register the Sample ActiveX control, you would type `regsvr32 sample.ocx`.

Incorrect answers: Regedit.exe opens the Registry Editor, allowing you to perform just about any configuration you can imagine in Windows, from the simple to the mega-complex. The MMC is the Microsoft Management Console; it is a blank console window that you can use to work with multiple other console windows simultaneously (for example, Computer Management and the Local Security Policy). MSTSC is the Command Prompt version of Remote Desktop Connection in Windows.

46. Answer: A

Explanation: The best option here is to create alerts to let any and all administrators know if a backup failure occurs. These alerts would either be created at the network-attached storage (NAS) device or at the individual servers to be backed up. If an admin receives an alert, that person will know to either rerun the backup or (more likely) fix the backup task and then run it. One of the issues here is that you might not know if a backup fails—without the alerts, that is.

Incorrect answers: Setting up scripts is a good idea for the backup processes them-selves, but you first need to be alerted to an issue before you can script a rerun of the failed backup jobs. In this case, the backups are being stored to a NAS device locally (on the LAN), so they are not being stored offsite. You should always test a backup the first time it runs and periodically afterwards; however, frequent restoration tests are very time-consuming, not to mention hardware-intensive to the NAS device. Restoring to a VM is a good way to test, but it's not a good way to ensure rapid recovery, nor is it where the backups are supposed to be restored to; the question says "physical servers."

47. Answer: D

Explanation: If your system's motherboard is equipped with a UEFI BIOS, you should definitely take advantage of the GUID Partitioning Table (GPT). It is superior to Master Boot Record (MBR) technology. It allows for up to 128 partitions, is not limited to the 2-TB maximum partition size of MBR, and stores multiple copies of itself on the system.

Incorrect answers: As mentioned, MBR is inferior to GPT and should be avoided; how-ever, you might service older systems that require it. FAT32 is not really a partitioning scheme, but rather a type of file system—and an older one at that. NTFS or exFAT is preferable. A dynamic drive is a drive in Windows that has been upgraded from basic; it allows a user to change the size of the volumes on the drive.

48. Answer: B

Explanation: You should disable System Restore on Windows systems just before attempting to remediate the system of malware. This is step 3 of the CompTIA A+ best practices/procedure for malware removal. The entire procedure is as follows:

1. Identify malware symptoms.

2. Quarantine infected system.

3. Disable System Restore (in Windows).

    4. Remediate infected systems.

        a. Update anti-malware software.

        b. Scan and removal techniques (safe mode, pre-installation environment).

    5. Schedule scans and run updates.

    6. Enable System Restore and create restore point (in Windows).

    7. Educate end user.

Incorrect answers: As you can see, the rest of the answers listed in the question come after (or during) "remediate infected systems."

49. Answers: A, D, and E

Explanation: If a mobile device cannot connect to the network, you should attempt to power cycle the device, forget and reconnect to the Wi-Fi network, and check if the correct SSID was entered in the first place. Perhaps the #1 method would be to power cycle Wi-Fi (not listed in the answers).

Incorrect answers: Re-pairing has to do with Bluetooth, not Wi-Fi. Re-pairing means that you remove the paired Bluetooth device, and then reconnect it again. A hard reset wipes the device of its data and returns it to factory condition. This is a very last resort; there are plenty of other things you can try before that. Changing the IP address is possible but usually not necessary because most mobile devices obtain their IP addresses dynamically.

50. Answer: A

Explanation: The Sync Center is a Windows feature that enables you to keep information synchronized between your computer and network servers. You can still access the files and modify them even if you don't have physical access to the server; in this case they are modified "offline" and are synchronized automatically when you return to the network. Some mobile devices are also compatible with Sync Center. The Sync Center can be configured within the Control Panel.

Incorrect answers: Windows Aero is a premium visual experience included in some versions of Windows 7. Windows Defender is the free Microsoft anti-malware program. HomeGroup is meant to quickly and easily share printers and media between Windows computers in a home network but was abandoned by Microsoft in Windows 10 (starting with version 1803).

51. Answer: A

Explanation: The technician should repeat the problem back to the customer to make sure that everyone is talking about the same thing and that both parties understand each other. Always clarify.

Incorrect answers: Having the customer call back later is just delaying the problem. Asking a person with an accent to stop speaking with an accent is like telling a dog to stop wagging its tail; it is probably futile. A technician needs to be culturally sensitive. If you seriously cannot understand the customer even after attempting to listen several times and repeating the problem back, you will have to get someone else involved who can help you or attempt to communicate with the person through email.

52. Answer: C

Explanation: Virtual private networks (VPNs) rely on a tunneling protocol such as Point-to-Point Tunneling Protocol (PPTP) or Layer 2 Tunneling Protocol (L2TP) to create a secure connection between a network and a remote computer or group of computers. The preferred method for Windows clients is to use Internet Key Exchange version 2 (IKEv2). You might also make use of a RADIUS server for authentication or use an always-on VPN solution such as OpenVPN.

Incorrect answers: WWAN is another name for cellular Internet access. 4G LTE is a wireless cellular service used over large geographic areas; most phones use this standard in the United States and many other countries. WLAN is the wireless LAN that is created when you implement a wireless access point or create an ad hoc network of devices.

53. Answer: C

Explanation: Entering %temp% at the Run prompt displays a folder with the current user's temporary files. For example, in Windows this would show: C:\Users\%username%\AppData\Local\Temp folder.

Incorrect answers: Nothing will be added, changed, or deleted. The folder will simply be displayed in a Windows Explorer or File Explorer window. The operating system's temporary folder is located at C:\Windows\Temp.

54. Answer: D

Explanation: The standard user cannot install software or make changes to the system without knowing an administrative login.

Incorrect answers: Administrators have full control over a system. Power users (way back in the Windows XP days) were able to install programs and device drivers but are found in newer versions of Windows only for backward compatibility with older applications. Remote Desktop users can remote into other machines to control them from another location.

55. Answer: A

Explanation: Chkdsk /R locates bad sectors and recovers the information from them.

Incorrect answers: /F fixes errors but doesn't locate bad sectors and recover the information from them. /C and /I skip certain checks of the volume (in this case C:), which ultimately reduces the time it takes to check the volume.

56. Answer: D

Explanation: Of the listed answers, a fingerprint is the best way to secure the smartphone. If the smartphone is lost or stolen, another person would have a difficult time unlocking the device (though not impossible). For a device that cannot be remote wiped (for various reasons), the best alternatives are the use of biometric authentication, in combination with a strong password (for MFA); plus encryption.

Incorrect answers: Passcodes and PINs can be cracked; doing so just takes time. Even a lengthy and complex password can be cracked given enough time.

57. Answer: A

Explanation: Every user profile gets a Desktop folder by default. This folder is located within the user profile folder, which is shown in the answer as a variable %username%.

Incorrect answers: In a standard Windows 10, 8, or 7 configuration, the Documents and Settings and System Volume Information folders are hidden and access is denied. Historically, the no-longer-supported Windows XP used Documents and Settings as the main user folder, but newer versions of Windows changed that by creating a junction from that folder to the Users folder. Now the Documents and Settings folder is protected, but you have limited access to the Users folder. The System32 folder is inside the Windows folder, not the Users folder.

58. Answers: A and D

Explanation: If a user cannot print to a brand-new printer, yet everyone else can print to it, you should check whether the printer is installed on that user's computer and if it is set as the default printer.

Incorrect answers: If the printer has not yet been installed, there will be no print queue to clear. However, if the printer has been installed, the next thing to check would be whether the print queue has failed. You could also check the Print Spooler. If the user was able to print to an older printer that was also shared by other users in the workgroup, you should not have to change the user's password or permissions.

59. Answer: D

Explanation: The best option in this scenario would be to deny read access to the Accounting folder for Bill through shared access security.

Incorrect answers: You would not use local access security because the folder is shared from a network server within your Active Directory domain. Also, if you remove Bill from all domain groups that have access to the accounting folder, Bill will probably lose access to other folders as well. If you deny read access to the accounting folder for any group that Bill is a member of, you will probably impact other users on the network negatively.

60. Answer: B

Explanation: The Disk Management component of Computer Management is displayed in the figure. You can tell because it shows each disk and the volumes within each disk.

Incorrect answers: The Event Viewer houses log information for the system, applications, and security auditing events. Gparted is a partitioning tool used with Linux. DiskPart is the command-line tool used to create and modify partitions on the hard drive.

61. Answer: C

Explanation: System Protection is a feature that creates and saves data about the computer's system files and settings. It does this by creating restore points. You access it by going to the System Properties dialog box and clicking the System Protection tab. External storage is not necessary for these restore points; they are automatically stored in the system volume.

Incorrect answers: `Msconfig` is used to modify the way Windows boots and the services that are loaded at startup. The Task Manager is used to view system performance, enable/disable applications, stop services, and kill processes. `Robocopy` is an advanced file copy tool that can be used to copy entire directory trees of data, but it doesn't copy settings.

62. **Answer: A**

Explanation: BitLocker is a type of whole-disk encryption, or WDE. It encrypts all of the contents that are created on it or copied to it in real time. It requires a trusted platform module (TPM) on the motherboard or an encrypted USB flash drive. Only select editions of Windows support BitLocker when used in this manner. Other lesser versions of Windows are compatible with BitLocker To Go for reading encrypted documents from USB flash drives.

Incorrect answers: A PKI is a public key infrastructure, which is an entire system of technologies and users dealing with encryption. The TPM can be required for this scenario, but it is not the encryption itself. Kerberos is an authentication protocol.

63. **Answer: B**

Explanation: The first thing you should do is identify the malware. (By the way, if the computer is on the network, disconnect it first.) Then you can research that malware and any possible cures by searching the Internet and accessing your AV provider's website.

Incorrect answers: Rolling back drivers should not be necessary, especially if you find it necessary to run a System Restore at some point. Remember your best practices procedure for malware removal!

64. **Answer: A**

Explanation: User A will end up having the Read Only level of access to the share. Generally, a user gets the more restrictive level of access. The only thing that is different between the share's permissions and the parent directory's permissions is the level of control for the Users group. Normally, a share will obtain its permissions from the parent folder—that is, unless that option is unchecked in the properties of the folder. Then the folder can be reconfigured for whatever permissions an admin wants to set for it. That must be what happened in this scenario.

Incorrect answers: Administrators get Full Control access to almost everything by default. And Guests get No Access to just about everything by default. So the only possibilities for this question are Change and Read Only. Again, in general, the typical Standard user account receives the more restrictive level of permissions.

65. **Answer: A**

Explanation: Before implementing the BitLocker solution in Windows, you should enable the trusted platform module (TPM) in the BIOS. This is the chip on the motherboard that includes the encryption code.

Incorrect answers: UAC is User Account Control, a separate security option in Windows that checks whether users have administrative permissions before allowing them to carry out administrative tasks. Defragmenting the hard drive is not necessary, but it can't hurt to at least analyze the drive and see if it needs to be defragged.

Defragging a drive that requires it can increase performance. BitLocker works on FAT16, FAT32, NTFS, and exFAT partitions, so you do not need to convert the file system.

66. Answer: D

Explanation: Use the Folder Options utility in the Control Panel of Windows 8.1. From there, you go to the View tab and then deselect the check box labeled "Hide protected operating system files (Recommended)." You might also deselect the "Hide extensions for known file types" check box to see which ones are .dll files. Note that this utility was removed from the Windows 10 Control Panel. Instead, you can access it with File Explorer Options or from the File Explorer program by choosing View > Options > Change Folder and Search Options. Or you can go to Run and type control folders.

Incorrect answers: The other Control Panel utilities do not apply here.

67. Answer: A

Explanation: The Recover command can recover readable information from a bad or defective disk. The disk should be attached (slaved) to a working computer to get back the data.

Incorrect answers: The Replace command replaces source and destination files but does not recover lost information. Convert changes a file system from FAT to NTFS without losing data. REM records comments in a batch file (.bat) or within config.sys, a root file not typically used in Windows.

68. Answer: A

Explanation: You should first verify that the installation is allowed under a company's licensing agreement. It probably isn't, but you should check first. Most organizations do not allow purchased software to be installed on an employee's home computer. If doing so is against organization policy, you should notify your supervisor. There are many types of licenses that you should be aware of, including end-user licensing agreements (EULA), digital rights management (DRM), commercial and enterprise licenses (such as client access licenses or CALs), open source versus closed source (that is, Android versus iOS), personal licenses, and so on. Again, be sure to follow and incorporate corporate end-user policies and security best practices when it comes to these types of licenses.

Incorrect answers: You would notify your supervisor/manager, not the company owner, unless it was a very small company. Verify whether the license is valid or allowed before advising any individuals. Calling law enforcement is premature because you have not yet verified the nature and validity of the license.

69. Answer: A

Explanation: If you see video issues such as pausing during game play, upgrade the video drivers. Make sure that you download the latest video driver from the manufacturer's website. Gamers cannot rely on Microsoft drivers.

Incorrect answers: Sometimes reinstalling a game is necessary but shouldn't be in this scenario. Replacing the hard drive and reinstalling the OS are drastic and unnecessary measures for this problem.

70. Answer: B

Explanation: The first thing you should do is export the user's certificate from the first laptop to the second laptop. You can do this by clicking Start and typing `certmgr.msc` in the Search box; then locate and export the correct Personal Certificate. The Certificates console window can also be added to an MMC. The Encrypting File System (EFS) is the standard single-file encryption method for Windows (if the version supports it).

Incorrect answers: Administrative privileges won't help immediately because the encryption would still be in effect, but an administrator can deal with the importing and exporting of certificates from one computer to another, whereas a typical user cannot. Networking need not be disabled, and you aren't sure which user is being referred to in the answers, but if the certificate has been exported, that user should be able to read the files. Partitions can be converted from FAT32 to NTFS but not vice versa.

71. Answer: B

Explanation: Authentication can be carried out by utilizing something a user is, such as a fingerprint; something a user knows, such as a password or PIN; something a user has, such as a smart card or token; and something a user does, such as writing a signature or speaking words.

Incorrect answers: A smart card is something the user *has* (a possession factor), not something the user knows. A PIN and a password are something the user knows (a knowledge factor), not something the user does. A signature is something the user does, not something the user has.

72. Answer: B

Explanation: You should configure the Enforce password history policy and set it to a number higher than zero. This way, when a user is prompted to change her password every 42 days (which is the default minimum password age), that user will not be able to use the same password. Password policies can be accessed in Windows within Local Security Policy window > Security Settings > Account Policies > Password Policy.

Incorrect answers: Minimum password length is the policy that states the fewest characters a password must contain. Eight is a decent setting, but to be full-on secure, many organizations require 15 minimum. There are several technical reasons for this, but the A+ exam does not go into that kind of depth. Complexity requirements policy, if enabled, forces a user to select a password that meets three of the following five categories: uppercase characters, lowercase characters, numbers, special characters (such as ! or #), and Unicode characters (not often implemented). As of 2017, the National Institute of Standards and Technology (NIST) has leaned toward lengthy passwords as opposed to complex passwords.

73. Answer: B

Explanation: When you add a second drive to a system that already has Windows installed, you will probably have to initialize the drive and format it in the Disk Management utility.

Incorrect answers: Rebooting the computer does not help the system see the drive. You can configure the drive in the BIOS to a certain extent, but that won't help Windows see the drive. When you format the drive, Disk Management asks you to assign a drive letter. You don't need to set the drive to active because this drive does not have an OS to be booted to.

74. Answer: D

Explanation: The most practical way to prevent intrusion to the network is to install a firewall. In fact, if this is a SOHO network, chances are the network is controlled by a multifunction network device that already acts as a switch and a router and probably has built-in firewall technology; it just has to be enabled. Usually, these are enabled by default, but perhaps someone inadvertently disabled this feature, and that's one of the reasons an attacker keeps trying to get into the network.

Incorrect answers: An intrusion-detection system (IDS) is usually more elaborate and costs more money, but it would help to prevent network intrusion. (Some devices combine IDS and firewall technologies, but usually not SOHO multifunction network devices.) Disabling the SSID helps to discourage the average user from accessing the wireless network, but any hacker worth his or her salt can get right past that; plus, the attacker could be trying to connect directly through the Internet connection. Antivirus software, regardless of where it is installed, does not repel attackers; it locates and quarantines malware. Disconnecting the Internet connection would work; the hacker wouldn't be able to get in, but none of the employees would be able to use the Internet. Not a good compromise.

75. Answers: A and C

Explanation: The most likely reasons the users cannot connect are because of denied permissions and mapped drives. If the data was moved to another computer, the folders will inherit new permissions from the parent (by default). That will most likely eliminate the current user access. Also, the path to the share will change (again by default). Either the server name/IP address, the sharename, or both will be different when the data is moved to another server. So, to fix the problem, the user and group permissions will have to be modified for the new share, and new mapped drives will need to be configured.

Incorrect answers: There is no evidence that the time of day restrictions have been changed for any users. Administrative shares (such as C$) are for admins only; the users are not trying to access these shares in the scenario. Disabling proxy settings is done at the client computer. It *might* make sense if this happened to one system, but because multiple users are affected, it is unlikely.

76. Answer: D

Explanation: Use `iwconfig` (or `ifconfig`) to analyze a wireless network adapter in the Linux terminal. (Note that `iwconfig` does not work in macOS, but `ifconfig` does.) Also, as of the writing of this book, the `ip a` command can be used as well.

Incorrect answers: `Ipconfig` is a similar tool in Windows. `Regedit` is the executable that opens the Registry Editor in Windows. `Apt-get` is used for installing and uninstalling applications in the command line in Linux.

77. **Answer: D**

Explanation: Use the shutdown command. It works in the Command Prompt and also works programmatically within batch files (.bat) or beyond. To set a shutdown to occur after a specific time period, use the /t xxx switch.

Incorrect answers: Taskkill ends processes from the Command Prompt. Down is not a command in Windows, but it has been used by other operating system manufacturers to initiate a shutdown. Kill is the older Windows NT predecessor to the taskkill command.

78. **Answer: C**

Explanation: /s copies subdirectories but skips any empty ones.

Incorrect answers: /E copies all subdirectories, including empty ones. /B copies files in backup mode. /DCOPY:T also copies timestamps of files and folders.

79. **Answers: A, C, and D**

Explanation: When dealing with prohibited content, there will always be a first responder who is required to identify the issue, report through proper channels, and preserve data and possibly devices used. This person will be in charge of starting the documentation process, which includes maintaining a chain of custody, tracking evidence, and maintaining a chronological log of that evidence.

Incorrect answers: You should always maintain a positive attitude and avoid distractions, but those concepts concern professional behavior, not first response and prohibited content.

80. **Answers: C and D**

Explanation: The HVAC system's primary responsibilities are to provide an appropriate ambient temperature for the equipment and to maintain appropriate humidity levels. This keeps the equipment from overheating and prevents electrostatic discharge (ESD).

Incorrect answers: HVAC equipment, by its very nature, is a producer of electromagnetic interference (EMI); it does not shield equipment from EMI—quite the reverse. HVAC equipment often needs to be shielded to reduce EMI after it is installed. Isolation can be provided by other methods such as the material used in the perimeter of the room. A separate ventilation system can be installed to vent fumes away from the server room; however, there shouldn't be any fumes. Products that contain fumes should be stored in a separate and specially secured area. And if a fire were to occur, the sprinkler system or special hazards system should end that threat, eliminating any fumes that were a result of the fire.

THAT WAS A LOT OF FUN!

That's the end of Exam C, and that's the last exam of the book. I hope you enjoyed reading it as much as I enjoyed writing it.

If you scored 90 percent or higher on this 220-1002 practice exam, you are in pretty good shape. Now complete the book, and then access the companion website and my website for more content.

CHAPTER TEN

Review of the Core (220-1002)

Great work! You have completed all of the 220-1002 practice exams. That is a feat in and of itself. But the real test is yet to come. We discuss that in the next chapter.

Now that you have completed the practice exams, let's do a little review of the 220-1002 domains, talk about your next steps, and look at some test-taking tips.

Review of the Domains

Remember that the 220-1002 exam is divided into four domains, shown in Table 10.1.

TABLE 10.1   220-1002 Domains

Domain	Percentage of Exam
1.0 Operating Systems	27
2.0 Security	24
3.0 Software Troubleshooting	26
4.0 Operational Procedures	23
Total	100

As you could see while taking the practice exams, Windows operating system and troubleshooting questions are the bulk of what you will see on the real exam. Troubleshooting questions are generally more difficult than the questions from the other domains. You have to place yourself within the scenario and imagine that you are actually fixing software problems step by step. The way to succeed at troubleshooting is to (1) know the system and (2) use a logical troubleshooting process.

Even if you are a solid troubleshooter and really know your Windows operating systems, that still leaves half of the test unaccounted for. So, Security and Operational Procedures become the pivotal domains. Without them, you could be in trouble; with them, you will have all the tools you need to rule the exam.

Everyone who takes the exam gets a different group of questions. Because the exam is randomized, one person may see more questions on a particular topic than the next person. The exam differs from person to person. To reduce your risk of failing, be ready for any question from any domain, and study all of the objectives.

Review What You Know

At this point you should be pretty well versed when it comes to the 220-1002 exam. I still recommend going back through all of the questions and making sure there are no questions, answers, concepts, or explanations you are unclear about. If there are, additional study is probably necessary. If something really just doesn't make sense, is ambiguous or vague, or doesn't appear to be technically correct, feel free to contact me at my website, https://dprocomputer.com, and I will do my best to clarify. Think through the issue carefully before you do so, though. Many questions are written in an ambiguous manner to replicate what you will see on the real exam.

Here are a few great ways to study further:

- ▶ **Take the exams in flash card mode**—Use a piece of paper to cover up the potential answers as you take the exams. This approach helps make you think a bit harder and aids in committing everything to memory. There are also free flash card applications that you can download to your computer to help you organize your studies.

- ▶ **Download the A+ 220-1002 objectives**—You can get these from https://certification.comptia.org/ or from my website (https://dprocomputer.com). Go through the objectives one by one and check each item that you are confident in. If you are unsure about any items in the objectives, study them hard. That's where the test will trip you up. It's a big document, so going through them will take awhile. But this approach really helps close any gaps in your knowledge and gives that extra boost for the exam.

- ▶ **Check out my website for additional materials**—My A+ Study Page is designed to help you get ready for the exam. You never know what you might find there!

▶ **Consider my other A+ products**—For example, consider the main A+ Exam Cram guide or my A+ Complete Video Course. You can find more information about them on my A+ Study Page, which you can find at https://dprocomputer.com/blog/?p=3030.

More Test-Taking Tips

I've mentioned this point several times already, but it bears repeating: Take your time on the exam. The thing is, you either know the content or you don't. If you know it, you will probably end up with time left over, so there is no rush. Rushing can cause you to miss some key word, phrase, or other tidbit of information that could cost you the correct answer. Take it slow, and read everything you see carefully.

While taking an exam, follow these recommendations:

▶ Use the process of elimination.

▶ Be logical in the face of adversity.

▶ Use your gut instinct.

▶ Don't let one question beat you.

▶ If all else fails, guess.

I expand on these points in the final chapter.

If you finish early, use the time allotted to you to review all of your answers. Chances are you will have time left over at the end, so use it wisely. Make sure that everything you have marked has a proper answer that makes sense to you. But try not to overthink! Give it your best shot and be confident in your answers.

Taking the Real Exam

Do not register until you are fully prepared. When you are ready, schedule the exam to commence within a day or two so that you don't forget what you have learned.

Registration can be done online. Register at Pearson VUE (https://home.pearsonvue.com/). The site accepts payment by major credit card for the exam fee. First-timers need to create an account with Pearson VUE.

Here are some good general practices for taking the real exams:

- ▸ Pick a good time for the exam.
- ▸ Don't overstudy the day before the exam.
- ▸ Get a good night's rest.
- ▸ Eat a decent breakfast.
- ▸ Show up early.
- ▸ Bring ear plugs.
- ▸ Brainstorm before starting the exam.
- ▸ Take small breaks while taking the exam.
- ▸ Be confident.

I embellish on these concepts in the final chapter.

Well, that's it for the 220-1002 portion of this book. Meet me at the final chapter for the wrap-up.

CHAPTER ELEVEN

Wrap-Up

This chapter provides the following tools and information to help you be successful when preparing for and taking the CompTIA A+ Core 1 (220-1001) and Core 2 (220-1002) exams:

▶ Getting Ready and the Exam Preparation Checklist

▶ Tips for Taking the Real Exam

▶ Beyond the CompTIA A+ Certification

> **EXAM ALERT**
>
> **Warning! Don't skip this chapter!**   I impart some of the most vital things you need to know about taking the real exams here.

Getting Ready and the Exam Preparation Checklist

Anyone can take the CompTIA A+ certification exams; there are no prerequisites, but CompTIA recommends one year of prior lab or field experience working with computers. For more information on the A+ certification, visit the A+ section of my website at https://dprocomputer.com.

To acquire your A+ certification, you need to pass two exams: 220-1001 and 220-1002. These exams are administered by Pearson VUE (https://home.pearsonvue.com/). You need to register with Pearson VUE to take the exams.

EXAM ALERT

I strongly suggest that you do not take both exams on the same day. Instead, take them a week or so apart (at least). Trust me on this.

Each exam consists of two types of questions:

▸ **Multiple-choice**—These pose a question to you and ask you to select the correct answer (or answers) from a group of four or more choices. They are quite similar to the questions you've seen throughout this book.

▸ **Performance-based**—These ask you to answer a question, complete a configuration, or solve a problem in a hands-on fashion. The questions might ask you to drag and drop information to the correct location or complete a simulation in a virtual system. (See the "Real-World Scenarios" document and supporting simulations and videos on the companion website.)

To master both types of questions, you need to have a deep understanding of the theory, but you also need to know the hands-on. So, practice on your actual computers as much as possible. This is, of course, imperative for the exams, but it is even more important for the real world. The more you install, configure, and troubleshoot real systems, the more you will be prepared for the job interview as well as whatever comes your way after you have acquired a position within an organization.

EXAM ALERT

You've been warned! Practice as much as possible on the following:
- Real desktop/laptop computer hardware and software
- A SOHO router
- Smartphone and tablet
- Printers, displays, and other peripherals

> **NOTE**
>
> **An important note regarding exam questions.**
>
> This book does not offer the exact questions that are on the exam. There are two reasons for this:
>
> 1. CompTIA reserves the right to change the questions at any time. Any changes, however, will still reflect the content within the current A+ objectives.
>
> 2. The contents of the CompTIA A+ exams are protected by a nondisclosure agreement (NDA); anyone who sits an exam has to agree to this before beginning a test. The NDA states that the questions within the exams are not to be discussed with anyone.
>
> Therefore, I cannot tell you exactly what is on the exams, but I do cover all of the objectives within this book to give you the best chance of passing the exams.

You must be fully prepared for the exams, so I created a checklist (see Table 11.1) that you can use to make sure you have covered all the bases. Go through the checklist twice, once for each exam. For each exam, place a check in the status column as you complete each item. Do this first with the 220-1001 exam and then again with the 220-1002 exam. I highly recommend completing each step in order and taking the 220-1001 exam first. Historically, my readers and students have benefited greatly from this type of checklist.

TABLE 11.1   Exam Preparation Checklist

Step	Item	Details	220-1001 Status	220-1002 Status
1.	Attend an A+ course.	(Optional): A hands-on A+ course can do so much for you when it comes to installing, configuring, and especially troubleshooting. Especially if you don't have the CompTIA recommended experience (12 months), consider an A+ class.		
2.	Review your study guide.	Whatever main study guide or guides you used, be sure to review them carefully.		
3.	Complete the practice exams in this book.	Take the 220-1001 exams and review them carefully. On the second runthrough of this checklist, take the 220-1002 exams and review them. Note: Also, take the bonus exams located on the companion website (print book only). If you score under 90 percent on any one exam, go back and study more.		

(Continued)

Step	Item	Details	220-1001 Status	220-1002 Status
		If you have any trouble at this stage, consider getting my A+ Exam Cram study guide, or another study guide of your choice, and read it very carefully.		
4.	Create your own cheat sheet.	See Table 11.2 for an example. The act of writing down important details helps to commit them to memory. Keep in mind that you will not be allowed to take this cheat sheet into the actual testing room.		
5.	Register for the exam.	Do not register until you have completed the previous steps; you shouldn't register until you are fully prepared. When you are ready, schedule the exam to commence within a couple of days so that you don't forget what you have learned. Registration can be done online. Register at Pearson VUE (https://home.pearsonvue.com/).		
		The site accepts payment by major credit card for the exam fee.		
		(You need to create an account to be able to sign up for exams.)		
6.	Review practice questions.	Keep reviewing practice questions until the day of the exam. Review your cheat sheet also if you created one.		
7.	Take the exam.	Check off each exam to the right as you pass it. Good luck!		

EXAM ALERT

Do not register for the exam until you are thoroughly prepared. Meticulously complete items 1 through 4 in Table 11.1 before you register.

Table 11.2 provides a partial example of a cheat sheet that you can create to aid in your studies. Fill in the appropriate information in the right column. For example, the first step of the six-step troubleshooting methodology is "Identify the problem."

TABLE 11.2   Example Cheat Sheet

Concept	Fill in the Appropriate Information Here
The six-step A+ troubleshooting methodology	1. 2. 3. 4. 5. 6.
Types of custom computers	
Cloud-based services	
The laser imaging process	
The malware removal process	
Windows log files	
Commands and descriptions (For example: ping – tests to see if other systems on the network are live.)	
* Etc.	

* Continue Table 11.2 in this fashion on paper. The key is to write down various technologies, processes, step-by-step procedures, and so on to commit them to memory. Make a separate cheat sheet for the 220-1001 and the 220-1002 exams.

Tips for Taking the Real Exam

Some of you will be new to exams. This section is for you. For other readers who have taken exams before, feel free to skip this section or use it as a review.

The exam is conducted on a computer and is multiple choice and performance-based. You have the option to skip questions. If you do so, be sure to mark or flag them for review before moving on. Feel free to mark any other questions that you have answered but are not completely sure about. This approach is especially recommended for the performance-based questions. In fact, you might choose to leave all of the performance-based questions until the end. That, of course, is up to you.

When you get to the end of the exam, you will find an item review section, which shows you any questions that you did not answer and any that you marked for review. Be sure to answer any questions that were not completed.

The following list includes tips and tricks that I have developed over the years. I've taken at least 20 certification exams over the past two decades, and the following points have served me well.

General Practices for Taking Exams

- ► **Pick a good time for the exam**—It appears that the fewest people are at test centers on Monday and Friday mornings. Consider scheduling during these times. Otherwise, schedule a time that works well for you, when you don't have to worry about anything else. Keep in mind that Saturdays can be busy. Oh, and don't schedule the exam until you are ready. I understand that sometimes deadlines have to be set, but in general, don't register for the exam until you feel confident you can pass. Things come up in life that can sometimes get in the way of your study time. Keep in mind that most exams can be canceled as long as you give 48 hours' notice. (To be sure, check that time frame when registering.)

- ► **Don't overstudy the day before the exam**—Some people like to study hard the day before; some don't. My recommendations are to study from your cheat sheet and maybe run through some quick Q&A, but in general, don't overdo it. It's not a good idea to go into overload mode the day before the exam.

- ► **Get a good night's rest**—A good night's sleep (seven to nine hours) before the day of the exam is probably the best way to get your mind ready for an exam.

- ► **Eat a decent breakfast**—Eating is good! Breakfast is number two when it comes to getting your mind ready for an exam, especially if it is a morning exam. Just watch out for the coffee and tea. Too much caffeine if you are not used to it can be detrimental to the thinking process.

- ► **Show up early**—The testing agency recommends that you show up 30 minutes prior to your scheduled exam time. This is important: Give yourself plenty of time, and make sure you know where you are going. Know exactly how long it takes to get to a testing center, and account for potential traffic and construction. You don't want to have to worry about getting lost or being late. Stress and fear are the mind killers. Work on reducing any types of stress the day of and the day before the exam. By the way, you do need extra time because when you get to the testing center, you need to show ID, sign forms, get your personal belongings situated, and be escorted to your seat. Have two forms of ID (signed) ready for the administrator of the test center. Turn off your cell phone or smartphone when you get to the test center; they'll check that, too.

▶ **Bring ear plugs**—You never know when you will get a loud testing center or, worse yet, a loud test-taker next to you. Ear plugs help block out any unwanted noise that might show up. Just be ready to show your ear plugs to the test administrator.

▶ **Brainstorm before starting the exam**—Write down as much as you can remember from the Cram and cheat sheets before starting the exam. The testing center is obligated to give you something to write on; make use of it! Getting all the memorization out of your head and on "paper" first clears the brain somewhat so that it can tackle the questions. I put *paper* in quotation marks because it might not be paper; it could be a mini dry-erase board or something similar.

▶ **Take small breaks while taking the exam**—Exams can be brutal. You have to answer a lot of questions (typically anywhere from 75 to 90) while staring at a screen for an hour or more. Sometimes these screens are old and have seen better days; these older flickering monitors can cause a strain on your eyes. I recommend small breaks and breathing techniques. For example, after going through every 25 questions or so, close your eyes and slowly take a few deep breaths, holding each one for five seconds and then releasing each one slowly. Think about nothing while doing so. Remove the test from your mind during these breaks. This technique takes only about half a minute but can help get your brain refocused. It's almost a Zen type of thing; but for me, when I have applied this technique properly, I have gotten a few perfect scores. It's amazing how the mind-set can make or break you.

▶ **Be confident**—You have studied hard, gone through the practice exams, created your cheat sheet—you've done everything you can to prep. These things alone should build confidence. But actually, you just have to be confident for no reason whatsoever. Think of it this way: You are great...I am great...(to quote Dr. Daystrom). But truly, there is no disputing this. That's the mentality you must have. You are not being pretentious about this if you think it to yourself. Acting that way to others...well, that's another matter. So build that inner confidence, and your mind-set should be complete.

Smart Methods for Difficult Questions

▸ **Use the process of elimination**—If you are not sure about an answer, first eliminate any answers that are definitely incorrect. You might be surprised how often this approach works. This is one of the reasons it is recommended that you not only know the correct answers to the practice exam questions but also know why the wrong answers are wrong. The testing center should give you something to write on; use it by writing down the letters of the answers that are incorrect to keep track. Even if you aren't sure about the correct answer, if you can logically eliminate anything that is incorrect, the answer will become apparent. To sum it up, the character Sherlock Holmes said it best: "When you have eliminated the impossible, whatever remains, however improbable, must be the truth." There's more to it, of course, but from a scientific standpoint, this method can be invaluable.

▸ **Be logical in the face of adversity**—The most difficult questions are when two answers appear to be correct, even though the test question requires you to select only one answer. Real exams do not rely on trick questions. Sometimes you need to slow down, think logically, and compare the two possible correct answers. Also, you must imagine the scenario that the question is a part of. Think through step by step what is happening in the scenario. Write out as much as you can. The more you can visualize the scenario, the better you can figure out which of the two answers is the best one.

▸ **Use your gut instinct**—Sometimes a person taking a test just doesn't know the answer; it happens to everyone. If you have read through the question and all the answers and used the process of elimination, sometimes this is all you have left. In some scenarios, you might read a question and instinctively know the answer, even if you can't explain why. Tap into this ability. Some test-takers write down their gut instinct answers before delving into the question and then compare their thoughtful answers with their gut instinct answers.

▸ **Don't let one question beat you!**—Don't let yourself get stuck on one question, especially the performance-based questions. Skip it and return to it later. When you spend too much time on one question, the brain gets sluggish. The thing with these exams is that you either know the content or you don't. And don't worry too much about it; chances are you are not going to get a perfect score. Remember that the goal is only to pass the exams; how many answers you get right after that is irrelevant. If you have gone through this book thoroughly, you should be well prepared. You should have plenty of time to go through all the exam questions with time to spare to return to the ones you skipped and marked.

▸ **If all else fails, guess**—Remember that the exams might not be perfect. A question might seem confusing or appear not to make sense. Leave questions like this until the end. After you have gone through all the other techniques mentioned, make an educated, logical guess. Try to imagine what the test is after and why it would be bringing up this topic, as vague or as strange as it might appear.

Wrapping Up the Exam

Review all your answers. If you finish early, use the time allotted to you to review the answers. Chances are you will have time left over at the end, so use it wisely. Make sure that everything you have marked has a proper answer that makes sense to you. But try not to overthink. Give the exam your best shot, and be confident in your answers. You don't want to second-guess yourself.

Beyond the CompTIA A+ Certification

A person who passes the CompTIA A+ exams will be certified for three years. To maintain the certification beyond that time, you must either pass the new version of the exams (before the three years is up), pass a higher level CompTIA exam (such as the Security+), or enroll in the CompTIA Continuing Education Program. This program has an annual fee and requires that you obtain Continuing Education Units (CEUs) that count toward the recertification. There are a variety of ways to accumulate CEUs. See CompTIA's website for more information: https://certification.comptia.org/continuing-education.

After you pass the exams, consider thinking about your technical future. Not only is it important to keep up with new technology and keep your technical skills sharp, but technical growth is important as well. Consider expanding your technical horizons by learning different technologies.

Usually, companies wait at least six months before implementing new operating systems and other applications on any large scale, but you will have to deal with new technology sooner or later—most likely sooner. Windows, macOS, Linux, Android, and iOS are always coming out with new versions. Consider keeping up with the newest versions and obtaining access to the latest software and operating systems. Practice installing, configuring, testing, securing, maintaining, and troubleshooting them.

To keep on top of the various computer technologies, think about subscribing to technology websites, RSS feeds, and periodicals, and read them on a regular basis. Check out streaming video tech channels on the Internet. Join computer Internet forums and attend technology conventions. After all, a technician's skills need to be constantly honed and kept up to date. Feel free to contact me for specific and current recommendations.

Information Technology (IT) technicians need to keep learning to foster good growth in the field. Consider taking other certification exams after you complete the A+. The CompTIA A+ certification acts as a springboard to other certifications. For example, the CompTIA Security+ certification takes this to another level, evaluating the technician's knowledge of how to secure networks, computers, and their applications. Now that you know exactly how to go about passing a certification exam, consider more certifications to bolster your resume.

The best advice I can give is for you to do what you love. From an IT perspective, I usually break it down by technology, as opposed to by the vendor or certification. For example, you might want to learn more about email systems or securing internetworks, or you might prefer to work on databases, build websites, develop apps—who knows! You are limited only by your desire. Whatever the field of technology, learn as much as you can about that field and all its vendors to stay ahead.

Final Note: I wish you the best of luck on your exams and in your IT career endeavors. Please let me know when you pass your exams. I would love to hear from you! Also, remember that I am available to answer any of your questions about this book via my website:

https://dprocomputer.com

Sincerely,

David L. Prowse

REGISTER YOUR PRODUCT at PearsonITcertification.com/register
Access Additional Benefits and SAVE 35% on Your Next Purchase

- Download available product updates.

- Access bonus material when applicable.

- Receive exclusive offers on new editions and related products.
  (Just check the box to hear from us when setting up your account.)

- Get a coupon for 35% for your next purchase, valid for 30 days. Your code will
  be available in your PITC cart. (You will also find it in the Manage Codes
  section of your account page.)

Registration benefits vary by product. Benefits will be listed on your account page
under Registered Products.

PearsonITcertification.com–Learning Solutions for Self-Paced Study, Enterprise, and the Classroom
Pearson is the official publisher of Cisco Press, IBM Press, VMware Press, Microsoft Press,
and is a Platinum CompTIA Publishing Partner–CompTIA's highest partnership accreditation.
At **PearsonITcertification.com** you can

- Shop our books, eBooks, software, and video training.
- Take advantage of our special offers and promotions (pearsonitcertifcation.com/promotions).
- Sign up for special offers and content newsletters (pearsonitcertifcation.com/newsletters).
- Read free articles, exam profiles, and blogs by information technology experts.
- Access thousands of free chapters and video lessons.

Connect with PITC – Visit PearsonITcertifcation.com/community
Learn about PITC community events and programs.

PEARSON IT CERTIFICATION

Addison-Wesley · Cisco Press · IBM Press · Microsoft Press · Pearson IT Certification · Prentice Hall · Que · Sams · VMware Press

ALWAYS LEARNING   PEARSON

To receive your 10% off
Exam Voucher, register
your product at:

www.pearsonitcertification.com/register

and follow the instructions.